1̄01̄ Investment Decision Tools

Investment Decision Tools

Barometers, Instruments, and Keys
(Where to find them and how they're used)

JAE K. SHIM

JOEL G. SIEGEL

JONATHAN LANSNER

International Publishing Corporation
Chicago, Illinois

Library of Congress Number: 93-80035.

ISBN: 0-942641-44-2

This publication is designed to provide accurate and authoritative information in regard to the subject matter covered. It is sold with the understanding that the authors and publisher are not engaged in rendering legal, accounting, or other professional service. If legal advice or other expert assistance is required, the services of a competent professional person should be sought. (From a declaration of principles jointly adopted by a committee of the American Bar Association and a committee of publishers.)

TABLE OF CONTENTS

ABOUT THE AUTHORS

Jae K. Shim, Ph.D., is Professor of Finance and Accounting at California State University, Long Beach, and President of National Business Review Foundation, an investment consulting and training firm. He is also Chief Investment Officer (CIO) of a Lawndale-based investment firm. Dr. Shim received his M.B.A. and Ph.D. degrees from the University of California at Berkley. He has published numerous articles in academic and professonal journals.

Dr. Shim has over 30 professional and college books to his credit, including *SOURCE: The Complete Guide to Investment Information, Where to Find It and How to Use It,* which he also co-authored with Joel G. Siegel, *Personal Finance, The Personal Finance Planning and Investment Guide, Encyclopedic Dictionary of Accounting and Finance, Financial Management, Managerial Finance, Dictionary of Personal Finance,* and the best-selling, *The Vest-Pocket MBA.*

Dr. Shim was the 1982 recipient of the *Credit Research Foundation Award* for his article on investment management.

Joel G. Siegel, Ph.D., CPA, is an active consultant in investment analysis and Professor of Finance and Accounting at Queens College of the City University of New York. Previous employers include Coopers, Lybrand, and Arthur Anderson. Dr. Siegel is a personal financial analyst and planning consultant. He has acted as an investment consultant to Citicorp, ITT, United Technologies, AICPAs, and Person-Wolinsky Associates.

Dr. Siegel is the author of more than 34 books and 200 articles on financial topics. His books have been published by International Publishing, MacMillan, Prentice-Hall, McGraw-Hill, Harper and Row, John Wiley, Barron's, and the AICPAs. He has been published in many financial journals, including the *Financial Analysts Journal, Financial Executive,* and the *CPA Journal.*

Jonathan Lansner is a professional journalist who works as an Assistant Business Editor for the *Orange County Register* (California), where he has edited and written banking and finance stories for seven years.

A graduate of the University of Pennsylvania's Wharton School he also spent seven years writing and editing for the Pittsburgh Press.

Lansner was among the first reporters to break stories on the savings & loan crisis and the scandal involving Lincoln Savings & Loan, Charles Keating, and five U.S. Senators.

Lansner has been nominated four times for the Pulitzer Prize for his investigative reporting and writing on complex economic issues in an easy-to-comprehend style.

ALPHABETICAL LISTING OF TOOLS

LIST OF FIGURES

INTRODUCTION

Decades ago, investors scrambled to get the smallest bit of "inside" knowledge from stock, bond, and other investment markets. Stock quotations had to be gleaned from a broker and yields were best found at the bank. A need for detailed statistics required either expensive subscriptions to market newsletters or a trip to the library—or both.

Today, the challenge is very different. The chore is to sort through the vast array of facts and figures available in the local newspaper, no less the national financial newspapers—*Investor's Business Daily*, the *Wall Street Journal*, *Barron's*, and investment magazines—*Forbe's*, *Money Magazine*, on television and on a home computer. Then, of course, there's what is contained in the many market advisory services that still thrive.

Consider this: A typical major city newspaper contains quotations on more than 10,000 stocks, bonds, and mutual funds and more than 100 indexes. Add to that expanded coverage of economic statistics or the added availability of such information on television, radio, and via on-line information services accessed by home computers. Most investors are not able to decipher what's up from what's down.

101 Investment Decision Tools: Barometers, Instruments, and Keys (Where to find them and how they're used) is designed to help the investor cut through all the statistical noise. It gets a reader quickly to the best financial barometers and helps him make informed investment decisions.

More than just an ordinary investment dictionary, *101 Investment Decision Tools* analyzes in a concise style various investment vanes—from stock indexes to measures of housing affordability to leading economic indicators. The reader will learn what these measures are, who's compiling them, where they are easily found (publications, media outlets, and more) and how they can, or cannot, be used to guide investment decisions. All in a handy, carry-along format.

In the ongoing complex investment climate we live in, those who understand and can use such investment tools will be the ones who succeed.

1. AMEX MAJOR MARKET INDEX (MMI)

What Is It? The American Stock Exchange (AMEX) Major Market Index is a price-weighted arithmetic average of 20 high-quality industrial NYSE securities.

How Is It Computed? The index is prepared by the AMEX but includes only stocks listed on the NYSE, 17 of which are included in the Dow Jones Industrial Average. High-priced issues have a greater impact on the index than low-priced issues. The base level of 200 was established in 1983. Figure 1 shows the components of this index.

Where Is It Found? The index appears in the financial pages of newspapers such as *Barron's* and the *Wall Street Journal*, and investment magazines.

How Is It Used for Investment Decisions? This index may be used to confirm market moves in other indexes containing blue chip stocks such as the Dow Jones Industrial Average.

Futures on this index as well as other indexes are traded on the Chicago Board of Trade.

Also See: AMEX MARKET VALUE INDEX (AMVI), DOW JONES INDUSTRIAL AVERAGE

Figure 1: AMEX Major Market Index (MMI) Components

Company	Ticker Symbol	Capitalization Weight (%)	Price as a Percent of Index
1. IBM*	IBM	15.03	9.80
2. Exxon*	XON	12.07	3.47
3. General Electric*	GE	8.69	3.57
4. American Telephone & Telegraph*	T	6.99	2.41
5. General Motors*	GM	5.69	6.90
6. Merck & Company*	MRK	5.23	4.92
7. Philip Morris*	MO	5.22	8.38
8. E.I. Du Pont de Nemours*	DD	4.87	7.55
9. Mobil Oil	MOB	4.00	3.60
10. Dow Chemical	DOW	3.73	7.43
11. Coca-Cola*	KO	3.55	3.68
12. Chevron*	CHV	3.41	3.70
13. Sears, Roebuck*	S	3.31	3.24
14. Eastman Kodak*	EK	3.20	3.68
15. Procter & Gamble*	PG	3.20	7.00
16. Minnesota Mining & Mfg.*	MMM	3.17	5.20
17. Johnson & Johnson	JNJ	3.13	6.93
18. American Express*	AXP	2.68	2.38
19. USX*	X	1.72	2.44
20. International Paper*	IP	1.12	3.74

* Components of the Dow Jones Industrial Average (17).

Source: Chicago Board of Trade; American Stock Exchange.

2. AMEX MARKET VALUE INDEX (AMVI)

What Is It? The AMVI is a market value-weighted index of more than 800 securities traded on the American Stock Exchange.

How Is It Computed? Nine major industries are represented in the calculation of the capitalization value of the issues included in the index. There is a weighting by industry group with no one company accounting for more than 7% of the total. Figure 2 shows the components of the index. The issues include common stock, warrants, and ADRs. The index assumes the reinvestment of cash dividends. It has a base level of 50 as of 1983.

Where Is It Found? The index may be found in the financial section of major newspapers such as *Barron's*, *Investor's Business Daily*, and the *Wall Street Journal*. It can also be found in the electronic on-line Prodigy. The AMEX index in the *Wall Street Journal* can be found under the heading Stock Market Data Bank.

How Is It Used for Investment Decisions? The index is used to gauge the performance and trading activity of the stocks on the AMEX. Therefore, an investor owning securities on this exchange will find the index of much interest. Furthermore, strength or weakness in the overall market is indicated.

Options on the AMVI are listed on the AMEX.

Also See: AMEX MAJOR MARKET INDEX (MMI)

Figure 2: AMEX Market Value Index (AMVI) Components

	Industry Sector	Approximate Weight (%)
1.	Natural resources	36
2.	High technology	15
3.	Service	12
4.	Consumer goods	10
5.	Capital goods	7
6.	Financial	5
7.	Housing, construction, land	5
8.	Retail	3
9.	Unclassified	7

Source: American Stock Exchange.

3. AMEX: OTHER INDEXES

COMPUTER TECHNOLOGY INDEX

What Is It? This is an index of computer hardware and software companies that reflect the financial health of this technology industry. The stocks are traded on all the exchanges.

How Is It Computed? The index is a capitalized weighted-average and is narrowly determined by looking at the market prices of stock of 30 large computer and semiconductor companies such as International Business Machines and Digital Equipment. The base year was 1983 at which time a value of 100 was assigned. Figure 3 shows the components of this index.

Where Is It Found? The AMEX and *Barron's* publish this index.

How Is It Used for Investment Decisions? The investor can use the index to gauge the performance of his investments in companies that produce computers and peripherals. Movement in the index must be monitored closely because technological issues can be subject to rapid and significant price swings.

The index also may be used to settle option contracts.

Figure 3: AMEX Computer Technology Index Components

Company	Ticker Symbol	Capitalization Weight (%)
1. IBM Corporation	IBM	44.20
2. Hewlett-Packard Company	HWP	8.26
3. Digital Equipment	DEC	8.04
4. Xerox Corporation	XRX	4.12
5. Motorola, Inc.	MOT	3.52
6. NCR Corporation	NCR	2.94
7. Apple Computer, Inc.	AAPL	2.89
8. Intel Corporation	INTC	2.84
9. Unisys Corporation	UIS	2.72
10. Tandy Corporation	TAN	2.58
11. Texas Instruments	TXN	2.05
12. Honeywell, Inc.	HON	1.93
13. Automatic Data Processing	AUD	1.88
14. Microsoft Corporation	MSFT	1.87
15. COMPAQ Computer Corporation	CPQ	1.79
16. Cray Research, Inc.	CYR	1.41
17. Amdahl Corporation	AMH	1.21
18. Tandem Computers	TDM	1.15
19. Wang Laboratories "B"	WAN.B	0.95
20. Control Data Corporation	CDA	0.58
21. Prime Computer	PRM	0.56
22. National Semiconductor	NSM	0.52
23. Computer Sciences	CSC	0.51
24. Advanced Micro Devices	AMD	0.45
25. Commodore International	CBU	0.37
26. Storage Technology	STK	0.31
27. Data General Corporation	DGN	0.30
28. Datapoint Corporation	DPT	0.03
29. NBI, Inc.	NBI	0.01
30. Quantel Corporation	BQC	0.01

Source: American Stock Exchange.

INSTITUTIONAL INDEX

What Is It? This index tracks the performance of 75 companies that have significant positions held by institutions.

How Is It Computed? This is a broad capitalized market value-weighted index of the shares of companies widely held by large institutional investors. Some of the companies included in the index are also included in the Dow Jones averages. To be eligible to be listed, a minimum of seven million shares must be traded and at least 200 institutional investors must hold the stock. Some companies included in the index are American Express, Chevron, Exxon, General Electric, and Boeing. A base level of 25 was assigned in 1986. The list of stocks is updated when appropriate.

Where Is It Found? Information on the index is available from the AMEX and *Barron's*.

How Is It Used for Investment Decisions? An investor may judge the performance of actively traded securities held in large measure by institutional investors. Institutions are considered "smart money" and a trend in the index may indicate changes in institutional perceptions of the overall stock market. The individual investor may want to follow institutional leads when they appear sound.

The index may be a proxy for an investor's "core" stock holdings. Stocks with large institutional holders tend to be conservative.

INTERNATIONAL MARKET INDEX

What Is It? The index looks at the market price of the shares of 50 high-quality companies located in Japan, Australia, and Europe. While nine countries are represented, most of the companies listed are Japanese. The stocks are traded as regular stock in the country's own exchange or as American Depository Receipts (ADRs) on one of the U.S. exchanges or over-the-counter (OTC) markets.

How Is It Computed? This is a narrowly determined index that is based on market value capitalization of ending stock prices. A base of 200 was established in 1987. Companies included in the index are Philips NV (Netherlands), Hitachi (Japan), British Petroleum (United Kingdom), Norsk Hydroelectric (Norway), Montedison (Italy), News Corporation (Australia), Banco Central (Spain), NOVO Industries (Denmark), and Volvo (Sweden).

The index will not include a foreign company's shares if its trading volume is less than 20,000, there are fewer than eight market makers for an over-the-counter issue, or the market value capitalization is less than $100 million.

Where Is It Found? Information on this index can be obtained in *Forbes*.

How Is It Used for Investment Decisions? The index indicates how foreign company stocks are performing. An investor wishing to diversify his portfolio internationally may use this index as a way to gauge the performance of overseas company stocks that trade in U.S. markets.

Also See: FOREIGN STOCK INDEXES: MORGAN STANLEY EAFE INDEX

OIL INDEX

What Is It? This is an index of the stock prices of top oil companies.

How Is It Computed? The index is a capitalized-weighted market value based on the market prices per share of 15 petroleum companies listed on the NYSE. These companies are involved in exploring, manufacturing, or developing oil products. In 1984, a base level of 125 was established. The index is heavily weighted by British Petroleum. Other petroleum companies included are Mobil, Texaco, and Royal Dutch.

Where Is It Found? The index is published by the AMEX. It can be found in brokerage research reports and petroleum industry trade publications.

How Is It Used for Investment Decisions? The investor may examine how high or low the index is as a basis for determining whether oil prices are overvalued or undervalued. This could be used as a basis for timing the purchase or sale of oil stocks. The trend in the index indicates the direction of crude oil prices.

The index is used as a price basis for settlement of petroleum option contracts.

4. ARBITRAGE

What Is It? Arbitrage is the process of simultaneously buying and selling the same securities in different markets. The investor takes advantage of the price differential of the same or comparable securities simultaneously trading on two different exchanges. The security is bought from the exchange having the higher-priced security while, at the same time, the investor sells the security on the lower-priced exchange. Brokerage commissions have to be paid on both the buy and sell. Arbitrage takes advantage of market inefficiencies while eliminating them in the process.

How Is It Computed? Arbitrage profit = $(Y_b - X_a) \times Q$

where

Y_b = Price of higher-priced comparable security on Exchange B
X_a = Price of lower-priced comparable security on Exchange A
Q = Quantity

Example: Stock ABC was trading on the NYSE for $4 per share and simultaneously trading on the London Exchange for $4.30 per share. An investor buys 10,000 shares of the stock on the NYSE and at the same time sells 10,000 shares on the London Exchange. The profit is:

Arbitrage profit = ($4.30 - $4) x 10,000 = $3,000

The arbitrage profit is $3,000 in this transaction. This transaction and similar transactions would increase the demand and therefore the price of the NYSE security while simultaneously lowering the price of the NYSE security traded on the London Exchange. This would continue until the prices of the two securities were in parity.

Where Is It Found? An investor can find the prices of a security on different exchanges by using a personal computer and telecommunications software to access an on-line database of price quotations. When price differences are noted, they must be taken advantage of instantly.

How Is It Used for Investment Decisions? The investor uses arbitrage when seeking to exploit the price variation between the same or comparable securities or commodities on two different exchanges. These opportunities exist for fleeting periods of time, and the investor must act quickly in order to take advantage of these differences.

Another arbitrage strategy is to purchase stock in a company soon to be taken over and sell the stock of the acquiring company.

Index arbitrage involves selling and simultaneously buying either a stock index or a basket of stocks making up that index. It is done when the market has "incorrectly" priced the index leaving a profit "margin" or "premium" for those willing to use this strategy. It is part of what is referred to as "program trading," where computerized systems follow indexes and execute index arbitrage when profit potential exists.

A Word of Caution: Arbitrage can result in losses if a sudden, unexpected adverse price occurs in the stock of a company.

5. ARMS INDEX (TRIN)

What Is It? The Arms Index, developed by Richard W. Arms, Jr., is a short-term trading index that offers the day trader as well as the long-term investor a look at how volume—not time—governs stock price changes. It is also commonly referred to by its quote machine symbols, TRIN and MKDS, or as just TRIN.

The Arms Index is designed to measure the relative strength of the volume associated with advancing stocks versus that of declining stocks. If more volume goes into advancing stocks than declining stocks, the Arms Index will fall to a low level under 1.00. Alternatively, if more volume flows into declining stocks than advancing stocks, the Arms Index will rise to a high level over 1.00.

It helps forecast the price changes of market indexes as well as of individual issues. You will find Arms indexes for the NYSE, the OTC market, the AMEX, and Giant Arms (a combined index for OTC and AMEX). There is also the Bond Arms Index, which helps forecast interest rates.

How Is It Computed? The Arms Index is calculated by dividing the ratio of the number of advancing issues to the number of declining issues by the ratio of the volume of advancing issues to the volume of declining issues. It is computed separately for the NYSE, the AMEX, and the National Association of Securities Dealers Automated Quotation System (NASDAQ).

Example: Using the data in Figure 4, reported in *Diaries* of the *Wall Street Journal*, TRIN is computed as follows:

Figure 4: Diaries for Arms Index (TRIN)

NYSE	THUR	WED	WK. AGO
Issues traded	2,531	2,547	2,532
Advances	1,130	1,196	597
Declines	775	761	1,412
Unchanged	626	590	523
New highs	85	93	73
New lows	15	24	16
zAdv vol (000)	166,587	238,087	105,901
zDecl vol (000)	78,016	70,598	156,632
zTotal vol (000)	279,550	340,157	289,856
Closing tick[1]	+358	+478	-329
Closing Arms[2] (trin)	.68	.47	.63
zBlock trades	6,278	7,705	6,490

Source: *Wall Street Journal*, May 21, 1993.

$$\frac{\dfrac{\text{Advances}}{\text{Declines}}}{\dfrac{\text{Advancing volume}}{\text{Declining volume}}} = \frac{1130/775}{166,587/78,016} = 0.70$$

Where Is It Found? It is found in *Barron's* and the *Wall Street Journal* and reported daily on television networks such as The Business Channel and CNBC.

A sample report is presented in Figure 5.

Figure 5: Arms Index

Daily	May 3	4	5	7
NYSE	.63	1.02	.93	1.09
AMEX	.87	.61	.47	.76
NASDAQ	.40	.40	.56	.69

Source: *Barron's*, May 10, 1993.

How Is It Used for Investment Decisions? A figure of less than 1.0 indicates that money is flowing into stocks (a bullish sign), while a ratio of greater than 1.0 shows that money is flowing out of stocks (a bearish sign).

One variation of the Arms Index that many technicians monitor is the Open 10 TRIN (also known as the Open 10 Trading Index). It is calculated by dividing a ratio of a ten-day total of the number of advancing issues to a ten-day total of the number of declining issues by a ratio of a ten-day total of the volume of advancing issues to a ten-day total of the volume of declining issues. In addition, a 30-day version of the Open 10 TRIN is frequently used.

High readings reflect an oversold condition and are generally considered bullish. Low readings reflect an overbought condition and are generally deemed bearish.

A Word of Caution: Many studies have been performed on the Arms Index with various conclusions. Many indicate that the Arms Index has relatively limited value for forecasting stock prices.

Also See: TICK AND CLOSING TICK

6. ASSET ALLOCATION

What Is It? Asset allocation measures the weighting of various types of investments in a portfolio. The changing of asset allocations is an attempt to maximize return while minimizing risks.

The calculation can be applied to professionally managed portfolios as well as to an individual's holdings. The most widely discussed asset allocation is some combination of stocks, bonds, and cash although other asset types can be used.

How Is It Computed? The mathematics can be simple. To determine his asset allocation mix, an investor can add his holdings of stocks, bonds, and cash, and divide each sum by the total value of the portfolio.

However, in today's complex investment world, determining what asset class certain investments belong to can be confusing. An investor will have to give some thought to how he allocates mixed investments such as balanced mutual funds that own both stocks and bonds or how he treats convertible securities, which are half-bond and half-stock.

The calculation can be done by hand or by using a spreadsheet software program. Personal finance software such as Meca's Managing Your Money can also help. The Dreyfus Group mutual funds and the Shearson Lehman Brothers brokerage will do the calculation for no charge.

Example: Such a grid serves as an easy way to calculate asset allocation. Figure 6 provides a filled grid as an example and a blank grid for your own use.

Figure 6: Asset Allocation Grids

INVESTMENT	(A) AMOUNT	(B) % STOCK	(C) % BOND	(D) % CASH	$ IN STOCK (A × B)	$ IN BONDS (A × C)	$ IN CASH (A × D)
BLT common	$10,000	100%	0	0	$10,000	0	0
Jaytown Balanced Fund	$15,000	60%	30%	10%	$9,000	$4,500	$1,500
Certificate of Deposit	$8,000	0	0	100%	0	0	$8,000
Burgh Water District Bond	$5,000	0	100%	0	0	$5,000	0
TOTAL	(E) $38,000				(F) $19,000	(G) $9,500	(H) $9,500
ASSET ALLOCATION					(F÷E) 50%	(G÷E) 25%	(H÷E) 25%

INVESTMENT	(A) AMOUNT	(B) % STOCK	(C) % BOND	(D) % CASH	$ IN STOCK (A × B)	$ IN BONDS (A × C)	$ IN CASH (A × D)
TOTAL	(E)				(F)	(G)	(H)
ASSET ALLOCATION					(F÷E) %	(G÷E) %	(H÷E) %

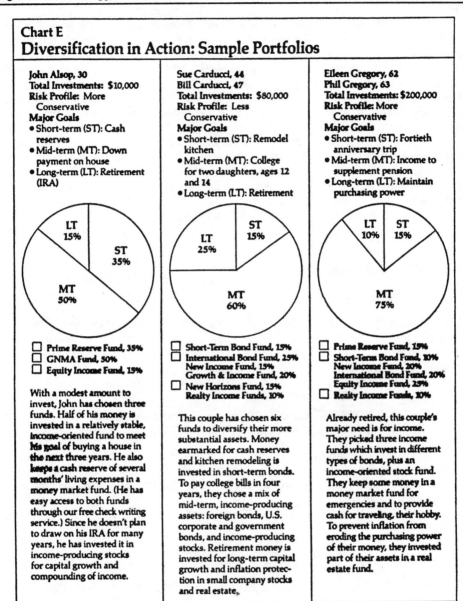

Chart E
Diversification in Action: Sample Portfolios

John Alsop, 30
Total Investments: $10,000
Risk Profile: More
  Conservative
Major Goals
- Short-term (ST): Cash
  reserves
- Mid-term (MT): Down
  payment on house
- Long-term (LT): Retirement
  (IRA)

LT 15%
ST 35%
MT 50%

☐ Prime Reserve Fund, 35%
☐ GNMA Fund, 50%
☐ Equity Income Fund, 15%

With a modest amount to invest, John has chosen three funds. Half of his money is invested in a relatively stable, income-oriented fund to meet his goal of buying a house in the next three years. He also keeps a cash reserve of several months' living expenses in a money market fund. (He has easy access to both funds through our free check writing service.) Since he doesn't plan to draw on his IRA for many years, he has invested it in income-producing stocks for capital growth and compounding of income.

Sue Carducci, 44
Bill Carducci, 47
Total Investments: $80,000
Risk Profile: Less
  Conservative
Major Goals
- Short-term (ST): Remodel
  kitchen
- Mid-term (MT): College
  for two daughters, ages 12
  and 14
- Long-term (LT): Retirement

ST 15%
LT 25%
MT 60%

☐ Short-Term Bond Fund, 15%
☐ International Bond Fund, 25%
  New Income Fund, 15%
  Growth & Income Fund, 20%
☐ New Horizons Fund, 15%
  Realty Income Funds, 10%

This couple has chosen six funds to diversify their more substantial assets. Money earmarked for cash reserves and kitchen remodeling is invested in short-term bonds. To pay college bills in four years, they chose a mix of mid-term, income-producing assets: foreign bonds, U.S. corporate and government bonds, and income-producing stocks. Retirement money is invested for long-term capital growth and inflation protection in small company stocks and real estate.

Eileen Gregory, 62
Phil Gregory, 63
Total Investments: $200,000
Risk Profile: More
  Conservative
Major Goals
- Short-term (ST): Fortieth
  anniversary trip
- Mid-term (MT): Income to
  supplement pension
- Long-term (LT): Maintain
  purchasing power

LT 10%
ST 15%
MT 75%

☐ Prime Reserve Fund, 15%
☐ Short-Term Bond Fund, 10%
  New Income Fund, 20%
  International Bond Fund, 20%
  Equity Income Fund, 25%
☐ Realty Income Funds, 10%

Already retired, this couple's major need is for income. They picked three income funds which invest in different types of bonds, plus an income-oriented stock fund. They keep some money in a money market fund for emergencies and to provide cash for traveling, their hobby. To prevent inflation from eroding the purchasing power of their money, they invested part of their assets in a real estate fund.

Source: T. Rowe Price.

Where Is It Found? Most major brokerages maintain a recommended asset allocation that is updated to keep with the investment climate (see Figure 7 above). Each quarter the *Wall Street Journal* tracks what Wall Street firms are suggesting and how the various brokerages' allocation recommendations have performed previously.

In addition, many market newsletters and money management firms also tell investors what they believe are good allocations for the times.

How Is It Used for Investment Decisions? Many professionals believe that asset allocation is among the most important decisons for investors, and many theories are applied to asset allocation selection.

One popular theory is pegged to an investor's time horizon. Longer-term portfolios can allow an investor to take on, with some comfort, more risk. That means he can increase the share allocated to stocks or real estate or other volatile investments. Changes in allocation would be likely to be made as the individual's time horizon narrows or as profits or losses change the portfolio's composition.

Another tactic is to try to time changes in asset allocation to investment market changes, hopefully, in step with market cycles. In bull markets, investors would want to be heavily into stocks, for example. When stocks are out of favor, cash, bond, or precious metal allocations would be high. There is great debate whether individuals or professionals can profitably time market swings.

Also See: *MONEY'S* SMALL INVESTOR INDEX

7. BARRON'S INDEXES

CONFIDENCE INDEX

What Is It? The index reflects the trading pattern of bond investors to determine the timing of buying or selling stock. It is generally assumed that bond traders are more knowledgeable than stock traders. Consequently, bond traders identify stock market trends sooner. The index is used in technical investment analysis.

How Is It Computed? *Barron's* Confidence Index equals:

$$\frac{\text{Yield on Barron's 10 top-grade corporate bonds}}{\text{Yield on Dow Jones 40 bond average}}$$

The numerator will have a lower yield than the denominator because it consists of higher-quality bonds (rated AAA or AA). Some high-quality bonds are those of AT&T, General Electric, and Procter & Gamble. The lower the risk of default, the lower the return rate is.

Assume the Dow Jones yield is 8% and the *Barron's* yield is 7%. The Confidence Index is:

$$\frac{7\%}{8\%} = .875 = 87.5\%$$

Where Is It Found? The index is published weekly in *Barron's*. See Figure 8.

Figure 8: *Barron's* **Confidence Index**

Confidence Index (High-grade index divided by intermediate-grade index; decline in latter vs. former generally indicates rising confidence, pointing to higher stocks.)

92.8	92.8	93.9

Source: *Barron's*, August 31, 1992.

How Is It Used and Applied? Because top-quality bonds have lower yields than lower-grade bonds, the index will be below 100%. Typically, the trading range is between 80% to 95%. When bond investors are bullish, yield differences between the high-grade bonds and low-grade bonds will be small. In such cases, the index may be close to 95%.

If the feeling is bearish, bond market investors will want to hold top-quality isssues. Some investors who continue to put their money in average- or lower-quality bonds will want a high yield for the increased risk. The Confidence Index will then decline, since the denominator will be getting larger. If confidence is high, investors are apt to purchase lower-grade bonds. As a result, the yield on high-grade bonds will decrease while the yield on low-grade bonds will increase.

How Is It Used for Investment Decisions? If an investor knows what bond traders are doing now, he or she may predict what stock traders will be doing in the future. The lead time between the Confidence Index and economic conditions and stock market performance is considered to be several months. This leaves ample time for an investment decision.

If bond traders are bullish, an investor may invest in stocks now before stock prices rise. On the other hand, if bond traders are bearish, an investor would not buy stocks or consider selling current holdings on the expectation that stock prices will fall.

A Word of Caution: Bond traders may be making the wrong investment decision, which could result in misleading inferences as to stock prices. The Confidence Index has a mixed track record in predicting the future. The index is deficient in that it considers investors' attitudes only on yields (demand function). It ignores the supply of new bond issues (supply pattern) as they affect yields. A large bond issue by a major corporation, for example, may result in increased high-grade bond yields. Such movement would occur despite prevailing investor attitudes that yields should be dropping.

50-STOCK AVERAGE

What Is It? *Barron's* 50-Stock Average is an unweighted average of 50 leading NYSE-listed issues, 20 of which are components of the Dow Jones 65-Stock Composite Average. The 50 comprise 42 industrial, 5 transportation, and 3 public utility stocks.

How Is It Computed? Each stock is given equal weight in determining the average. It is an unweighted price average—calculated from the closing prices each Thursday—that includes both earnings and dividends of the 50 issues, and assumes that the same dollar investment is made in each component company instead of one share of each company.

Therefore, for example, although Merck's price is higher than most, a 5% move would have no more effect on the 50-Stock Average than a 5% move in a lower-priced stock.

Where Is It Found? It is found in *Barron's*. A sample is presented in Figure 9.

How Is It Used for Investment Decisions? The main value of this index is that it offers comparisons to projected quarterly and annual earnings. This average is intended to be used as a yardstick in deciding whether the market at any given time is reasonably priced, overvalued, or undervalued in view of what the investor believes to be the most probable course of the business cycle.

A Word of Caution: Like the Dow Jones Industrial Average, it is not a broad market index. It should not be interpreted as such.

Also See: DOW JONES INDUSTRIAL AVERAGE

Figure 9: *Barron's* 50-Stock Average

	May 6 1993	Apr. 29 1993	May 1992
Average price index	1864	1850	1769
Projected quarterly earn	20.33	20.33	18.75
Annualized projected earn	81.32	61.32	75.00
Annualized projected P/E	22.9	22.7	23.6
Five-year average earn	95.73	95.73	99.80
Five-year average P/E	19.5	19.3	17.7
Year-end earn	78.11	78.11	71.25
Year-end P/E	23.9	23.7	24.8
Year-end earns yield, %	4.2	4.2	4.0
Best grade bond yields, %	7.33	7.34	8.34
Bond yields/stock ylds, %	1.75	1.75	2.08
Actual year-end, divs	51.53	51.53	49.86
Actual yr-end divs, yld, %	2.76	2.78	2.81

Source: *Barron's*, May 10, 1993.

LOW-PRICED STOCK INDEX

What Is It? *Barron's* low-priced index is a weekly index of a group of 20 more speculative, poorer-quality low-priced stocks that tend to vacillate more in price than the blue chip stocks that comprise the Dow averages. Twelve of the issues are on the NYSE and eight are on the AMEX.

How Is It Computed? The index is market-value-capitalization-weighted.

Where Is It Found? It is found in *Barron's* under the column heading Trading Activity.

How Is It Used for Investment Decisions? The investor should track the index to determine if the risk-return tradeoff justifies investing in speculative securities. Perhaps the potential return justifies the increased risk. A comparison should be made over time of speculative versus quality issues.

A Word of Caution: What is considered speculative is judgmental and subjective. Furthermore, a speculative issue in one year may not be speculative next year.

8. BETA FOR A MUTUAL FUND

What Is It? Beta is a measure of uncontrollable risk that results from forces outside the mutual fund's control. Purchasing power, interest rate, and market risks fall into this category. This type of risk is measured by *beta*.

How Is It Computed? In measuring a fund's beta, an indication is needed of the relationship between the fund's return and the market return (such as the return on the Standard & Poor's 500 Stock Index). This relationship is statistically computed, which is not covered here.

Where Is It Found? Betas for mutual (stock) funds are widely available in many investment publications and directories. Examples are *Business Week, Forbes, Fortune, The Individual Investor's Guide to No-load Mutual Funds, Lipper Analytical Service's Report, Money, Morningstar Mutual Funds, S & P's Stock Guide,* and *Wiesenberger Investment Service's Report.* Financial advisory services such as Morningstar and Lipper Analytical Service, which are widely subscribed to, provide their own risk-adjusted rating systems developed based on beta and return. A sample report is presented in Figure 10 on pages 16-17.

How Is It Used and Applied? Beta measures a stock fund's volatility relative to an average fund. In assessing the risk or instability of a mutual fund, beta is widely used. Beta shows how volatile a mutual fund is compared with the market as a whole, as measured by the Standard & Poor's 500 index of the most widely held stocks.

For example, if the S&P goes up 10% and an investor's fund increases in the same period, the fund has a beta of 1. But if the fund goes up 20%, it has a beta of 2, meaning that it is twice as volatile as the market. The higher the beta, the greater the risk.

Beta	What It Means
1.0	A fund moves up and down just as much as the market.
>1.0	The fund tends to climb higher in bull markets and dip lower in bear markets than the S&P index.
<1.0	The fund is less volatile (risky) than the market.

How Is It Used for Investment Decisions? Beta of a particular fund is useful for predicting how much the fund will go up or down, provided that investors know the direction of the market. Beta helps to figure out risk and expected (required) return.
Expected (required) return = risk-free rate + beta x (market return - risk-free rate)

The higher the beta for a fund, the greater the return expected (or demanded) by the investor.

Example: XYZ Fund actually returned 25%. The risk-free rate (for example, a return on a T-bill) = 6%, market return (for example, return on the S&P 500) = 12%, and XYZ's beta = 2. The return on the XYZ Fund required by an investor would then be
Expected (required) return= 6% + 2 (12% - 6%) = 6% + 12% = 18%.

Since the actual return (25%) is significantly above the required return (18%), an investor would be willing to buy the shares of the fund.

A Word of Caution: An investor should cover at least three years of beta to get an accurate idea about the risk and instability of the fund.

Beta should be considered along with other selection criteria such as net asset value (NAV), alpha, R-squared, and standard deviation.

Also See: LIPPER MUTUAL FUND RANKINGS, MUTUAL FUNDS: ALPHA FOR A MUTUAL FUND, MUTUAL FUNDS: NET ASSET VALUE, MUTUAL FUNDS: R-SQUARED, MUTUAL FUNDS: STANDARD DEVIATION, TOTAL RETURN

9. BETA FOR A SECURITY

What Is It? Many investors hold more than one financial asset. The portion of a security's risk (called unsystematic risk) can be controlled through diversification. Unsystematic risk is unique to a given security. Nondiversifiable risk, more commonly referred to as systematic risk, results from forces outside of the company's control and are

Vista Growth & Income

Objective Growth/Inc.	Load 4.75%	Yield 1.1%	SEC Yield 0.89%	Assets ($mil) 575.1	NAV 30.11

Vista Growth and Income Fund seeks long-term capital appreciation; current income is secondary.

The fund normally invests at least 80% of its assets in common stocks with a broad range of capitalization. The fund selects common stocks that are currently out of favor with investors. These undervalued securities display relatively low P/E ratios, low ratios of market price to book value, or underlying asset values that are not fully reflected in the current market price.

The fund does not apply a sales charge on purchases made in a fiduciary capacity and certain transactions effected by an investment advisor.

Historical Profile

Return:	High
Risk:	Below Avg
Rating:	★★★★ Highest

Performance

Relative Strength

Load-Adj Return
1 Yr	16.65
5 Yr	25.63
10 Yr	...

Alpha	8.9
Beta	1.05
R²	71
Std Dev	16.00
Mean	20.60
Sharpe Ratio	1.00

Performance Quartile (Within Objective)

Total Returns

	1st Qtr	2nd Qtr	3rd Qtr	4th Qtr	Total
1987	...	...	...	0.00	...
1988	7.22	24.92	6.59	-1.88	40.08
1989	9.05	17.75	14.26	6.91	56.85
1990	3.38	8.93	-13.65	3.01	0.17
1991	33.98	1.82	8.45	7.52	59.07
1992	5.95	-3.13	2.33	9.60	15.11
1993	5.71	3.30	...	...	...

Income — Paid Quarterly

	1st Qtr	2nd Qtr	3rd Qtr	4th Qtr	Total
1991	0.07	0.03	0.06	0.07	0.23
1992	0.06	0.10	0.08	0.08	0.32
1993	0.08	0.09	...	...	0.17

Capital Gains — Paid Annually

	1st Qtr	2nd Qtr	3rd Qtr	4th Qtr	Total
1991	0.00	0.00	0.00	1.59	1.59
1992	0.00	0.00	0.00	0.62	0.62
1993	0.00	0.00	...	...	0.00

Performance/Risk: 06/30/93

	Total Return %	+/- S&P 500	% Rank All	% Rank Obj	Growth of $10,000
3 Mo	3.30	2.83	35	7	10,330
6 Mo	9.20	4.33	22	12	10,920
1 Yr	22.47	8.86	12	4	12,247

History

	1982	1983	1984	1985	1986	1987	1988	1989	1990	1991	1992	06/93
NAV	...	...	...	...	...	10.00	12.67	18.02	16.83	24.93	27.73	30.11
Total Return %	...	...	...	...	...	...	40.08	56.85	0.17	59.07	15.11	9.20
+/- S&P 500	...	...	...	...	...	...	23.47	25.16	3.28	28.59	7.49	4.33
Income Return	...	...	...	...	...	...	2.62	5.05	3.66	1.05	1.28	0.62
Capital Return	...	...	...	...	...	...	37.46	51.80	-3.50	58.02	13.82	8.58
Total Rtn % Rank All Funds								1	54	5	10	22
% Rank Objective							1	1	16	2	10	12
Income						0.00	0.32	0.71	0.66	0.23	0.32	0.17
Capital Gains						0.00	1.02	1.06	0.57	1.59	0.62	0.00
Expense Ratio							0.00	0.00	1.09	1.25	1.43	1.39
Income Ratio							2.64	4.56	3.65	1.24	1.19	1.02
Turnover Rate							109	319	160	103	56	...
Net Assets ($mil)							1.2	9.1	18.9	45.4	190.2	575.1

Portfolio — Total Stocks: 130 as of 04/30/93

Investment Style

	Portfolio Average	Relative S&P
Price/Earnings Ratio	18.8	0.95
Price/Book Ratio	2.8	0.81
5-Yr Earnings Gr %	5.7	0.83
Return on Assets	4.7	0.68
Debt % Total Cap	42.3	1.23
Med Mkt Cap ($mil)	3976	0.30

3 Yr Avg	21.15	9.72	3	1	17,784
5 Yr Avg	26.86	12.65	1	1	32,053
10 Yr Avg	...				
15 Yr Avg	...				

	Mstar Risk % Rank		Mstar Return	Mstar Risk	Mstar Risk-Adj Rating
	All	Obj	1.00 = Equity Average		
3 Yr	72	80	2.11	0.84	★★★★
5 Yr	60	27	2.82	0.70	★★★★★
10 Yr	...				

Percentile Ranks: 1=highest, 100=lowest
Except Mstar Risk: 1=lowest, 100=highest

Style: Size Large/Med/Small — Style Value/Blend/Growth

Average Historical Rating: 4.9 ★s over 34 months

Analysis by Jennifer Newport 07/09/93

Vista Growth and Income Fund has a program for success.

This fund has posted astounding long-term results following the direction of its quantitative stock-ranking model. The model ranks about 1600 stocks according to five valuation measures, three earnings-momentum considerations, and a macro-economic model. The proprietary measures are weighted equally because, while it's easy to look at which factors have been the best at finding good stocks in the past, it's impossible to tell which will be the best in the future, says manager Mark Tincher.

The model doesn't do it all, though. Tincher takes a closer look at the fundamentals of the stocks that make up the model's top 20%. In addition to relative value and strong earnings growth, Tincher also looks for an earnings catalyst. For example, the fund has recently added Tribune Company. The stock is cheap, and the firm has restructured, which included getting out of the unprofitable Canadian newsprint business. Tincher also adds a top-down spin, emphasizing industries that are experiencing above-average earnings growth. He currently favors finance, technology, and capital goods.

Under Tincher's watchful eye, the model's blend of growth and value has allowed the fund's returns to soar in a variety of market environments. The fund has shown great performance both in growth-oriented years, such as 1989 and 1991, and when value has been in favor, as in 1988. Even when market favor flip-flopped between styles, as in 1992, this fund has landed near the top.

Overall, this fund's results have been outstanding—both before and since Tincher came aboard in late 1991. For the trailing five years this fund has racked up the highest annualized total returns of any fund in Morningstar's database: an amazing feat for a below-average-risk vehicle.

Address	Vista Service Center P.O. Box 419392
	Kansas City, MO 64179
Telephone	800-348-4782
Portfolio Manager	Mark A. Tincher (9/91)
Advisor	Chase Manhattan Bank
Subadvisor	None
Distributor	Vista Broker-Dealer Services
Ticker	VGRIX
States Available	All

Sales Fees	4.75%L, 0.25%B, 0.10%A
Management Fee	0.40% flat fee
3-,5-,10-yr Expense Projections	$90, $121, $209
Annual Brokerage Cost	0.28%
Min IRA Purchase	$2500 (Addt'l: $25)
Min Auto Invest Plan	$250
Shareholder Report Grade	$500
Date of Inception	B
	09/23/87

Share Change (10/92)	Amount	Stock	Value $000	% Net Assets
100000	100000	TRIBUNE	5475	1.34
40000	70000	FNMA	5434	1.33
125000	125000	CHRYSLER	5156	1.26
100000	175000	GENERAL MOTORS CL H	4878	1.19
240000	300000	SANTA FE PACIFIC	4763	1.16
30000	60000	CAPITAL HOLDING	4733	1.16
100000	100000	TEXTRON	4700	1.15
65000	100000	FIRST UNION	4625	1.13
70000	90000	APPLE COMPUTER	4613	1.13
100000	100000	PRIMERICA	4600	1.12
80000	100000	FIRST FIDELITY BANCORP (NJ)	4488	1.10
20000	200000	TYSON FOODS CL A	4450	1.09
180000	180000	ECHLIN	4433	1.08
60000	110000	WR GRACE	4318	1.06
55000	100000	SUNDSTRAND	4200	1.03
120000	150000	RYDER SYSTEM	4163	1.02
65000	100000	TRITON ENERGY	4088	1.00
35000	75000	WHIRLPOOL	4088	1.00
75000	75000	BANK OF NEW YORK	4031	0.99
20000	60000	ALLIEDSIGNAL	3915	0.96
75000	75000	PARAMOUNT COMMUNICATIONS	3900	0.95
125000	125000	SPRINT	3875	0.95
42500	50000	GOODYEAR TIRE & RUBBER	3731	0.91
100000	100000	REEBOK INTERNATIONAL	3663	0.90
45000	50000	MOTOROLA	3650	0.89

Stock Exchange/Index Allocation
% of equity assets in:

NYSE	86.6
AMEX	0.8
NASDAQ	9.6
Foreign	3.0

Dow 30	8.1
S&P 500	75.6
S&P Mid-Cap 400	14.4
U.S. Small Cap	8.1

Composition % as of 03/31/93

Cash	6.2	Preferreds	1.0
Stocks	79.8	Convertibles	2.6
Bonds	10.4	Other	0.0

Sector Weightings

	Portfolio %	Relative S&P
Utilities	9.7	0.65
Energy	9.0	0.87
Financials	16.4	1.51
Industrial Cyclicals	16.3	1.44
Consumer Durables	16.0	2.25
Consumer Staples	3.6	0.29
Services	9.4	1.21
Retail	4.9	0.65
Health	3.1	0.39
Technology	11.7	1.19

Tax Analysis

	Tax-Adj Historical Return	% Pre-Tax Return
3 Yr Avg	19.21	90.8
5 Yr Avg	23.97	89.3
10 Yr Avg	...	...

Estimated Current Tax Liability (% of assets): 9%

449

Source: Reprinted by permission of Morningstar, Inc., Chicago, IL.

therefore not unique to the given security. Purchasing power, interest rate, and market risks fall into this category. This type of risk is measured by beta.

How Is It Computed? In measuring an asset's beta, an indication is needed of the relationship between the asset's return and the market return (such as the return on the Standard & Poor's 500 Stock Index). This relationship is statistically computed, which is beyond the scope of this book.

Where Is It Found? Betas for stocks are widely available in many investment newsletters and directories. Examples are *Value Line Investment Survey* and *S&P's Stock Guide*. Figure 11 shows a list of some selected betas.

Figure 11: Selected Betas

Companies	Betas
Apple Computer	1.25
Bristol-Meyers	1.00
IBM	0.95
Neiman-Marcus	1.65
Mead Corporation	1.45
Mobil Corporation	0.85

Source: *Value Line Investment Survey*, October 8, 1992.

How Is It Used for Investment Decisions? Beta measures a security's volatility relative to an average security. Put another way, it is a measure of a security's return over time to that of the overall market.

For example, if ABC's beta is 2.0, if the stock market goes up 10%, ABC's common stock will go up 20%. If the market goes down 10%, ABC will go down 20%.

Here is a guide for how to read betas:

Beta	What It Means
0	The security's return is independent of the market. An example is a risk-free security such as a T-bill.
0.5	The security is only half as responsive as the market.
1.0	The security has the same responsiveness or risk as the market (*i.e.*, average risk). This is the beta value of the market portfolio such as Standard & Poor's 500.
2.0	The security is twice as responsive, or risky, as the market.

Beta of a particular stock is useful in predicting how much the security will go up or down, provided that investors know which way the market will go. Beta helps to figure out risk and expected (required) return.

Expected (required) return = Risk-free rate + beta x (market return - risk-free rate)

The higher the beta for a security, the greater the return expected (or demanded) by the investor.

Example: ABC stock actually returned 8%. Assume that the risk-free rate (for example, the return on a T-bill) is 5.5%, market return (for example, the return on the S&P 500) is 9%, and ABC's beta is 1.2. The return on ABC stock required by investors would then be:

Expected (required) return $= 5.5\% + 1.2 \, (9\% - 5.5\%)$
$$= 5.5\% + 4.2\%$$
$$= 9.7\%$$

Since the actual return (8%) is less than the required return (9.7%), an investor would not be willing to buy the stock.

A Word of Caution: An investor should look at beta for at least three years to determine the stability of the security.

Beta should be considered along with other selection criteria such as dividend yield, earnings growth, and price-earnings (P/E) ratio.

Also See: BETA FOR A MUTUAL FUND, *INVESTOR'S BUSINESS DAILY'S* "INTELLIGENT" TABLES, SHARE PRICE RATIOS: PRICE-EARN-EINGS MULTIPLE RATIO, YIELD ON AN INVESTMENT: DIVIDEND PAYOUT RATIO

10. BOND MARKET INDEXES

BOND BUYER INDEXES

What Are They? *The Bond Buyer* is a daily newspaper that principally covers the municipal bond market. It publishes several benchmark averages for the municipal bond market. Its two best known indexes are its "40" and "20" indexes.

How Are They Computed? The Bond Buyer 40 consists of 40 actively traded, higher-rated general obligation, municipal bonds of varying maturities. Each bond's price is converted through a complex formula to find at what price the bond would yield 8 %. The 40 converted prices are then averaged and put through another "conversion" designed to account for changes made in the index over the years.

The Bond Buyer 20 is an index that tracks the average prices of 20 higher-rated municipal bonds that have 20-year maturities.

Where Are They Found? The indexes appear in *Barron's*, the *Bond Buyer* and the *Wall Street Journal*. See Figure 12 for one example.

Figure 12: Tax-Exempt Securities

High	Low	(12-mos)	Close	Net Chg	% Chg	12-mos	% Chg	from 12/31	% Chg
103-8	93-13	Bond Buyer Municipal	100-18 +	-1 +	-.03 +	4-8 +	4.41 +	2-28 +	2.94
161.70	140.23	New 10-yr G.O. *(AA)	158.35 +	0.63 +	0.40 +	17.20 +	12.19 +	7.79 +	5.17
176.93	145.89	New 20-yr G.O. *(AA)	173.62 +	1.06 +	0.61 +	25.42 +	17.15 +	14.30 +	8.98
201.56	168.01	New 30-yr revenue *(A)	197.59 +	1.39 +	0.71 +	28.68 +	16.98 +	16.63 +	9.19

Source: *Wall Street Journal*, May 21, 1993. *Merril Lynch Indexes.

How Are They Used for Investment Decisions? Investors can look to these indexes for a measurement of how prices of municipal bonds are moving. This is an often underwatched area because many investors buy municipal bonds strictly for their yields and credit ratings.

Rising indexes are a bullish sign for those investors motivated to maximize their total return—both principal appreciation as well as coupon yields. Conversely, a falling index may indicate that the bond's tax-free status may not be worth the risk.

A Word of Caution: The municipal bond market is very fragmented with hundreds of very small issues, many with peculiar characteristics. Thus, analysts say that it is difficult for any one index to prove to be a good benchmark.

In addition, the municipal bond market can have wide price swings between trading houses for the same bond. To correct that, *The Bond Buyer* surveys five dealer institutions to obtain an average price for each of the issues in its Bond Buyer 40.

DOW JONES BOND AVERAGES

What Is It? This is an average of bond prices for major industrial companies and utilities.

How Is It Computed? The bond average is based on 20 bonds and represents an equal number of industrials and utilities. There is also a separate average for each of the industrial and utility bonds (10 each). It is a simple arithmetic average based on ending market prices of the bonds. Some utilities included in the average are Consolidated Edison, Philadelphia Electric, and American Telephone and Telegraph. Some industrials are Ford Motor, General Electric, and Eastman Kodak. Figure 13 shows the components of the Dow Jones Bond Average.

Figure 13: Components—Dow Jones 20 Bond Average

Public Utilities (10)			Industrials (10)		
Name	Coupon	Maturity	Name	Coupon	Maturity
Alabama Pwr	9 3/4%	2004	BankAm	7 7/8%	2003
Comwlth Ed	8 3/4%	2005	Beth Steel	6 7/8%	1999
Cons Ed	7.9%	2001	Champion Intl	6 1/2%	2011
Detroit Edison	9%	1999	Eastman Kodak	8 5/8%	2016
Duke Power	8 1/8%	2007	Exxon	6%	1997
Duquesne Light	8 3/8%	2007	General Elec	8 1/2%	2004
Ill Bell Tel	8%	2004	GM Accept	10 3/8%	1995
Mich Bell	7%	2012	IBM	9 3/8%	2004
Pac G&E	7 3/4%	2005	Pep Boys	6%	2011
Phil Elec	8 3/8%	2001	Union Carbide	7 1/2%	2012

Source: *Barron's*, August 31, 1992.

Where Is It Found? The average is published in *Barron's* and the *Wall Street Journal* and also is available via Prodigy and Dow Jones News/Retrieval on-line database services.

Figure 14 is a listing of the Dow Jones 20 Bond Average as it appears in *Barron's*. Figure 15 on page 21 shows the Dow Jones Bond Averages from *Barron's*.

Figure 14: Dow Jones 20 Bond Average

High and low range for the Dow Jones 20 Bond Average

Year	High	Date	Low	Date
1992	102.43	Aug. 14	98.41	Mar. 20
1991	98.93	Dec. 31	91.30	Jan. 16
1990	93.04	Jan. 3	88.44	Sept. 24
1989	94.15	Aug. 2	87.35	Mar. 23
1988	91.25	Mar. 3	86.92	Jan. 4
1987	95.51	Feb. 9	81.26	Oct. 19
1986	93.65	Dec. 19	83.73	Jan. 14
1985	83.73	Dec. 30	72.27	Mar. 20
1984	72.92	Dec. 30	64.81	May 30

Source: *Barron's*, August 31, 1992.

How Is It Used for Investment Decisions? As interest rates decrease, bond prices increase because investors withdraw their money from bank accounts and place it in bonds.

The bond average gives the investor a clue as to how corporate bonds are performing in the marketplace on which he can base an intelligent investment decision. If bond prices seem very low and the investor expects as upward movement, bonds may be bought.

Also See: BOND RATINGS, YIELD CURVE, YIELD TO MATURITY

Figure 15: Dow Jones Bond Averages

Dow Jones Bond Averages

	4/26	4/27	4/28	4/29	4/30
20 Bonds	106.89	106.89	106.81	106.89	107.23
10 Util	104.05	104.18	104.21	104.05	103.98
10 Ind	109.74	109.61	109.51	109.73	110.49

Dow Jones Weekly Bond Averages

	First	High	Low	Last	Chg.
20 Bonds	106.89	107.23	106.81	107.23 +	.35
10 Util	104.05	104.21	103.98	103.98 −	.13
10 Ind	109.74	110.49	109.51	110.49 +	.84

Dow Jones Bond Averages for 1993

	First	High	Low	Last	Chg.	%
20Bds	103.74	107.23	103.49	107.23 +	3.34	+ 3.21
10Util	102.48	104.34	102.30	103.98 +	1.34	+ 1.31
10Ind	104.99	110.49	104.58	110.49 +	5.35	+ 5.09

Source: *Barron's*, May 3, 1993. Reprinted by permission of *Barron's*, ©1993 Dow Jones & Company, Inc. All Rights Reserved Worldwide.

LEHMAN BROS. TREASURY BOND INDEX

What Is It? The index gauges market performance of U.S. Treasury bonds and notes.

How Is It Computed? The bond index is weighted based on current market values. There are two components of the index comprised of the Intermediate Treasury Index and the Long Treasury Index. The former consists of U.S. Treasury issues with maturities of less than ten years while the latter is comprised of issues with maturities of ten years or more. A base value of 100 was assigned in 1980.

Where Is It Found? The indexes can be found in *Barron's* and the *Wall Street Journal*. Bond market information is published in the *Wall Street Journal* under the Bond Market Data Bank column.

How Is It Used for Investment Decisions? A conservative investor who wants to protect his principal by buying U.S. guaranteed obligations but is willing to take temporary price risk may find U.S. Treasury securities attractive. The investor can compare the performance of U.S. Treasury notes and bonds to alternative investments.

MOODY'S BOND INDEXES

What Are They? The indexes apply to bonds issued by companies and government. There are bond averages determined for Corporate Composite, Industrial , Public Utility, and Railroad—Aa, A, and Baa.

How Are They Computed? The Moody's Corporate Bond Index is on a total return, price-weighted basis. It includes more than 75 nonconvertible, coupon corporate bonds. These taxable bonds mature in no more than five years. Price information for $1 million transactions are obtained from bond dealers. The base level of 100 was established in 1979.

Where Are They Found? Index and average information can be obtained from Moody's Investors Service and *Barron's*. Figure 16 shows bond rating changes for Moody's as they appeared in *Barron's*.

How Are They Used for Investment Decisions? The investor can use bond average and index information to determine the performance of bonds and bond mutual funds. If bonds have been doing well and they are expected to continue doing so, the bonds may be bought.

Also See: BOND MARKET INDEXES: DOW JONES BOND AVERAGES, BOND MARKET INDEXES: SALOMON BROTHERS BROAD INVESTMENT-GRADE BOND INDEX, BOND MARKET INDEXES: STANDARD & POOR'S JUNK BOND INDEXES

RYAN LABS TREASURY INDEX

What Is It? The Ryan Index is an unweighted average of total return based on the prices of the most recently auctioned Treasury notes and bonds with maturities of two years to 30 years. It was developed by the Ryan Financial Strategies Group and is made up of the current 2-, 3-, 4-, 5-, 7-, 10-, and 30-year Treasury issues that are auctioned by the Treasury on a periodic schedule. Newly auctioned Treasury notes have maturities that range from 2 to 10 years; Treasury bonds have 30-year maturities.

Figure 16: Moody's Bond Rating Changes

	Moody's	
UPGRADE	*FROM*	*TO*
First Interstate Bancorp		
euro, note, med-term note	Baa2	Baa1
sub note, convert sub deb	Baa3	Baa2
pref stk	baa3	baa2
New York State Elec & Gas		
1st mrt bd	Baa1	A3
unsec rev bd	Baa2	Baa1
DOWNGRADE	*FROM*	*TO*
Cleveland Electric Illum		
pref stk	baa2	baa3
Coca-Cola Co.		
Euro, note, med-term note	Aa2	Aa3
Wang Laboratories Inc.		
conv. sub. deb.	Caa	Ca
conv sub Swiss bd	Caa	Ca

Source: *Barron's*.

How Is It Computed? Price and income return are calculated for each maturity on the basis of market price changes and actual accrued interest. Each of the seven activematurities comprises a subindex. These are averaged to obtain the composite Ryan Index level, whose base level was set at 100 on December 31, 1979.

Where Is It Found? It is published weekly in *Barron's*. A sample report is presented in Figure 17.

Figure 17: Ryan Labs Treasury Index

Apr.	26	439.61
	27	437.70
	28	437.57
	29	438.81
	30	437.67

Source: *Barron's*, May 3, 1993.

How Is It Used for Investment Decisions? The index should be compared with similar indexes for different securities (such as Lipper convertible securities indexes) for yield comparisons.

A Word of Caution: When comparing indexes, the investor should note the difference in the base period. The detection of a trend is important.

SALOMON BROTHERS BROAD INVESTMENT-GRADE BOND INDEX

What Is It? This is a comprehensive index of bond prices for securities that have a minimum value of $25 million. It is the key benchmark to gauge a money manager's performance in the bond market.

How Is It Computed? The index reflects the total return rate earned on corporate, mortgage, and Treasury securities with a maturity of 1 year or more.

Total return = Capital appreciation (depreciation) + interest.

The index includes about 3,750 mortgages and bonds predominantly comprised of corporate issues. The index is updated monthly for changes in its component issues and revised bond ratings.

Its base value of 100 was assigned in 1979.

Where Is It Found? The index is published in the Salomon Brothers publications that track bond issues.

How Is It Used for Investment Decisions? The index indicates how well bonds are doing overall in the marketplace. A low index may indicate that poor returns are currently being earned and may signal a time to reallocate funds out of bonds and into a higher return alternative. On the other hand, a low index may indicate the time to buy bonds at a low price with the expectation of selling when prices are higher.

Also See: BOND MARKET INDEXES: MOODY'S BOND INDEXES, BOND MARKET INDEXES: SALOMON GOVERNMENT/CORPORATE YIELD SPREAD, STANDARD & POOR'S GOVERNMENT BOND AVERAGES AND INDEXES

SALOMON GOVERNMENT/CORPORATE YIELD SPREAD

What Is It? The index compares yields earned on government bonds and corporate bonds of the same maturity. Further, a yield comparison may be made separately for short-term, intermediate-term, and long-term government and corporate bonds.

How Is It Computed? Yield spread on similar maturity bond =

Yield on corporate bond - yield on government bond

Example 1: If the yields on corporate bonds and government bonds are 7% and 6% respectively, the yield spread is 1%.

Where Is It Found? The yield spread is published in *Barron's* and Salomon Brothers publications.

How Is It Used for Investment Decisions? The yield spread is the difference between the returns to maturity on government and corporate bonds. Government bonds have no default risk while corporate bonds do have default risk. Therefore, a wider yield spread indicates greater default risk with the corporate security. Further, the longer the maturity of a bond, the greater the uncertainty and, consequently, the greater the yield may be.

Example 2: Let us assume that the yield spread on similar maturity long-term government and corporate bonds is normally 2%. Yet for the current period this spread has widened to 5%. There will be a tendency to regress to narrow the range. The wide spread in this example could indicate a buying opportunity for corporate bonds. It is likely the gap will narrow in one of three ways: (1) corporate rates will go down while government rates remain flat; (2) corporate rates will go down while government rates will increase; or (3) corporate rates will remain flat while government rates rise. As a result, the corporate bonds will outperform the government bonds on a total return basis. In this example, the investment strategy is to buy corporate bonds and sell government bonds.

STANDARD & POOR'S GOVERNMENT BOND AVERAGES AND INDEXES

What Are They? Indexes and averages are provided for U.S. Treasury bonds in terms of yield and price. They include long-term, intermediate-term, and short-term Government Yield Averages as well as Prices Indexes.

How Are They Computed? Long-term issues for the yield average and price index are 10 years and 15 years, respectively. Intermediate-term issues for the yield average and price index are 6 to 9 years and 7.5 years, respectively. Short-term issues for the yield average and price index are 2 to 4 years and 3.5 years, respectively.

The yield average is the arithmetic average of four typical issues.

Where Are They found? Price and yield indexes are found in *Barron's* and the *Wall Street Journal*.

How Are They Used for Investment Decisions? Government Bond Price and Yield Averages are important in investment decisions of whether to buy or sell government issues, and if so which type (short-term, intermediate-term, or long-term). The index information will indicate what return the investor can expect on his money and whether that rate of return is attractive.

Also See: BOND MARKET INDEXES: SALOMON BROTHERS BROAD INVEST-MENT-GRADE BOND INDEX

STANDARD & POOR'S JUNK BOND INDEXES

What Are They? Junk bonds are high-risk, high-return corporate bonds. They are considered poor quality with substantial gain potential. There are two Standard & Poor's indexes of junk bonds—BB–rated and B–rated.

How Are They Computed? The BB Rated Junk Bond Index represents the average yield of six BB rated bonds. These bond components include Union Carbide 8 1/2% debentures due in 2005 and Bally's Grand 11 1/2% notes due in 1996.

The B Rated Junk Bond Index looks at the average yield of seven B rated bonds including Armco's 9.2% debentures due in 2000 and Colt Industries 12 1/2% debentures due in 2001.

The indexes were started in 1988.

Where Are They found? These indexes are published in *Investor's Business Daily*.

How Are They Used for Investment Decisions? The indexes measure the performance of junk bonds. An investor willing to assume substantial risk may invest in junk bonds to achieve high return. However, significant losses may occur.

The indexes can be used to compare yields on individual issues of like-quality to the average.

Also See: BOND MARKET INDEXES: BOND BUYER INDEXES, BOND MARKET INDEXES: SALOMON BROTHERS JUNK BOND INDEXES

11. BOND RATINGS

What Are They? Bonds and preferred stock issues are rated by various agencies for investment safety.

The major agencies are Standard & Poor's of New York, Moody's of New York, Fitch of New York, and Duff & Phelps of Chicago. These firms' analysts weigh the probability that interest payments will continue and the chances for repayment of principal.

Ratings help investors evaluate risks and aid the market in setting prices for various securities. Higher-rated securities attract more investors and thus trade at higher prices with lower yields. Low-rated paper, in turn, comes with lower prices and loftier yields.

How Are They Computed? Each rating agency has different criteria and scales to weigh the credit risks of various securities. Bond and preferred stock issues are rated at initial offerings and then reviewed on a regular basis and after major economic events hit the issuer. Many rating systems' reviews, resulting in the bond rating, parallel grade-school gradings—A's are the best and C's and D's are the worst. All ratings assume that securities of the U.S. Treasury, in other words those that are backed by the full faith and credit of the U.S. government, warrant the highest rating for credit safety. Figure 18 shows how the rating systems of the two largest agencies, S&P and Moody's, compare (Moody's uses the numbers 1 through 3 to denote quality levels within a ranking; S&P uses pluses or minuses).

Where Are They Found? All the agencies publish their ratings on a regularly. Credit ratings are also an important part of brokerage reports and commentary on interest-bearing

Figure 18: S&P and Moody's Rating Systems

CREDIT RISK	MOODY'S	S&P
Prime	Aaa	AAA
Excellent	Aa	AA
Upper medium	A-1, A	A
Lower medium	Baa-1, Baa	BBB
Speculative	Ba	BB
Very speculative	B, Caa	B,CCC,CC
Default	Ca, C	D

investments. *Barron's* publishes a weekly update on credit-rating changes (see Figure 16, page 23).

How Are They Used for Investment Decisions? Investors can use credit ratings to help match their risk tolerance to their fixed-income investments.

Those investors who prefer high safety to higher yields should choose securities with credit gradings near the top of the scale. Those who can stand some degree of credit risks, often have their risk-taking rewarded with higher yields.

In addition, the overall level of rating changes is seen as one indicator of the nation's economic health. Each agency compiles a periodic report summarizing its recent rating actions. More upgrades than downgrades is a positive signal. When downgrades prevail, it's an ominous sign.

A Word of Caution: Credit risk is only one potential pitfall for fixed-income investors. Too many savers look at credit quality only and ignore another large risk—length of maturity. Price changes due to changes in interest rates can deeply affect longer-term investments.

Also See: DURATION

12. BREADTH (ADVANCE-DECLINE) INDEX

What Is It? The Breadth (Advance-Decline) Index, used in technical analysis, computes for each trading day the net advances or declines in stocks on the NYSE. A strong market exists when there are net advances while a weak market exists when there are net declines. Of course, the magnitude of strength depends on the excess number of advancing issues versus declining ones. On the other hand, if declining stocks outnumber advancing stocks by 3 to 1, a significant market weakness exists.

How Is It Computed?

$$\text{Breadth Index} = \frac{\text{Number of net advances or declines in securities}}{\text{Number of securities traded}}$$

Example: Assume net advancing issues are 230. Securities traded are 2,145. The Breadth index equals:

$$\frac{\text{Net Advancing issues}}{\text{Number of issues traded}} = \frac{230}{2,145} = +0.107$$

The higher the plus percentage, the better since more stocks are increasing in price relative to those decreasing in price.

Zweig Breadth Advance/Decline Indicator equals:

$$\frac{\text{10-day moving average of advancing issues}}{\text{10-day moving average of declining issues}}$$

Where Is It Found? The Breadth Index may be computed easily by referring to the financial pages of a newspaper. The market diary section of the paper will provide the number of advancing and declining issues along with the number of issues unchanged. The total number of issues traded are the sum of these and is provided as well. Some financial advisory publications calculate the index, relieving the investor from performing the computation. Martin Zweig's Breadth Advance/Decline Indicator is published in the *Zweig Forecast*. The financial news program CNBC reports it daily. Figure 19 shows the totals for market advances and declines as published in *Barron's*. Figure 20 shows the NYSE Composite Daily Breadth. Figure 21 lists a bond diary, including advances and declines, from *Barron's*.

How Is It Used and Applied? Breadth analysis emphasizes change rather than level. The Breadth Index should be compared to popular market averages. Typically, there is consistency in their movement. In a bull market, an investor should be on guard against an extended disparity of the two. An example is when the Breadth Index gradually moves downward to new lows while the Standard & Poor's 500 Index reaches new highs.

A comparison also may be made of the Breadth Index over a five- to ten-year period. The Breadth Index also may be compared to a base year or included in a 150-day moving average.

Figure 19: Trading Diary—Market Advance/Decline Totals

Weekly Comp.	NYSE	AMEX	NASDAQ
Total Issues	2,497	887	4,180
Advances	938	275	1,306
Declines	1,193	420	1,875
Unchanged	366	192	1,066
New Highs	130	35	144
New Lows	136	54	277

Source: *Barron's.*

Figure 20: NYSE Composite Daily Breadth

	Aug 24	25	26	27	28
Issues Traded	2,345	2,335	2,318	2,328	2,318
Advances	399	719	1,013	1,087	955
Declines	1,490	1,002	732	662	749
Unchanged	456	614	573	579	614
New Highs	23	25	26	47	56
New Lows	75	56	28	20	22
Blocks	3,630	4,446	3,850	4,176	3,406
Total (000)	210,592	246,485	210,905	219,159	187,506

Source: *Barron's.*

Figure 21: NYSE Bond Diary

	Aug 24	25	26	27	28
Total	536	513	497	525	486
Advances	130	159	183	243	130
Declines	279	238	192	159	165
Unchanged	127	116	122	123	141
New Highs	25	22	25	26	30
New Lows	9	8	11	8	7
Sales th$	39,220	45,910	44,310	46,250	39,610

Source: *Barron's.*

How Is It Used for Investment Decisions? The investor is interested in market direction to identify strength or weakness. Advances and declines usually follow in the same direction as standard market averages (*e.g.,* Standard & Poor's 500 Index and the

Dow Jones Industrial Average). However, they may go in the opposite direction at a market peak or bottom.

The investor can be confident of market strength when the Breadth Index and a standard market index are increasing. Securities may be bought since a bull market is indicated. If the indexes are decreasing, market weakness is indicated. Securities should not be bought in a bear market. In fact, securities held should be sold.

A Word of Caution: Historically, stock advances have exceeded declines. However, a sudden reversal can occur in the future and a net decline may in fact occur.

13. BRITISH POUND

What Is It? The currency of one of the United States' top allies and trading partners, the British pound is one of the world's most important currencies. Its relationship to the U.S. dollar is a key to the global marketplace and is seen as a barometer of the United Kingdom's economic strength versus that of the United States'.

How Is It Computed? It is typically quoted in newspapers and financial reports on television and radio in terms of its relationship to the U.S. dollar. If the pound is at 1.4, that means each U.S. dollar buys 1.4 pounds. To figure out what 1 pound equals in U.S. currency, this formula is used:

$$1 \text{ pound} = \frac{\$1 \text{ U.S.}}{\text{Pound-to-dollar rate}}$$

Example: If $1 buys 1.4 pound, then 1 pound is equal to $1 divided by 1.4 or 71.4 cents.

Where Is It Found? Currency rates are listed daily in most major metropolitan newspapers as well as national publications such as the *New York Times*, the *Wall Street Journal*, and *USA Today* and on computer services such as Prodigy. See Figure 22.

How Is It Used for Investment Decisions? For American investors buying British securities, the pound's movement is a key part of the profit potential in the investment. If the pound rises after an investment in British securities is made, the value of those stocks or bonds to a U.S. investor will get a boost from the currency. That is because when the

Figure 22: Currency Rates

	Dollar	Pound	SFranc	Guilder	Yen	Lira	D-Mark	FFranc	CdnDlr
Canada	1.2673	1.9707	.86387	.69908	.01145	.00086	.78364	.23264	....
France	5.4475	8.471	3.7134	3.0050	.04923	.00369	3.3685	....	4.2985
Germany	1.6172	2.5147	1.1024	.89210	.01462	.00110	....	.29687	1.2761
Italy	1475.1	2293.7	1005.51	813.70	13.331	....	912.12	270.78	1164.0
Japan	110.65	172.06	75.426	61.038	....	.07501	68.421	20.312	87.31
Netherlands	1.8128	2.8189	1.2357	....	.01638	.00123	1.1209	.33278	1.4304
Switzerland	1.4670	2.2812	....	.80925	.01326	.00099	.90712	.26930	1.1576
U.K.	.64309	....	.43837	.35475	.00581	.00044	.39765	.11805	.50745
U.S.	....	1.5550	.68166	.55163	.00904	.00068	.61835	.18357	.78908

Source: Telerate. *Barron's.*

investment is sold, the stronger pound will generate more dollars when the proceeds are converted to the U.S. currency. Conversely, a weak pound will be a negative to a British investment for a U.S. investor. In some cases, the movement of the pound can also be viewed as an indicator of British economic health. A strong pound can signal a buoyant economy, a possible indication to buy British stocks. The pound's strength, however, should be verified not only against the U.S. dollar but against other major currencies.

A Word of Caution: The pound's strength versus the dollar can be distorted by prevailing interest rates in each country. For example, a movement by the British central bank to slow down the economy by boosting British interest rates—two potential negatives for stock prices—might also increase the pound's price versus the dollar if U.S. rates are stagnant or falling. This scenario of a rising pound might give an incorrect reading on the potential of buying British securities.

Widely quoted currency rates are typically for transactions of $1 million or more. Consumers attempting use such figures to determine currency rates for foreign travel should expect to get somewhat less favorable exchange rates.

Also See: GERMAN DEUTSCHE MARK, JAPANESE YEN

14. BULLISHNESS INDICATORS

What Are They? They are numerous surveys of investors seeking to determine whether these market watchers and players are likely to be buyers (bulls) or sellers (bears) of stocks in the near-term.

How Are They Computed? Various groups conduct polls of various sets of investors, ranging from professional traders to the small stockholder. Typically, they ask the survey sample one key question: Are you bullish on the stock market? The survey then adds up the percentage of those polled who say they are "bullish". A "bullish" reading can be anything over 50% or, after a prolonged market drop, a turn from increasing bearishness to increasing bullishness.

Where Are They Found? *Barron's* publishes four such surveys each week: a poll of investment advisers and/or traders by Investors Intelligence of New Rochelle, NY, Consensus Inc. of Kansas City, MO, and Market Vane, plus a poll of small investors by the American Association of Individual Investors of Chicago. The Fidelity mutual funds of Boston, in conjunction with the University of Michigan, produces an investors confidence index each month much like the university's well-known consumer confidence poll. Coverage of the Fidelity index appears in some daily newspapers.

How Are They Used for Investment Decisions? Such polls can be used to measure the market trend's true strength, often in a contrarian way. In a rising market or one near its peak, growing bearish feelings may indicate the market may be headed higher since healthy skepticism abounds. But a hot market with strong bullish feelings could be a signal or overheated investor expectation. That might be a sell signal. In a falling market or one near a possible bottom, the slightest turn to bullishness could be a buying signal. At such a low point for stocks, watch for any hint that bearish sentiment is ebbing.

A Word of Caution: Such surveys often give conflicting signals, leading to tricky analysis. And do not tend to lean towards the surveys of pro traders in such cases. Remember that many studies show that Mom and Pop Investors often do quite well on their own.

15. CASH INVESTMENTS

CERTIFICATE OF DEPOSIT YIELDS

What Are They? Yields on certificates of deposit provide a gauge of what bankers are paying on short-term, fixed-maturity savings accounts. CDs are popular investments for small and deep-pocketed savers to stash their cash holdings.

How Are They Computed? Several different organizations track bank deposit rates. Bank Rate Monitor, 100 Highest Yields of Florida, and Banxquote of New York poll banks and savings institutions about rates offered to consumers across the nation. They publish weekly reports on how savings rates have changed, both nationwide and in major U.S. cities.

The Federal Reserve also compiles weekly averages of so-called jumbo CDs, which are deposits of $100,000 and more, placed mainly by institutional investors. The Telerate service reports daily on rates paid on these savings accounts.

Where Are They Found? Many daily newspapers—both national and local—carry information on CD rates. The *New York Times* and the *Wall Street Journal* both write weekly stories on changes in savings rates. Telerate's institutional CD rate information is published in the financial tables of many newspapers.

How Are They Used for Investment Decisions? Certificates of deposits are popular savings tools for the small investor. When these rates are high or rising, such investors are unlikely to be actively buying stocks or bonds. That can be a negative signal to those markets.

Conversely, when CD rates are low or falling, small savers tend to look to markets like stocks, real estate, or bonds to improve their returns.

CD rates also can signal the banking industry's outlook for the economy. The movement of CD rates, particularly when compared to broader market interest rates, can suggest how bankers expect interest rates to move. The aggressiveness of the bankers' moves can show a willingness to lend if they're pushing up rates or the lack of good loans if CD rates are plunging.

A Word of Caution: CDs are relatively illiquid unless a saver wants to pay early withdrawal fees. That expense can dramatically affect the yield on a CD investment.

GUARANTEED INVESTMENT CONTRACT YIELDS

What Are They? Guaranteed investment contracts (GICs) are a popular fixed-income investment offered by insurance companies. The contracts act much like bankers' certificates of deposit, promising a fixed rate of return over a specified time. In employer retirement savings' plans that offer GICs to workers, GICs on average take in more than half the money in the plan.

How Are They Computed? Average GIC yields are compiled by several firms such as T. Rowe Price of Baltimore and Fiduciary Capital Management of Woodbury, Connecticut that survey major insurance companies to see what yields and maturities they are offering. GICs run in excess of $1 million.

Where Are They Found? The Rowe Price report on GICs appears daily in the *Wall Street Journal* while Fiduciary Capital's review is published weekly in *Barron's*. An example appears in Figure 23.

Figure 23: Guaranteed Investment Contracts (GICs)

	1 YEAR		2 YEARS		3 YEARS		4 YEARS		5 YEARS	
	RATE	CHG	RATE	CHG	RATE	CHG	RATE	CHG	RATE	CHG
High	3.61%	+0.10	4.72%	+0.10	5.25%	+0.09	5.80%	+0.10	6.27%	+0.07
Low	2.60	+0.05	3.69	+0.10	4.02	unch	4.60	unch	5.40	+0.09
Index	3.13	+0.04	4.17	+0.07	4.72	+0.06	5.32	+0.05	5.90	+0.05

TOP QUARTILE RANGE

	3.61%	-3.38%	4.72%	-4.35%	5.25%	-4.85%	5.80%	-5.51%	6.27%	-6.03%

SPREAD vs. TREASURIES

-0.04	+0.16	+0.16	+0.17	+0.36

Source: T. Rowe Price GIC Index.

How Are They Used for Investment Decisions? An investor can review GIC yields to see how his employer's retirement plan offering compares to that offered elsewhere.

Changes in GIC yields also can be used as an indicator of how insurance company executives see the outlook for interest rates much like certificate of deposit rates signal bankers' intentions.

If, for example, GIC rates are falling faster than other similar rates, that can be viewed as a sign that insurers want to lock in low rates before an upturn begins. Conversely, if GIC rates are steady while other competing rates fall, that can be viewed as a bet by insurers that rates may eventually go higher. When rates do go higher, insurance companies will have profited by locking in those lower rates.

A Word of Caution: Although GICs look and sound like bank products, they do not have the same safety, as many savers learned recently. The only guarantee backing GIC investments is the promise of the insurance company or companies underwriting the contract. A bank account, by comparison, is insured by the U.S. government up to $100,000.

MONEY MARKET FUND AVERAGE MATURITY

What Is It? This is information reported weekly on the maturity of securities held by money market mutual funds.

How Is It Computed? The figures reflect the average of all securities held by money funds and is tracked by IBC/Donoghue weekly. Money funds are restricted to securities of no more than one year in maturity and cannot have an average maturity more than 90 days.

Where Is It Found? Many newspapers such as the *Orange County Register* and the *Boston Globe* run both fund and industrywide figures weekly as does *Barron's* (see Figure 24). The information on individual funds also can be obtained from the fund's management.

Figure 24: Money Fund Report

MONEY MARKET FUNDS

	Last Week	Prev. Week	Year Ago
Asset Levels, Bil $	487.8	490.5	496.0
Avg. maturity, days	63	63	59
Avg. 7-day comp yld, %	2.65	2.66	3.66
Avg. 7-day simple yld, %	2.61	2.63	3.59
Avg. 30-day comp yld, %	2.67	2.69	3.73
Avg. 30-day simple yld, %	2.65	2.65	3.66

TAX-EXEMPT FUNDS

	Last Week	Prev. Week	Year Ago
Asset Levels, Bil $	99.4	100.8	94.2
Avg. maturity days	48	49	48
Avg. 7-day comp yld, %	2.04	1.97	3.11

Source: IBC/Donoghue's Money Fund Report.

How Is It Used for Investment Decisions? Changes in the average maturity can be seen as an indication of where shortest-term interest rates are headed.

When managers believe that rates are headed lower, they extend their maturities to lock in what they believe are currently higher rates. When fund managers think rates are headed higher, they shorten the average maturity so they can have the most money available to buy the expected higher-yielding paper in the near future. The IBC/Donoghue industrywide average serves as a consensus for the overall leanings of all fund managers.

When comparing individual funds, relative maturities can show which fund or funds will better respond to such rate moves. Longer maturity funds should do best if rates fall. Shorter maturity funds excel when rates rise. Of course, with a maximum maturity of 90 days, such advantages will diminish quickly.

Also See: CASH INVESTMENTS: MONEY MARKET FUND YIELDS

MONEY MARKET FUND YIELDS

What Are They? These are a measurement of the return on money market mutual funds, which are popular alternatives to bank accounts and other cash investments. Money funds are managed to maintain a stable $1 per share price.

How Are They Computed? The money fund yield is typically viewed in three ways: a 7-day yield compounded over a year; a 30-day yield compounded over a year; and a 12-month total return.

The 7-day and 30-day yields reflect dividends the money funds have collected in a recent week and month, respectively, less costs such as management fees. Those returns are then annualized, that is, assumed to be collected at the same rate for a year.

The annual return figure reflects both dividends collected as well as any capital gains earned minus any expenses. Accounting rules allow those capital gains to be shown to investors as yield enhancements rather than per-share price changes.

Where Are They Found? IBC/Donoghue's 7-day yields are published weekly in many daily newspapers such as *Dallas Morning News*, the *Los Angeles Times*, the *New York Times* (see Figure 25). The 30-day yield and total return figures are typically what is quoted by mutual fund companies in sales literature.

Figure 25: Money Market Fund Yields

Fund	This week	Last week	6 mos. ago
Merrill Lynch CMA Money Fund	2.94%	2.98%	3.67%
American Express Daily Dividend	3.08%	3.14%	3.79%
Vanguard Money Market Prime	3.27%	3.32%	4.04%
Fidelity Cash Reserves	3.22%	3.26%	4.07%
Dean Witter/Sears Liq. Assets	2.95%	2.97%	3.70%
Merrill Lynch Ready Assets	2.94%	2.98%	3.61%
Prudential MoneyMart Assets	2.99%	3.01%	3.83%
Dreyfus Worldwide Dollar	3.37%	3.44%	4.23%
Merrill Lynch Ret Res MF	3.00%	3.08%	3.74%
Dreyfus Liquid Assets	3.05%	3.10%	3.69%
Avg. of 550 taxable money funds	2.90%	2.95%	3.72%

Source: IBC/Donoghue's Money Fund Report.

How Are They Used for Investment Decisions? IBC/Donoghue's average of all money fund yields are used as both an indicator of what very short-term investments are returning and a barometer to measure all funds' performance.

An investor must be careful, however, when comparing yields of funds.

Although these funds are managed very conservatively, there are some subtle safety differences that should be reviewed. Some funds own a mixture of corporate, banking, and government obligations. Others take a slightly less risky path, holding only U.S.-backed issues. Such funds tend to pay out less.

A Word of Caution: Many fund management companies temporarily waive money fund fees—which can cut as much as a full percentage off the yields—as an inducement to invest. These discounts can be misleading, so investors are advised to check out a high-paying fund carefully. An investor should query whether the fund is offering such a discount, how long the discount will last, and what the fund would have yielded if the full fees were charged.

Also See: CASH INVESTMENTS: MONEY MARKET FUND AVERAGE MATURITY, INTEREST RATES: DISCOUNT, FED FUNDS, AND PRIME, INTEREST RATES: THREE-MONTH TREASURY BILLS

16. CHANGES: UP AND DOWN

What Is It? This is a listing—usually daily—of the stocks having the highest percentage increase in price and the highest percentage decrease in price for the trading period. The stocks are listed in the order of their percentage change. Typically, ten advancing stocks and ten declining stocks are listed. There is a separate listing for the NYSE, AMEX, and NASDAQ issues.

How Is It Computed? A tabulation is made of the stocks on each exchange and over-the-counter market in terms of their percentage increase or decrease in market price. The tables use only stock prices above $1.

Where Is It Found? The up changes and down changes appear in the financial pages of newspapers and magazines such as *Barron's*, the *New York Times*, and the *Wall Street Journal*. Figure 26 is a sample listing of NYSE, AMEX, and NASDAQ Stocks with the largest percentage changes up and down.

Figure 26: Stock Listing of Ups and Downs

MARKET DIARY

	Yesterday	Prev. Day
Advanced	955	1087
Declined	749	662
Unchanged	614	579
Total Issues	2318	2328
New Highs	56	47
New Lows	22	20

MOST ACTIVE: SHARE VOLUME

	Vol. (100s)	Last	Chg.
Merck	26003	49 3/8	- 1/2
GnMotr	24187	33 1/2	- 1/4
Shoney	22989	17 1/2	- 5/8
BakrHu	19688	25 1/8	+ 1 5/8
Glaxo	18405	28 3/8	+ 3/8
Maxus	18181	7 1/4	+ 1/4
FPL Gp	15480	35 7/8	- 5/8
GlobM	15470	2 1/8	+ 1/8
FlaPrg	15415	32 3/4	- 1/4
NatnsBk	15349	44 1/4	- 1/2
ToyRU	14686	39 1/8	+ 3/4
RJR Nab	13520	8 5/8	...
FordM	13458	39 3/4	- 5/8
BlockE	13147	13 1/2	+ 1/2
Halbtn	12873	35 1/2	+ 2 3/4

Continued.

Figure 26: Stock Listing of Ups and Downs (*continued*)

CHANGES: UP

	Last	Chg.	Pct.
AmShipB	1 3/8	+ 3/8	37.5
USG	1 3/8	+ 3/8	37.5
CompreCre	1 1/2	+ 1/4	20.0
MHI Group	1 1/2	+ 1/4	20.0
UnitCp	2 3/8	+ 3/8	18.8
LL&E Roylty	3 3/4	+ 1/2	15.4
Mesalnc n	10	+ 1 1/8	12.7
FtCtyBcp	1 1/8	+ 1/8	12.5
GitanoGp	3 3/8	+ 3/8	12.5

CHANGES: DOWN

	Last	Chg.	Pct.
Dycom	6 3/8	- 1 1/8	15.0
SizelerPty	9 3/4	- 1 1/4	11.4
LTV Cp pfA	2	- 1/4	11.1
DataDesign	1 1/8	- 1/8	10.0
AHealthPr	22 3/4	- 2 3/8	9.5
FurrsBsh pf	1 1/4	- 1/8	9.1
CarlislePts	4	- 3/8	8.6
Shoneys	17 1/2	- 1 5/8	8.5
GenRad	1 1/2	- 1/8	7.7
WheelPitts wt	1 1/2	- 1/8	7.7

Source: *New York Times.*

How Is It Used for Investment Decisions? In looking at price increases or decreases, consideration should be given to the trading volume. For example, a price increase on heavy volume is a stronger indicator of movement than a price increase on low volume.

If a stock appears frequently under both the up changes and down changes listings, it is a volatile issue since it fluctuates in price drastically. This is typically associated with a speculative issue that implies risk.

The investor must determine whether a stock with a significant price increase can sustain its upward momentum. If it can, the stock might be attractive. On the other hand, if the sharp increase in price cannot be sustained and is temporary, the market price of the stock might fall because it is overvalued. In such a case, the investor should not buy the stock.

If there is a sharp decline in the market price of a stock, the investor should ascertain whether the issue is in a downward trend or whether it is now undervalued and should be bought. Further, a sharp move in stock price may be due to specific good or bad news.

A Word of Caution: A company experiencing a significant percentage increase in price in a given day may be vulnerable to a price decline the next day because the stock may be overvalued. Further, stocks that significantly change in price are volatile issues that involve risk.

17. CHARTING

What Is It? Charts are used to evaluate market conditions including the price and volume behavior of the overall stock market and of individual securities.

How Is It Prepared? The three basic types of charts are line, bar, and point-and-figure. On line charts (see Figure 27) and bar charts (see Figure 28), the vertical line shows price and the horizontal line shows time.

Figure 27: Line Chart

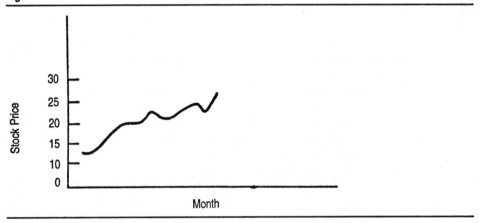

Figure 28: Bar Chart

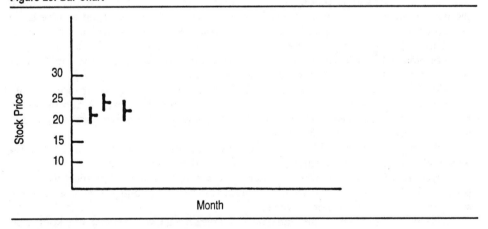

On a line chart, ending prices are conected by straight lines. On a bar chart, vertical lines appear at each time period, and the top and bottom of each bar shows the high and low prices. A horizontal line across the bar marks the ending prices.

Point-and-figure charts (see Figure 29) show emerging price patterns in the market in general and for specific stocks. Typically, only the ending prices are charted. An increase in price is denoted by an X while a decrease in price is shown as an 0.

Figure 29: Point-and-Figure Chart

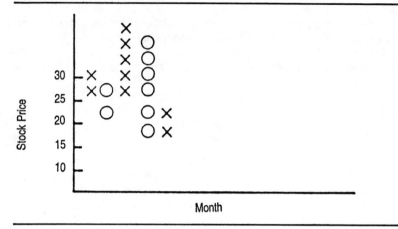

There is no time dimension in Figure 29. A column of X's shows an upward price trend while a column of 0's reveals a downward price trend.

In point-and-figure charts, there is a vertical price scale. Plots on the chart are made when a price changes by a predetermined amount.

Significant price changes and their reversal are depicted. What is significant is up to the individual investor. The investor can use either ending prices or inter-day prices, depending on time constraints. The usual predetermined figures are 1 or 2 points for medium-priced stocks, 3 or 5 points for high-priced stocks, and 1/2 point for low-priced stocks. Most charts contain specific volume information.

The investor should plot prices representing a trend in a single column, moving to the next column only when the trend is reversed. He will usually round a price to the nearest dollar and start by plotting a beginning rounded price. Nothing new appears on the chart if the rounded price does not change. If a different rounded price occurs, the investor plots it. If new prices continue in the same direction, they will appear in the same column. A new column begins when there is a reversal.

Where Is It Found? Standard & Poor's *Trendline* gives charting information on many securities. Other financial services, financial magazines and newspapers, and brokerage research reports also provide charts. The Telescan Analyzer from Telescan Inc. prepares graphs for technical and fundamental indicators.

Figure 30 shows a graph of stock indexes as published in *Investor's Business Daily,* which also publishes many other charts of stock and market performance.

How Is It Used and Applied? A chart pattern may be studied to predict future stock prices and volume activity. Charts may cover historical data of one year or less for active stocks or several years for nonactive stocks.

Point-and-figure charts provide data about resistance levels (points). Breakouts from resistance levels indicate market direction. The longer the sideways movement before a break, the more the stock can increase in price.

How Is It Used for Investment Decisions? The investor may use charts to analyze formations and spot buy and sell indicators.

The investor can use these charts to determine whether the market is in a major upturn or downturn and whether the trend will reverse. The investor also can see what price may be accomplished by a given stock or market average. Further, these charts can help the investor predict the magnitude of a price swing.

A Word of Caution: Historical trends in prices may not result in future price trends because of changing circumstances in the current environment.

Also See: JAPANESE CANDLESTICK CHARTS

Figure 30: Stock Indexes

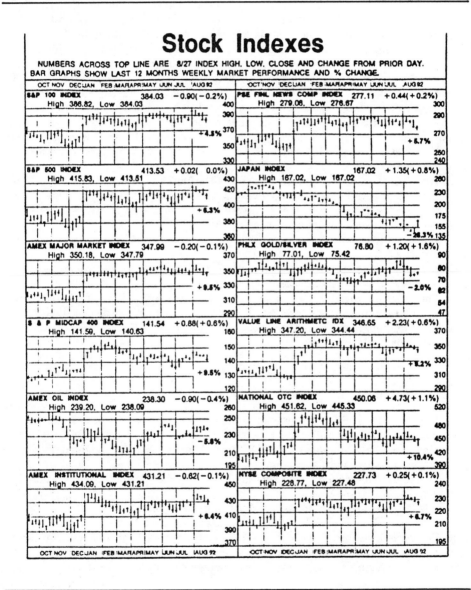

Source: *Investor's Business Daily.*

18. COLLECTIBLES

SOTHEBY'S ART INDEX

What Is It? Developed by Jeremy Eckstein, the Sotheby's Art Index tracks price trends in the worldwide art and antique market. The index is based on the aggregate prices (including buyers' premium) in auction sales by Sotheby's Holdings Inc. of London and its affiliated companies of arts-related items and other relevant information. The index downplays dealer sales. However, the index may have little correlation to most artwork.

How Is It Computed? The index is comprised of more than 400 individual items in 12 market classifications. These classifications are old master paintings, 19th century European paintings, Impressionist and post-Impressionist paintings, modern paintings (from 1900 through 1950), American paintings (from 1800 to before World War II), continental ceramics, Chinese ceramics, English silver, continental silver, American furniture, French and continental furniture, and English furniture. The index is a weighted-average of the prices of these 12 categories based on the dollar volume of each in proportion to the total market dollar volume. A base price of 100 was assigned in 1975.

Where Is It Found? The Sotheby's Art Index is published in *Barron's* and the *Wall Street Journal*.

How Is It Used for Investment Decisions? The investor should refer to the Sotheby's Art Index before deciding whether to invest in art and antiques. If the index is at a very low point and the investor feels that prices are going to increase, art may be bought. The particular art item will have to be decided upon.

While returns from art investing can be high, prices are subject to wide variation. It is a risky investment.

Before art is bought it should be appraised by an expert to determine its market value. Forgery is also a major concern.

The purchase price for art is expensive and resale may be difficult. There are high transaction fees and insurance costs. Small investors do not have sufficient funds to buy art other than lithographic prints. A deficiency of the index is that it does not adjust for changing price levels.

STAMP INDEXES

What Are They? Stamp indexes track the prices of stamps. The Scott Index and the U.S. Stamp Market Index are two.

How Are They Computed? The U.S. Stamp Market Index is a weighted-average of U.S. 19th– and 20th–century stamp and air mails.

Where Are They found? The Scott Index is published by Scott Philatelic Corporation, an affiliate of Scott Publishing.

The U.S. Stamp Market Index is published in *Linn's Stamp News*.

How Are They Used for Investment Decisions? The values of "fine" stamps are used as a basis for comparison in a study of quality-adjusted rates of return in stamp auctions. The trend in stamp prices indicates how the stamp collector is faring. If there are temporarily depressed prices, stamps may be bought for future appreciation.

19. COMMODITY INDEXES

COMMODITY RESEARCH BUREAU INDEXES

What Are They? The Commodity Research Bureau (CRB) has two indexes: the *CRB Spot Price Index* and the *CRB Futures Price Index.*

The CRB Spot Price Index is based on prices of 23 different commodities, representing livestock and products, fats and oils, metals, and textiles and fibers, and it serves as an indicator of inflation.

The CRB Futures Price Index is the composite index (1967 = 100) of futures prices that tracks the volatile behavior of commodity prices. It is the best-known commodity index. The CRB index, produced by Knight-Ridder Financial Publishing, was designed to monitor broad changes in the commodity markets. The CRB index consists of 21 commodities.

In addition to the CRB Futures Index, nine subindexes are maintained for baskets of commodities representing currencies, energy, interest rates, imported commodities, industrial commodities, grains, oil-seeds, livestock and meats, and precious metals. All indexes have a base level of 100 as of 1967, except the currencies, energy, and interest rates indexes, which were set at 100 in 1977.

How Are They Computed? The CRB Futures Index can be thought of as a three-dimensional index. In addition to averaging the prices of all 21 components, the index also incorporates an average of prices over time for each commodity. The price for each commodity is the simple average of the futures price for a nine-month period.

Example: The average price for wheat contracts traded on the Chicago Mercantile Exchange in July 1992 would be determined as the average for the following five contract months: August, October, December, 1992, and February and April, 1993. Mathematically,

$$\text{Wheat average} = \frac{\text{Aug '92 + Oct '92 + Dec '92 + Feb '93 + Apr '93}}{5}$$

For other commodities, there may be more or less than five contract months in the average.

The average prices of the 21 component commodities are then geometrically averaged and the result is divided by 53.0615 (the 1967 base-year average for these commodities); multiplied by 0.95035 and by 100. Mathematically,

$$\text{CRB Futures Index} = \sqrt{\frac{\text{Cattle avg. x . . . x Wheat avg.}}{53.0615}} \times 0.95035 \times 100$$

The factor 0.95035 amounts for an adjustment necessitated by the index's changeover (on July 20, 1987) from 26 commodities averaged over 12 months to 21 commodities averaged over nine months. The index is multiplied by 100 in order to convert its level into percentage terms. In other words, the CRB Futures Index involves both geometric and arithmetic averaging techniques.

Where Are They Found? The *Wall Street Journal* displays monthly charts of the CRB Futures Index and also provides a one-year perspective on prices of gold, oil, wheat, and steers and thus an idea on inflationary trends. The CRB chart frequently appears on the cable network CNBC. Figure 31 is an example from *Commodity Price Charts* (219 Parkade, Cedar Falls, IA 50613).

Figure 31: Commodity Prices Over Time

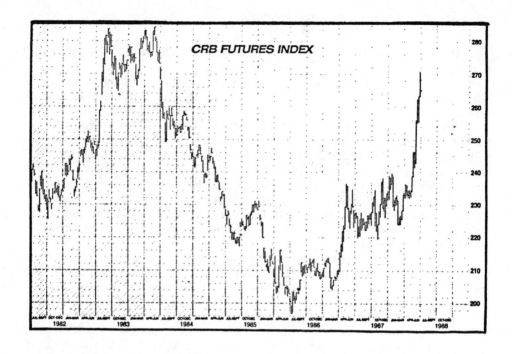

Source: *Commodity Price Charts.*

How Are They Used for Investment Decisions? The CRB Futures Index serves as the basis for cash-settled futures contracts that are traded on the New York Futures Exchange (NYFE) under the commodity code CR. Higher commodity prices, for example, can signal inflation, which in turn can lead to higher interest rates and yields and lower bond prices. Higher interest rates tend to depress the stock market as well.

A Word of Caution: In order to gauge inflation pressure, an investor should also look at popular price indexes such as the Producer Price Index (PPI).

Also See: ECONOMIC INDICATORS: INFLATION, ECONOMIC INDICATORS: INTEREST RATES

THE ECONOMIST *COMMODITIES INDICATORS*

What Are They? The indicators gauge commodity spot prices and their movements.

How Are They Computed? The indicators include 28 commodities including foods and industrial products. Examples are metals, timber, cotton, coffee, cocoa, and sugar. There is a weighting of the commodities based on their values. The commodities are typically expressed in special drawing rights (SDRs), which is a weighted-average of the market value of the currencies used by the International Monetary Fund. This consists of the currencies of the United States, United Kingdom, Germany, France, and Japan.

Where Are They Found? The indicators are published in *The Economist* (United Kingdom). Figure 32 shows the components of the index.

How Are They Used for Investment Decisions? The commodity price indicators may be used by investors in commodities to appraise current prices, trends in prices, and price fluctuation. The information may be helpful in buying or selling commodity futures contracts. The indicators also may serve as barometers of global inflation and global interest rates.

Figure 32: *The Economist* **Commodity Index Components**

Sector/Commodity			(%) Weight (3/12/88)
Industrial materials	50.2%		
Metals (6)		29.3%	
Aluminum			12.25%
Copper			8.32
Zinc			2.90
Nickel			2.70
Tin			1.85
Lead			1.28
Nonfood agriculturals (12)		20.9%	
Timber			5.60
Cotton			4.23
Rubber			2.97
Hides			2.34
Wool 64s			2.19
Wool 48s			2.19
Soybeans			0.92
Palm oil			0.15
Coconut oil			0.13
Soybean oil			0.08
Sisal			0.06
Jute			0.04
Foods (14)	49.8%		
Coffee			16.68
Cocoa			5.33
Soybeans†			5.13
Maize			4.23
Sugar			4.03
Soybean meal			3.78
Beef			3.34
Wheat			2.34
Tea			1.49
Lamb			1.05
Palm oil*			0.80
Coconut oil*			0.70
Soybean oil*			0.55
Groundnut oil			0.35
Total: 28 commodities			
*Also included in Nonfood agriculturals			

Source: *The Economist.*

REUTERS INDEX

What Is It? The index applies to British staple commodities prices, but inferences may be made to international commodities prices.

How Is It Computed? The index is a geometric weighted-average based on the significance in international trade of spot prices of 17 major commodities. The commodities include wheat, cotton, sugar, zinc, and coffee. The prices are stated in U.K. pounds sterling or U.S. dollars. There is a translation at the applicable foreign currency exchange rate. The base year was 1931 at which time a base value of 100 was assigned.

Where Is It Found? The index information may be obtained from Reuters Economic Services.

How Is It Used for Investment Decisions? The index may be used as a reflection of worldwide commodities prices, enabling the investor to determine the attractiveness of specific commodities. The investor may enter into futures contracts.

20. CONTRARIAN INVESTING

CONTRARY OPINION RULE

What Is It? Contrary opinion is a sentiment indicator in which after finding out what most investors are doing, the investor does the opposite. The rationale is that popular opinion is usually wrong. The rule presumes that the crowd is typically incorrect at major market turning points.

Where Is It Found? The majority opinion is normally reflected in the news media including reports, articles, and television network news items. Popular magazines to be referred to include *Business Week, Forbes, Fortune, Newsweek,* and *Time.* Other sources include financial books for lay people and financial television news programs.

How Is It Used and Applied? Published and televised news usually has been reflected in the price of securities. Therefore, the publicizing of the news is probably the end instead of the beginning of a move.

If most investors are bullish, they have probably fully invested their available funds—contributing to a stock market peak. If most investors are bearish, they have probably sold their shares—contributing to a stock market bottom.

How Is It Used for Investment Decisions? An investor following a contrarian strategy does the opposite of what most investors are doing. If everyone is pessimistic, the investor concludes that it is probably the time to buy. If everyone is optimistic, the investor believes that it is probably the time to sell.

The investors should compare the news stories with other technical and fundamental indicators.

The investor may find good buys for company stocks that are out of favor because of an oversold situation. However, these stocks should possess fundamental values based on the company's financial condition.

A Word of Caution: There may be instances in which what most investors are doing is the right strategy. The investing public may be buying securities during what is, in fact, a bull market.

Also See: TRADING VOLUME GAUGES: ODD-LOT THEORY

What Is It? The index is based on a reversal of the recommendations of investment advisory services as contained in their market letters. Such services are considered to be a proxy for "majority" opinion. This index operates according to the contrary opinion rule: Whatever the investment advisory services recommend, the investor should do the opposite. It is a technical investment analysis tool. Investors Intelligence believes that advisory services are trend followers rather than anticipators. They recommend equities at market bottoms and offer selling advice at market tops.

How Is It Computed?

$$\text{Index} = \frac{\text{Bearish investment advisory services}}{\text{Total number of investment advisory services}}$$

Investors Intelligence believes that when 42% or more of the advisory services are bearish, the market will go up.

On the other hand, when 17% or fewer of the services are bearish, the market will go down.

Where Is It Found? The Index of Bearish Sentiment is published by Investors Intelligence (New Rochelle, New York 10801). It can be found in *Barron's*. The index was originally developed by A.W. Cohen of Chartcraft.

Example: Of 200 investment advisory services, 90 of them are bearish on the stock market. The Index equals .45 (90/200).

Since 45% of the advisory services are pessimistic about the prospects for stock, or more than the 42% benchmark, the investor should buy securities.

How Is It Used for Investment Decisions? A movement toward 10% means that the Dow Jones Industrial Average is about to go from bullish to bearish. When the index approaches 60%, the Dow Jones Industrial Average is headed from bearish to bullish.

The investor should use this index in predicting the future direction of the securities market based on contrary opinion. If bearish sentiment exists, a bull market is expected, and the investor should buy stock. If bullish sentiment exists, a bear market is likely, and the investor may consider selling securities owned.

A Word of Caution: Other measures of stock performance should be used in conjunction with this index.

21. CRUDE OIL SPOT PRICE

What Is It? The market price for a barrel of unrefined petroleum, typically a high-quality grade oil, is called the crude oil spot price. Crude oil prices are carefully watched as a barometer of everything from global political tensions to inflation to oil company profits. Investors also can invest directly in oil by buying futures and options contracts.

How Is It Computed? The often-quoted spot price for crude oil is the per-barrel price on the most current Light Sweet Crude futures contracts that trade on the New York Mercantile Exchange. Each futures contract calls for delivery of 1,000 barrels of oil but its price is quoted per barrel. The NYMEX, as it is known, also trades futures for sour crude oil, natural gas, and two refined products—unleaded gasoline and heating oil.

Where Is It Found? The crude oil spot price appears in commodity futures listings in such newspapers as *Barron's, Investor's Business Daily,* the *New York Times,* and the *Wall Street Journal,* and on computerized databases such as Prodigy.

How Is It Used for Investment Decisions? Swings in crude oil prices can have a dramatic impact on the world economy and investment markets. Rising oil prices can hurt both stock and bond prices.

Stock investors fear the effect of high oil prices, crippling both to demand as consumers pay more for gasoline and to corporate bottom lines at firms (notably airlines) that are heavy petroleum users. The bond market dislikes any sign of inflation, particularly from oil prices—a holdover from the Arab oil embargoes of the 1970s. Inflation erodes the buying power of the cash stream, which is generated by long-term, fixed-income investments.

Rising oil prices can be good for a handful of investments. Oil company stocks enjoy a high-priced environment because profits soar for most petroleum drillers, refiners, and sellers. In addition, short-term cash investments such as money market mutual funds could see their yields improve as higher oil prices likely bump up interest rates.

A Word of Caution. There are major risks associated with investing in commodity futures and options. These securities provide huge leverage—that is, the chance to control a huge amount of petroleum products for a fraction of the cost. But the wrong bet can be financially devastating. Option players can lose only their entire investment while futures speculators can be liable for more than they originally invested if they're far wrong on their hunches.

22. CURRENCY INDEXES

FEDERAL RESERVE TRADE-WEIGHTED DOLLAR

What Is It? The index reflects the currency units of more than 50% of the U.S. principal trading countries.

How Is It Computed? The index measures the currencies of ten foreign countries: the United Kingdom, Germany, Japan, Italy, Canada, France, Sweden, Switzerland, Belgium, and the Netherlands. The index is weighted by each currency's base exchange rate, and then averaged on a geometric basis. This weighting process indicates relative significance in overseas markets. The base year was 1973.

Where Is It Found? The index is published by the Federal Reserve System and is found in its *Federal Reserve Bulletin.* It also appears in the *Wall Street Journal.*

How Is It Used for Investment Decisions? The investor should examine the trend in this index to determine foreign exchange risk exposure associated with his investment portfolio.

Also, the Federal Reserve trade-weighted dollar is the basis for commodity futures on the New York Cotton Exchange.

Also See: BRITISH POUND, GERMAN DEUTSCHE MARK

GRANT'S FINANCIAL DOLLAR

What Is It? This is a financial index of currencies based on their relative importance in world trade.

How Is It Computed? The index is weighted by the currency units of the United Kingdom, West Germany, Japan, and Switzerland. The currencies are weighted based on the assets of the associated central banks. The currencies have been converted to U.S. dollars using the relevant exchange rates.

Where Is It Found? The index can be found in *Grant's Interest Rate Observer* published by James Grant.

How Is It Used for Investment Decisons? The index can be used by the investor to appraise the effect of changes in foreign exchange rates on U.S. dollars. This will indicate the dollar impact on the investment due solely to revaluation.

MORGAN GUARANTY DOLLAR INDEX

What Is It? The index measures the value of currency units versus dollars.

How Is It Computed? The index is a weighted-average of 15 currencies including that of France, Italy, United Kingdom, Germany, Canada, and Japan. The weighting is based on the relative significance of the currencies in world markets. The base of 100 was established for 1980 through 1982.

Where Is It Found? The index appears in the *Wall Street Journal*.

How Is It Used for Investment Decisions? The index highlights the impact of foreign currency units in U.S. dollar terms. The investor can see the effect of foreign currency conversion on U.S. dollar investment.

23. DOLLAR-COST AVERAGING

What Is It? Dollar-cost averaging is an investment strategy that attempts to spread out investment risk over time. It does so by requiring small and periodic set dollar amount purchases of an asset over a lengthy period. It is often recommended for small investors who have little investment monies at their disposal or who are unable or unwilling to follow investment markets regularly.

How Is It Computed? Investors seeking to use this strategy must figure out how much they can afford to contribute systematically to a dollar-cost averaging account each month and/or quarter.

Example: Figure 33 shows a once-a-month purchase plan in a no-load mutual fund.

Where Is It Found? The biggest promoters of dollar-cost averaging have been mutual funds, whose typically small investment minimums allow investors to implement this strategy easily in a cost-effective way. Many funds and brokerages make this process easy by allowing automatic purchases through direct deductions from investors' checking accounts or paychecks.

Investors may unknowingly be using this strategy as part of employer-sponsored savings plans such as 401(k) retirement programs. Many of these benefit plans routinely make equal purchases of assets at set periods, quietly accomplishing dollar-cost averaging.

How Is It Used for Investment Decisions? Dollar-cost averaging attempts to eliminate one investment decision: Timing.

By distributing purchases over a lengthy period, an investor lowers the risk of purchasing a large amount of an investment at the highest possible price. By using a set dollar amount, when prices are high, this strategy tells an investor to buy fewer shares.

Figure 33: Mutual Fund Purchase Plan

Date	Invest	Price	Shares
1/15	$1000	$25	40.0
2/15	$1000	$23	43.4
3/15	$1000	$21	47.6
4/15	$1000	$20	50.0
5/15	$1000	$19	52.6
6/15	$1000	$18	55.5
7/15	$1000	$18	55.5
8/15	$1000	$19	52.6
9/15	$1000	$20	50.0
10/15	$1000	$21	47.6
11/15	$1000	$23	43.4
12/15	$1000	$25	40.0

Total invested: $12,000
Total shares purchased: 578.2
Average price per share: $12,000 ÷ 578.2 = $20.75
Final investment value: 578.2 × $25 = $14,455
Net profit: $14,455 - $12,000 = $2,445 or 20.4%

When prices are low, the investor would accumulate more, discounted shares. Therefore, the strategy screens out whims that could result in the investor buying high and selling low.

Dollar-cost averaging will work as long as prices of the assets targeted by the strategy rise over the long haul.

A Word of Caution: Dollar-cost averaging can result in high transaction costs that can lower returns over time. That is why mutual funds, which often charge either no sales fee or a flat commission, are a popular way to implement this strategy.

Such plans also can create a nightmare at tax time after the investment is sold. Each of the systematic purchases should be separately accounted for on the tax return.

Also See: VALUE AVERAGING

24. DOW JONES INDUSTRIAL AVERAGE

What Is It? Dating back to 1885, the Dow Jones Industrial Average or DJIA is the most widely watched benchmark for U.S. stock markets. This index is synonymous with the market's fortunes. When someone says, "The market's up 20," they mean the point change in the Dow index.

How Is It Computed? The Dow industrial index took its current form of tracking 30 major companies' stocks in October 1928. The current 30 stocks are: Allied Signal, Alcoa, American Express, AT&T, Bethlehem Steel, Boeing, Caterpillar, Chevron, Coca-Cola,

Disney, Du Pont, Eastman Kodak, Exxon, General Electric, General Motors, Goodyear, IBM, International Paper, McDonald's, Merck, Minnesota Mining & Manufacturing, J.P. Morgan, Philip Morris, Procter & Gamble, Sears, Texaco, Union Carbide, United Technologies, Westinghouse, and Woolworth.

Each stock's price is multiplied by the same amount, known as the divisor, to arrive at the index each day. For example, summer of 1992's divisor of 0.5463 meant that a $1 movement in any of those 30 stocks would move the index 1.83 points. Thanks to computers, the index is calculated constantly throughout the trading day.

Where Is It Found? The Dow 30 is found just about everywhere from virtually every daily newspaper, no matter how small, to reports on television and radio. The *Wall Street Journal* not only prints charts of how the Dow 30 has fared in recent weeks, it also details how it did hour-by-hour during the previous trading day. It also can be found on computer databases such as Prodigy.

How Is It Used for Investment Decisions? Despite its name recognition the Dow 30 is seen today as a poor indicator of how the U.S. stock market is doing. Many experts prefer to watch the Standard & Poor's 500 stock index because of its wider reading of stock performance. But since the Dow 30's movement is so widely watched, it cannot be ignored even when it may be giving off incorrect signals about the stock market. The Dow 30 still has powerful impact on investor psychology. Sharp movements in the Dow 30, regardless of whether they are quickly followed by broader indexes, are closely monitored.

A Word of Caution: The Dow can be actually misleading. Throughout much of the first half of 1992, the Dow was far outdistancing other U.S. stock benchmarks. The Dow was setting new highs while other indexes languished. The main culprit was one stock: Disney, which often enjoys great investor enthusiasm no matter what the economic climate.

Also See: DOW JONES TRANSPORTATION AVERAGE, DOW JONES UTILITIES AVERAGE, RUSSELL 1000, 2000, 3000, STANDARD & POOR'S (S&P) INDEXES

25. DOW JONES INDUSTRY GROUPS

What Are They? Dow Jones publishes statistics of the performance of industries in the following categories: basic materials, energy, industrial, consumer (cyclical), consumer (noncyclical), technology, financial, and utilities.

How Are They Computed? This is a weighted group of industries based on market capitalizations. The base of 100 was established as of June 30, 1982. The percentage volume change is the change from a previous 65-day moving average.

The historical information is compiled by Dow Jones and Shearson Lehman Brothers.

Where Are They Found? The performance of industry groups, including those leading and lagging, may be found in *Barron's* and the *Wall Street Journal*. Strongest and weakest companies in each group also may be found in publications such as in *Business Week*.

How Are They Used for Investment Decisions? The investor may examine the index of each major industry, along with 52-week highs and lows, to identify those industries that appear overvalued or undervalued. For example, if the investor concludes that an industry is undervalued and the prospects for that industry are bright, he may buy stocks in that industry. Further, industry groups are good to consider as a performance indicator of individual stocks within the industry group. A peer comparison can be quite useful.

A Word of Caution: Some companies may be doing well financially even though they are in a depressed industry.

26. DOW JONES: OTHER INDEXES

COMMODITY SPOT PRICE INDEX

What Is It? This is an index of the prices of food and fiber, grain, wood, metal, and livestock.

How Is It Computed? The index is based on an equal weighted-average of commodity prices. A 100 base value was assigned in 1974. Figure 34 lists the components of the index as it appears in *Barron's*.

Where Is It Found? The index appears in *Barron's*. Figure 35 shows commodity indexes appearing in *Investor's Business Daily*.

How Is It Used for Investment Decisions? The index can be used to examine the difference between the spot prices on commodities and the prices of short-term future commodity contracts. The wider the difference, the greater the risk. It also may be used as a gauge of future inflation.

Figure 34: Components-Dow Jones Commodity Futures Index

Cattle	Cotton	Silver
Coffee	Gold	Soybeans
Copper	Hogs	Sugar
Corn	Lumber	Wheat

Source: *Barron's*, August 31, 1992.

Figure 35: Commodity Indexes

Thursday, August 27, 1992

	Close	Net Chg.	Yr. Ago
Dow Jones Futures	115.67	+ 0.12	121.61
Dow Jones Spot	116.26	unch	117.28
Reuter United Kingdom	1517.3	- 1.5	1655.1
C R B Futures*	200.29	- 0.40	210.15
*Division of Knight-Ridder.			

Source: *Investor's Business Daily*, August 28, 1992.

EQUITY MARKET INDEX

What Is It? This is a capitalized weighted index of the prices of companies.

How Is It Computed? This is a broad, capitalized-weighted index of market prices of securities of about 750 businesses. Companies included in the index constitute a large percentage of capitalized market values in the marketplace and are represented by issues traded on the major stock exchanges and NASDAQ. This index is broken down into 82 industry segments. Its base year is 1992.

Where Is It Found? The index appears in *Barron's*, the *New York Times* and the *Wall Street Journal*. Figure 36 shows the component sectors of the index. Figure 37 shows the Dow Jones Equity Market Index as it appears in *Barron's*. Reference may be made to the Dow Jones News/Retrieval Service.

How Is It Used for Investment Decisions? The investor can use the index to see the overall direction of the stock market. It is a barometer of market conditions. The investor should examine industry segment charts.

Figure 36: Dow Jones Equity Market Index Component Sectors

Sectors/Number of Companies

1. Basic materials (66)
2. Energy (45)
3. Industrial (97)
4. Consumer, cyclical (116)
5. Consumer, noncyclical (85)
6. Technology (94)
7. Financial services (112)
8. Utilities (90)
9. Conglomerates (7)

Total: 712 companies

Source: *Wall Street Journal.*

Figure 37: Dow Jones Equity Market Index

Daily	Aug 24	25	26	27	28
Close	386.34	386.93	388.77	389.19	390.32
Change	-4.13	+0.59	+1.84	+0.42	+1.13

Source: *Barron's*, August 31, 1992.

FUTURES INDEX

What Is It? It is a U.S.-based measure of commodity prices.

How Is It Computed? The index weights prices of various commodities and is determined by Dow Jones.

Where Is It Found? This index of commodity prices may be obtained directly from Dow Jones. It also appears in financial publications such as *Barron's*.

How Is It Used for Investment Decisions? The index is an indicator for overall commodity price movements. The trend in the index may help identify a basic trend reversal by looking at past trend lines and price patterns. For example, if the investor believes that commodity prices have reached their lows, a buying opportunity may be indicated. The investor should track the individual commodities that make up the index, since a specific category of commodities may be attractive at a given time.

PRECIOUS METALS INDEX

What Is It? This is a narrow index of mining companies and is a component of the Dow Jones Equity Market Index.

How Is It Computed? This is a capitalized weighted market price based average of four precious metal companies listed on the NYSE. The companies included are ASA Limited, Hecla Mining, Battle Mountain Gold, and Homestake Mining. The base level of 100 was assigned in 1982.

Where Is It Found? The index is published in the *Wall Street Journal*. It also may be found in the Dow Jones News/Retrieval on-line database.

How Is It Used for Investment Decision? The index enables the investor to determine the price trend and current prices of companies involved in gold, silver, and platinum. Precious metals do well in times of inflation and worldwide unrest. If the investor finds that the index is low and expects times of economic and political uncertainties, an investment in precious metal companies may be suitable.

Also See: DOW JONES EQUITY MARKET INDEX

27. DOW JONES TRANSPORTATION AVERAGE

What Is It? This is a widely watched benchmark for the movement of U.S. transportation stocks. These issues are viewed by many analysts as highly cyclical, thus their performance can be seen as an indicator of future economic activity.

How Is It Computed? The Dow transportation index comprises 20 major transportation companies' stocks—from airlines to railroads. As of August 1992, the list comprised: AMR, Airborne Freight, Alaska Air, American Presidential, Burlington Northern, CSX, Carolina Freight, Consolidated Freight, Consolidated Rail, Delta Air, Federal Express, Norfolk Southern, Roadway, Ryder Systems, Santa Fe Pacific, Southwest Air, UAL, U.S. Air, Union Pacific, and Xtra. Each stock's price is multiplied by the same fixed amount to arrive at the index each day. That means that movement in any of those 20 stocks will have an equal impact on the index's final tally.

Where Is It Found? The Dow Transportation Average is published in most daily newspapers such as the *Los Angeles Times* and *Washington Post* with listings of its better known sister index, the Dow Jones Industrial Average. *Barron's* includes detailed information on the index and its component stocks. It also can be found on computer databases such as Prodigy.

How Is It Used for Investment Decisions? The Dow Transportation Average can be used to weigh how the stock market values transportation-related issues. A rising index can signal investors' sentiment swinging toward these cyclical transportation issues. Conversely, a falling index can be viewed as a negative sign.

The Dow Transportation Average is also a component of the broader Dow Jones Composite Index, which also includes shares in the Dow industrial and Dow utilities index. The composite index is seen by some analysts as a good indicator for the general market's success.

A Word of Caution: These stocks were once seen as a key indicator of the health of the U.S. economy. But the age of deregulation has beaten down many of these companies and their share prices. Some analysts now question whether this index can be used as a barometer of future economic activity.

Also See: DOW JONES INDUSTRIAL AVERAGE, DOW JONES UTILITIES AVERAGE

28. DOW JONES UTILITIES AVERAGE

What Is It? This is a closely viewed benchmark for U.S. utility stocks, which are a popular investment for conservative, income-oriented investors. Both its price movement and the yield on the average are watched by investors.

How Is It Computed? The Dow Utilities Index comprises shares in 15 large publicly owned utilities that provide consumers with everything from gas to water to electricity. As of August 1992, the index comprised: American Electric, Arkla, Centerior, Commonwealth Edison, Con Edison, Consolidated Natural Gas, Detroit Edison, Houston Industries, Niagara Mohawk, Pacific Gas & Electric, Panhandle Eastern, Peoples Energy, Philadelphia Electric, Public Service Enterprises, and SCEcorp.

Each stock's price is multiplied by the same amount to arrive at the index each day. That means that movement in any of those 15 stocks will have an equal impact on the index's result.

The Dow Utility Index's yield is found by totaling all dividends paid by the companies comprising the index and dividing that sum by the combined share price of the 15 utilities.

Where Is It Found? Daily price changes in the Dow Utilities Index can be located in most daily newspapers such as the *Baltimore Sun*, the *New York Times*, and the *Wall Street Journal*. It is usually found alongside listings of its better known sister index, the Dow Jones Industrial Average. The index's yield is somewhat more difficult to locate. It appears daily in the *Wall Street Journal* and weekly in *Barron's*, which contains detailed information on the index and its component stocks. It also can be found on computer databases such as Prodigy.

How Is It Used for Investment Decisions? The Dow Utilities Index can be used to evaluate the direction of utility stocks and how their yield compares to other income-oriented investments.

A rising index is a signal that investors are buying utility stocks. This occurs notably in two situations: One, when interest rates are falling and utility stock yields become attractive. Two, when the economy is picking up, translating to higher sales to industrial users of utility services.

Conversely, a falling index can be a sign that investors fear that interest rates will rise or that a weak economy may slow industrial outputs.

The Utilities Index's yield can be used to gauge the overall attractiveness of such stocks to an income-oriented investor. In addition, it can help measure how a single utility's dividend payout compares to its peers'.

A Word of Caution: Utility prices are not moved by national economics only. Other items that impact utility share prices are regulatory and environmental concerns, factors that have less significance to the broad investment outlook. An investor must determine if such noneconomic factors are figuring into the index's movement before making an investment based on a Dow Utilities Average's trend.

Also See: DOW JONES INDUSTRIAL AVERAGE, DOW JONES TRANSPORTATION AVERAGE, ECONOMIC INDICATORS AND BOND YIELDS

29. DURATION

What Is It? Duration is a way to measure the risk of price change due to interest rate fluctuations in a bond or a portfolio of bonds. While rarely discussed in the media, it is the top figure that professional money managers watch when reviewing a bond portfolio.

How Is It Computed? Duration is a complex calculation that includes evaluating the income stream that a bond or a bond portfolio generates. That cash flow is then discounted, creating a present value of that interest payment stream. The calculation also includes an estimate of the chances for the bond or bonds to be called back by the issuer.

As an example, a 30-year U.S. Treasury bond has a duration of approximately ten years.

The results are stated as figures in years. Simply translated, that means that for each year of duration, that bond or portfolio will lose or gain 1% of principal value for each 1 percentage point move in interest rates.

As an example, an investor who owns a 30-year U.S. Treasury (duration: ten years) would lose 15% of his principal if 30-year interest rates were to rise 1.5 percentage points.

The calculation is somewhat subjective and can sometimes misstate the bondholders' risks if certain incorrect assumptions are used.

Example: McCaulay's duration is a popular method. First, the present value of a bond's income stream must be determined. Second, that present value must be calculated as a percentage of the bond's price. Finally, that percentage must be multiplied by the corresponding year's number. The sum of the products equals the duration. Figure 38 shows an example for a new, ten-year bond with a $1,000 face value yielding 6.5%.

Where Is It Found? Duration is rarely discussed in the media although it is the most common measure of interest rate risk used by bond traders. Typically, a bond's stated maturity or a portfolio's average maturity (a simple calculation of weighing bond maturity and prices) is quoted. Such maturity figures do not as clearly outline the interest risks involved.

Owners of bond portfolios, such as mutual funds, probably can get duration figures from the management company. Such requests, however, are often poorly answered.

How Is It Used for Investment Decisions? Duration is a powerful tool that shows investors how much price risk exists in holding longer-term bonds just from interest rate swings. Bond prices fall as rates rise, and values increase when rates drop. And the price swings can be dramatic.

An investor comparing two bond portfolios with equal yields but different durations might choose the one with the longer duration if he believed that interest rates were going

Figure 38: Example of Duration

Year	Cash flow	Present value of cash flow	Present value as percentage of bond price	Year x PV percentage
1	65	$61.03	0.06	0.06
2	65	$57.31	0.06	0.12
3	65	$53.81	0.05	0.16
4	65	$50.53	0.05	0.20
5	65	$47.44	0.05	0.24
6	65	$44.55	0.05	0.27
7	65	$41.83	0.04	0.29
8	65	$39.28	0.04	0.31
9	65	$36.88	0.04	0.33
10	1,065	$567.35	0.57	5.67
				Duration:
				7.66

to fall. That portfolio would likely produce more capital gains if rates did go lower. However, if an investor thought rates were going to rise, or if the investor simply wanted to lower his risk-taking, he should choose the portfolio with the shorter duration.

A Word of Caution: Duration is not a static figure. Movements in interest rates alone will change a portfolio's duration. It will be further changed if a manager then takes actions in response to market movements. This means that an investor relying on duration to watch, for example, a bond mutual fund must make sure that his information is up-to-date. If rates were rising, an investor might want to prune a long-duration fund from his portfolio. However, the investor would first want to check to see if the fund's manager had already taken defensive moves and lowered the fund's duration.

Also See: ECONOMIC INDICATORS AND BOND YIELDS, YIELD ON A BOND, YIELD ON AN INVESTMENT: CURRENT

30. ECONOMIC INDICATORS AND BOND YIELDS

What are they? The investor makes an analysis of the economy primarily to determine his investment strategy. It is not necessary for him to formulate his own economic forecasts. The investor can rely on published forecasts in an effort to identify the trends in the economy and adjust his investment position accordingly.

The investor must keep abreast of the economic trend and direction and attempt to see how they affect bond yields and bond prices. Unfortunately, there are too many economic indicators and variables to be analyzed. Each has its own significance. In many cases, these variables could give mixed signals about the future of the economy and therefore mislead the investor.

How Are They Computed? Various government agencies and private firms tabulate the appropriate economic data and calculate various indexes.

Where Are They Found? Sources for these indicators are easily subscribed to at an affordable price or can be found in local public and college libraries. They include daily local newspapers and national newspapers such as *Investor's Business Daily*, the *Los Angeles Times*, the *New York Times*, *USA Today*, and the *Wall Street Journal*.

Many periodicals, such as *Barron's, Business Week, Forbes, Fortune, Kiplinger's Personal Finance Magazine, Money, Nation's Business, Smart Money, U.S. News and World Report*, and *Worth* also publish relevant information.

How Are They Used for Investment Decisons? Figure 39 provides a concise and brief list of the significant economic indicators and how they affect bond yields.

A Word of Caution: Figure 39 merely serves as a handy guide and should not be construed as accurate in all cases.

Also See: ECONOMIC INDICATORS AND THE SECURITIES MARKET

31. ECONOMIC INDICATORS AND THE SECURITIES MARKET

What Are They? The investor makes an analysis of the economy primarily to determine his investment strategy. It is not necessary for him to formulate his own economic forecasts. The investor can rely on published forecasts in an effort to identify the trends in the economy and adjust his investment position accordingly.

The investor must keep abreast of the economic trend and direction and attempt to see how they affect the security market. Unfortunately, there are too many economic indicators and variables to be analyzed. Each has its own significance. In many cases, these variables could give mixed signals about the future of the economy and therefore mislead the investor.

How Are They Computed? Various government agencies and private firms tabulate the appropriate economic data and calculate various indexes.

Where Are They Found? Sources for these indicators are easily subscribed to at an affordable price or can be found in local public and college libraries. They include daily local newspapers and national newspapers such as *Investor's Business Daily*, the *Los Angeles Times*, the *New York Times*, *USA Today*, and the *Wall Street Journal*.

Many periodicals, such as *Barron's, Business Week, Forbes, Fortune, Kiplinger's Personal Finance Magazine, Money, Nation's Business, Smart Money, U.S. News and World Report*, and *Worth* also publish relevant information.

How Are They Used for Investment Decisons? Figure 40 on page 58 summarizes the types of economic variables and their probable effect on the security market and the economy in general.

A Word of Caution: Figure 40 merely serves as a handy guide and should not be construed as accurate at all times.

Also See: ECONOMIC INDICATORS AND BOND YIELDS

Figure 39: Probable Effects of Economic Variables on Bond Yields*

Indicators**	Effects on Bond Yields***	Reasons
Business Activity		
GNP and industrial production falls	Fall	As economy slows, Fed may ease credit by allowing rates to fall
Unemployment rises	Fall	High unemployment indicates lack of economic expansion. Fed may loosen credit
Inventories rise	Fall	Inventory levels are good indicators of duration of economic slowdown
Trade deficit rises	Fall	Dollar weakens
Leading indicators	Rise	Advance signals about economic health; Fed may tighten credit
Housing starts rise	Rise	Growing economy due to increased new housing demand; Fed may tighten; mortgage rates rise
Personal income rises	Rise	Higher income means higher consumer spending, thus inflationary; Fed may tighten
Inflation		
Consumer Price Index rises	Rise	Inflationary
Producer Price Index rises	Rise	Early signal for inflation
Monetary Policy		
Money supply rises	Rise	Excess growth in money supply is inflationary; Fed may tighten
Discount rate rises	Rise	Causes increase in business and consumer loan rates; used to slow economic growth and inflation
Fed buys (sells) bills	Rise (fall)	Adds (deducts) money to the economy; interest rates may go down (up)
Required reserve rates	Rise	Depresses bank lending

*This table merely serves as a handy guide and should not be construed as accurate at all times.
**Fall in any of these indicators will have the opposite effect on bond yields.
***Note: The effects are based on yield and therefore wil have the opposite effect on bond prices.

Source: Jae K. Shim and Joel G. Siegel, *SOURCE: The Complete Guide to Investment Information, Where to Find It and How to Use It,* International Publishing Corporation, 1992.

32. ECONOMIC INDICATORS: FACTORY ORDERS-PURCHASING MANAGERS' INDEX

What Is It? The factory order series presents new orders received by manufacturers of durable goods other than military equipment. (Durable goods are defined as those having

Figure 40: Economic Variables and their Impacts on the Economy and the Security Market

Economic Variables Market	Impact on Security
Real growth in GNP	Positive (without inflation)
Industrial production	Consecutive drops are a sign of recession
Inflation	Detrimental to equity and bond prices
Capacity utilization	A high performance is positive, but full capacity is inflationary
Durable goods orders	Consecutive drops are a sign of recession
Increase in business investment, consumer confidnece, personal income, etc.	Positive
Leading indicators	The rise is bullish for the economy and the market; consecutive drops are a sign of bad times ahead
Housing starts	The rise is positive; vice versa
Corporate profits	Strong corporate earnings are positive for the market; vice versa
Unemployment	Unfavorable for the market and economy
Increase in business inventories	Positive for the inflationary economy; Negative for the stable economy
Federal deficit	Typically inflationary and negative though positive for the depressed economy
Deficit in trade and balance of payments	Negative
Weak dollar	Negative; inflationary and shows foreign doubt about U.S. economy
Interest rates	Rising rates depress the value of fixed income securities such as bonds which tend to fall; vice versa

Source: Jae K. Shim and Joel G. Siegel, *SOURCE: The Complete Guide to Investment Information, Where to Find It and How to Use It*, International Publishing Corporation, 1992.

a useful life of more than three years.) Nondefense equipment represents about 1/5 to 1/3 of all durable goods production. The series includes engines, construction, mining, and materials handling equipment; office and store machinery; electrical transmission and distribution equipment and other electrical machinery (excluding household appliances and electronic equipment); and railroad, ship and aircraft transportation equipment. Military equipment is excluded because new orders for such items do not respond directly to the business cycle.

The National Association of Purchasing Management releases its monthly *Purchasing Index,* which describes buying intentions of corporate purchasing agents.

How Is It Computed? The factory order series is released by the Department of Commerce. Each month, approximately 2,300 companies are asked to file a report covering orders, inventories, and shipments.

As for the *Purchasing Index*, the National Association of Purchasing Agents conducts a survey that polls purchasing managers from 20 industries.

Where Is It Found? They are reported in daily newspapers and business dailies such as *Investor's Business Daily* and the *Wall Street Journal*. Figure 41 shows how the former reports this data.

How Is It Used for Investment Decisions? Economists typically count on factory production, particularly of "big ticket" durable goods ranging from airplanes to home appliances, to help lift the economy from a downturn. A decline in this series suggests that factories are unlikely to hire new workers. A drop in the backlog of unfilled orders is also an indication of possible production cutbacks and layoffs. Alternately, the wider dispersal of gains in many types of goods is looked upon as a favorable sign for the economy. The broader the dispersal of order increases, the broader the rehiring.

The purchasing managers are responsible for buying the raw materials that feed the nation's factories. Their buying patterns are considered a good indication of the direction of the economy. A reading of 50% or more indicates that the manufacturing economy is generally expanding. A reading above 44.5 percent over a period of time indicates that the overall economy is augmenting.

A Word of Caution: Again, in order to make an overall assessment of the economy, the investor must look to other important economic indicators.

Also See: ECONOMIC INDICATORS AND BOND YIELDS, ECONOMIC INDICATORS AND THE SECURITIES MARKET

Figure 41: Factory Orders Report

	Feb. 1989	Jan. 1989	% Chg.
All industries	230.68	236.68	- 2.3
Durable goods	124.20	128.48	- 3.3
Nondurable goods	106.48	107.60	- 1.0
Capital goods industries	45.40	47.17	- 3.7
Nondefense	37.06	40.35	- 8.2
Defense	8.34	6.82	+ 22.4
Total shipments	227.61	231.49	- 1.7
Inventories	359.09	357.46	+ 0.5
Backlog of orders	476.52	473.45	+ 0.6

Source: *Wall Street Journal*, March 31, 1989.

33. ECONOMIC INDICATORS: GROSS DOMESTIC PRODUCT (GDP)

What Is It? Gross Domestic Product (GDP) measures the value of all goods and services produced by the economy within its boundaries and is the nation's broadest gauge of economic health. GDP is normally stated in annual terms, though data are compiled and released quarterly.

How Is It Computed? The Department of Commerce compiles GDP.

Where Is It Found? GDP is reported quarterly and appears in daily newspapers including the *Wall Street Journal.*

A sample report is presented in Figure 42.

How Is It Used for Investment Decisions? GDP is often a measure of the state of the economy. For example, many economists speak of recession when there has been a decline in GDP for two consecutive quarters. The GDP in dollar and real terms is a useful economic indicator. An expected growth rate of 5% in real terms would be very attractive for long-term investment and would affect the stock market positively. Since inflation and price increases are detrimental to equity prices, a real growth of GDP without inflation is favorable and desirable.

The following diagram charts a series of events leading from a rising GDP to higher security prices.

GDP up → Profits up → Dividends up → Stock prices up

Generally speaking, too much or too little is inflationary and thus negative for the security market. (When companies are producing "flat out," they need workers desperately and are willing to pay big wage increases to attract new workers and keep them.) But these wage increases raise business costs and lead firms to raise prices and must be avoided. Too little production is undesirable as well. Low levels of production mean layoffs, unemployment, low incomes for workers, and tend to depress the security market.

A Word of Caution: GDP fails the timely release criterion for useful economic indicators. It is also weak on the criterion of relevance to investors, since it includes many sectors of the economy in which there is no private investment.

Unfortunately, there is no way of gauging whether we are in a recession or prosperity currently, based on the GDP measure. Only after the quarter is over can it be determined if there was growth or decline.

In addition, an increasing number of analysts say the GDP criteria for a recession are no longer valid. Experts review other measures such as unemployment rate, industrial production, durable orders, corporate profits, retail sales, and housing activity to look for a sign of recession.

Also See: ECONOMIC INDICATORS AND BOND YIELDS, ECONOMIC INDICATORS AND THE SECURITIES MARKET, ECONOMIC INDICATOR: RECESSION

34. ECONOMIC INDICATORS: HOUSING STARTS AND CONSTRUCTION SPENDING

What Are They? Housing starts are an important economic indicator followed by investors and economists that offers an estimate of the number of dwelling units on which construction has begun during a stated period. It covers construction of new homes and apartments. When an economy is going to take a downturn, the housing sector is the first to decline. Housing starts indicate the future strength of the housing sector of the economy. At the same time, it is closely related to interest rates and other basic economic factors. The statistics for construction spending cover homes, office buildings, and other construction projects.

How Are They Computed? Both housing starts and construction spending figures are issued monthly by the Department of Commerce.

Where Are They Found? *Investor's Business Daily* and the *Wall Street Journal* report these data whenever released.

Figure 42: Sample Economic Indicators Report

Tracking the Economy   August 24, 1992

Consumers concerned about their jobs and financial stability continue to express a lack of confidence in the economy.

An index of consumer confidence published by the Conference Board, New York, probably moved up to 61.8% in August, slightly ahead of July's 61% reading, but far short of 81.1% peak registered after the Persian Gulf War, says Gary Ciminero, chief economist for Fleet Financial Group.

The index, measured against a 1985 base of 100, has been behaving like a "descending roller coaster" since the Gulf War, rising and falling but on an overall downward path, Mr. Ciminero says.

"It's been a case of up and down with lower peaks and deeper troughs," he says.

An 11.6-point decline in the July index wiped out nearly half of the cumulative gain in the index recorded during the spring months.

"Confidence remains warily low, giving little encouragement for a consumer-led recovery," Mr. Ciminero says.

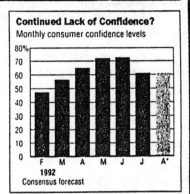

Continued Lack of Confidence?
Monthly consumer confidence levels

1992
Consensus forecast

Low consumer confidence has confounded the Federal Reserve Board, which has dropped interest rates sharply in an attempt to get people spending again and bolster the economic recovery.

"Interest rates are not doing it," Mr. Ciminero says. "The concerns about jobs and financial stability... never recovered after the war." Some 5,000 households nationwide are surveyed for the index.
—*Alan Yonan Jr.*

Statistics to Be Released This Week

ECONOMIC INDICATOR	PERIOD	RELEASE DATE	PREVIOUS ACTUAL	TECHNICAL DATA CONSENSUS FORECAST
New Car Sales (ann. rate)	Mid-August	Aug. 25	5.7 million	6.2 million
Durable Goods	July	Aug. 26	+2.7%	0.0%
Gross Domestic Product	2nd qtr. prelim.	Aug. 27	+1.4%	+1.5%
Initial Jobless Claims	Week to Aug. 15	Aug. 27	474,000	400,000
Money Supply: M1	Week to Aug. 17	Aug. 27	+$5.9 billion	+$2.6 billion
Money Supply: M2	Week to Aug. 17	Aug. 27	+$9.1 billion	+$3.8 billion
Money Supply: M3	Week to Aug. 17	Aug. 27	+$6.0 billion	+$3.0 billion
Consumer Confidence	August	Aug. 28	61.0%	61.8%
Personal Income	July	Aug. 28	unchanged	+0.2%
Personal Consumption	July	Aug. 28	+0.5%	+0.3%

Statistics Released Last Week

Housing starts (ann. rate) July	1.119 million −2.8%	Merchandise Trade Deficit June	$6.59 billion

Source: Technical Data

How Are They Used for Investment Decisons? Housing is a key interest rate-sensitive sector that usually leads the rest of the economy out of the recession. Also, housing is vital to a broader economic revival, not only because of its benefits for other industries but also because it signals consumers' confidence about making long-term financial commitments.

A Word of Caution: For the housing sector to be sustained, housing start figures need to be backed by building permits. Permits are considered a leading indicator of housing starts.

Also See: ECONOMIC INDICATORS AND BOND YIELDS, ECONOMIC INDICATORS: INTEREST RATES, ECONOMIC INDICATORS AND THE SECURITIES MARKET, REAL ESTATE RETURNS: HOME PRICE STATISTICS

35. ECONOMIC INDICATORS: INDEX OF LEADING INDICATORS

What Is It? The Index of Leading Indicators is the economic series of indicators that tend to predict future changes in economic activity. Its official name is the Composite Index of 11 Leading Indicators. The series is the government's main barometer for forecasting business trends. Each of the series has shown a tendency to change before the economy makes a major turn—hence, the term "leading indicators." The index is designed to forecast economic activity—direction of the economy—in the next six to nine months (1982 = 100).

The index consists of 11 indicators and is subject to revision. For example, petroleum and natural gas prices were found to distort the data from crude material prices and were subsequently dropped from that category.

How Is It Computed? This series is calculated and published monthly by the Department of Commerce. It consists of:

1. Average workweek of production workers in manufacturing
    Employers find it much easier to increase the number of hours current employees work in a week than to hire more employees.
2. Initial claims for unemployment insurance
    The number of people who sign up for unemployment benefits signals changes in present and future economic activity.
3. Change in consumer confidence
    It is based on the University of Michigan's survey of consumer expectations. The index measures consumers' optimism regarding the present and future state of the economy and is based on an index of 100 in 1966. Consumer spending buys two-thirds of the country's Gross Domestic Product or GDP (all goods and services produced in the economy), so any sharp change could be an important factor in an overall turnaround.
4. Percent change in prices of sensitive crude materials
    Rises in prices of such critical materials as steel and iron usually mean that factory demands are going up, which means that factories plan to step up production.
5. Contracts and orders for plant and equipment
    Heavier contracting and ordering usually leads economic upswings.
6. Vendor performance
    Vendor performance represents the percentage of companies reporting slower deliveries. As the economy grows, firms have more trouble filling orders.

7. Stock prices

A rise in the common stock index indicates expected profits and lower interest rates. Stock market advances usually precede business upturns by three to eight months.

8. Money supply

A rising money supply means easy money that sparks brisk economic activity. This usually leads recoveries by as much as fourteen months.

9. New orders for manufacturers of consumer goods and materials

New orders mean more workers hired, more materials and supplies purchased, and increased output. Gains in this series usually lead recoveries by as much as four months.

10. Residential building permits for private housing

Gains in building permits signal business upturns.

11. Factory backlogs of unfilled durable goods orders

Backlogs signify business upswings.

Where Is It Found? It is found in *Business Conditions Digest* published by the Bureau of Economic Analysis of the U.S. Department of Commerce and is also easily available in daily newspapers including *Investor's Business Daily* and the *Wall Street Journal*.

How Is It Used for Investment Decisions? If the index is consistently rising, even only slightly, the economy is chugging along and a setback is unlikely. If the indicator drops for three or more consecutive months, investors can look for an economic slowdown and possibly a recession in the next year or so.

A rising (consecutive percentage increases in) indicator is bullish for the economy and the stock market, and vice versa.

A Word of Caution: These 11 components of the index are adjusted for inflation. Rarely do these components of the index all go in the same direction at once.

Each factor is weighted. The composite figure is designed to tell only in which direction business will go. It is not intended to forecast the magnitude of future ups and downs.

Also See: ECONOMIC INDICATORS AND BOND YIELDS, ECONOMIC INDICATORS AND THE SECURITIES MARKET

36. ECONOMIC INDICATORS: INDUSTRIAL PRODUCTION-CAPACITY UTILIZATION

What Is It? The index of industrial production, more precisely the Federal Reserve Board Index of Industrial Production, measures changes in the output of the mining, manufacturing, and gas and electric utilities sectors of the economy. Detailed breakdowns of the index provide a reading on how individual industries are faring.

Industrial production is narrower than GDP since it omits agriculture, construction, wholesale and retail trade, transportation, communications, services, finance, and government.

Another way to view the performance of the real economy is to look at industrial production relative to the production capacity of the industrial sector. The actual production level as a percentage of the full capacity level is called the rate of capacity utilization. This monthly rate is limited to manufacturing industries.

How Is It Computed? Data for the index are drawn from 250 data series obtained from private trade associations and internal estimates. To construct the index, the base year of 1977 was selected to serve as a benchmark and assigned a value of 100.

Example: If the index was 151.0 in 1992, then the level of industrial production in real terms was 51% higher than in 1977.

Where Is It Found? This monthly Index of Industrial Production, which is released only two weeks into the next month, is published by the Federal Reserve Board. The rate of capacity utilization is announced every month by the Fed, one day after the Index of Industrial Production. Both are published in the *Federal Reserve Bulletin* and appear in major daily newspapers such as *Investor's Business Daily, USA Today,* the *Wall Street Journal.*

A sample report as it appears in the *Wall Street Journal* is presented in Figure 43.

Figure 43: Industrial Production Report

	% change from	
	Jan. 1989	Feb. 1988
Total	0.0	5.0
Consumer goods	0.1	5.8
Business equipment	0.8	8.5
Defense and space	- 0.2	- 5.4
Manufacturing only	0.0	5.7
Durable goods	0.1	6.1
Nondurable goods	- 0.1	5.0
Mining	- 1.8	0.0
Utilities	1.9	1.2

The industrial production index for February stood at 141.1% of the 1977 average.

Source: *Wall Street Journal,* March 17, 1989.

How Is It Used for Investment Decisions? A rising index is a sign that the economy will strengthen and that the stock market should turn up. A falling industrial production should be a concern for the economy and the investor. Regardless of the state of the economy, however, detailed breakdowns of the index provide a reading on how individual industries are faring and on what industries should be attended by investors. A rising rate of capacity utilization is positive for the economy and the security market; a falling rate is an indication of a sinking economy and thus negative for the security market.

A Word of Caution: Industrial production is more volatile than GDP because GDP, unlike industrial production, includes activities that are largely spared cyclical fluctuations, such as services, finance, and government.

Also See: ECONOMIC INDICATORS AND BOND YIELDS, ECONOMIC INDICATORS: FACTORY ORDERS—PURCHASING MANAGER'S INDEX, ECONOMIC INDICATORS AND THE SECURITIES MARKET

37. ECONOMIC INDICATORS: INFLATION

What Is It? Inflation is the general rise in prices of consumer goods and services. The federal government measures inflation by comparing prices today—measured in terms of price indexes such as the Consumer Price Index (CPI), Producer Price Index (PPI), and/or Gross Domestic Product (GDP) Deflator—to a two-year period, 1982 to 1984.

How Is It Computed? Price indexes are designed to measure the rate of inflation of the economy. Various price indexes are used to measure living costs, price level changes, and inflation. They are:

Consumer Price Index (CPI) The Consumer Price Index (CPI), the most well-known inflation gauge, is used as the cost-of-living index, which labor contracts and social security are tied to. The CPI measures the cost of buying a fixed bundle of goods (approximately 400 consumer goods and services) that would be representative of the purchase of the typical working-class urban family. The fixed basket is divided into the following categories: food and beverages, housing, apparel, transportation, medical care, entertainment, and other. Generally referred to as a cost-of-living index, it is published by the Bureau of Labor Statistics of the U.S. Department of Labor. The CPI is widely used for escalation clauses. The base period for the CPI index was 1982 to 1984 at which time it was assigned 100.

Producer Price Index (PPI) Like the CPI, the PPI is a measure of the cost of a given basket of goods priced in wholesale markets, including raw materials, semifinished goods, and finished goods at the early stage of the distribution system. The PPI is published monthly by the Bureau of Labor Statistics of the Department of Commerce. (Since the PPI does not include services, caution should be exercised when the principal cause of inflation is service prices.) For this reason, the PPI and especially some of its subindexes, such as the index of sensitive materials, serve as one of the leading indicators that are closely watched by policymakers. It is the one that signals changes in the general price level, or the CPI, some time before they actually materialize.

GDP Deflator (Implicit Price Index) The GDP implicit deflator is the third index of inflation that is used to separate price changes in GDP calculations from real changes in economic activity. The GDP Deflator is a weighted average of the price indexes used to deflate the components of GDP. Thus, it reflects price changes for goods and services bought by consumers, businesses, and governments. The GDP deflator is found by dividing current GDP in a given year by constant (real) GDP. Because it covers a broader group of goods and services than the CPI and PPI, the GDP Deflator is a very widely used price index that is frequently used to measure inflation. The GDP deflator, unlike the CPI and PPI, is available only quarterly—not monthly. It also is published by the U.S. Department of Commerce.

Where Is It Found? Price indexes appear in daily newspapers and business dailies such as *Investor's Business Daily* and the *Wall Street Journal*. A sample as appearing in the *Wall Street Journal* is presented in Figure 44.

How Is It Used for Investment Decisions? Rising prices is Public Enemy Number One for stocks and bonds. Inflation usually hurts stock prices since higher consumer prices lessen the value of future corporate earnings, which makes shares of those companies less appealing to investors. By contrast, when prices rocket ahead, investors often flock to long-term inflation hedges such as real estate and gold. Investors should check to see whether the inflation rate has been rising—a negative, or bearish, sign for stock and bond investors—or falling, which is bullish.

The following diagram charts a chain of events leading from lower rates of inflation to increased consumer spending and possibly an up security market.

CPI down → Real personal income up → Consumer confidence up → Consumer spending up (Retail sales up + Housing starts up + Auto sales up) → Security market up

A Word of Caution: Most likely, the Federal Reserve will tighten the money supply and raise interest rates (such as the discount rate or federal fund rate). The rationale is that if it is too expensive to borrow money, then there will be less demand for products, which in turn pushes prices down. The following diagram shows how inflation affects the security prices.

Inflation → Fed raises discount rate → Interest rates up → Demand for money down → Demand for products down → Corporate profits down → Security prices down

Figure 44: Consumer Prices Report

Here are the seasonally adjusted changes in the components of the Labor Department's consumer price index for February:

	% change from	
	Jan. 1989	Feb. 1988
All items	0.4	4.8
Minus food & energy	0.4	4.8
Food and beverage	0.5	6.0
Housing	0.3	3.9
Apparel	- 0.2	4.6
Transportation	0.6	4.5
Medical care	0.8	7.2
Entertainment	0.4	5.1
Other	0.6	7.4

Consumer price indexes (1982-1984 equals 100), unadjusted for seasonal variation, together with the percentage increases from 1988 were:

All urban consumers	121.6	4.8
Urban wage earners & clerical	120.2	4.8
Chicago	122.2	4.8
Detroit	120.1	5.6
Los Angeles	125.5	4.8
New York	127.6	5.4
Philadelphia	125.4	5.1
San Francisco	124.0	5.2
Dallas-Fort Worth	117.5	3.1
Detroit	120.1	5.6
Houston	112.7	4.4
Pittsburgh	117.9	4.1

Source: *Wall Street Journal*, March 22, 1989.

In economic theory, interest rates are no more than a reflection of what expectations are for inflation. Inflation therefore means higher interest rates.

Also See: COMMODITY INDEXES: COMMODITY RESEARCH BUREAU INDEXES, ECONOMIC INDICATORS AND BOND YIELDS, ECONOMIC INDICATORS AND THE SECURITIES MARKET

38. ECONOMIC INDICATORS: MONEY SUPPLY

What Is It? This is the level of funds available at a given time for conducting transactions in an economy, as reported by the Federal Reserve. The Federal Reserve System can influence money supply through its monetary policy measures. There are several definitions of the money supply: M1 (which is currency in circulation, demand deposits, traveler's checks, and those in interest-bearing NOW accounts), M2 (the most widely followed measure, it equals M1 plus savings deposits, money market deposit accounts, and money market funds), and M3 (which is M2 plus large CDs).

How Is It Computed? The Federal Reserve System computes these measures.

Where Is It Found? The weekly money supply figures are released on Thursday afternoons by the Federal Reserve Board and reported in daily newspapers including *Barron's* and the *Wall Street Journal*. A sample is presented in Figure 45.

Figure 45: Money Supply Report

Money Supply (Bil., seas. adj.)	Latest Week	Previous Week	Year Ago Week
M1 (One Week Ended July 24)	776.2	777.5	781.8
M2 (One Week Ended July 24)	3121.2	r3122.7	3024.6
M3 (One Week Ended July 24)	4004.3	r4008.9	3822.4

Monetary Aggregates (Bil. seas. adj.)	Latest Week	Previous Week	Year Ago Week
M1 (Month Ended June)	770.7	773.4	776.5
Currency	217.4	216.4	204.7
Travelers' checks	7.2	7.3	7.3
Demand Deposits	275.2	278.3	289.8
Other checkable deposits NOWs, Super NOWs	271.0	271.4	274.7
M2 (M1 plus:) (Month Ended June)	r3089.2	r3072.4	3013.1
Savings deposits	402.3	404.9	427.6
Small time deposits	1119.8	1106.1	975.7
Overnight RPs	59.8	57.9	63.7
Overnight Euro$	14.9	14.7	17.2
Money market funds	266.2	259.9	228.9
Money market deposit accounts	457.0	457.0	523.2
M3 (M2 plus:) (Month Ended June)	r3973.4	r3953.5	3795.6
Large time deposits	569.9	569.7	504.8
Inst. money funds	95.1	91.6	86.3
Term RPs	127.9	127.6	124.3
Term Euro$	100.2	101.4	93.9

Source: *Barron's*.

How Is It Used and Applied? A rapid growth in money supply is viewed as inflationary; in contrast, a sharp drop in the money supply is considered to be recessionary. Moderate growth is thought to have a positive impact on the economy. Economists attempt to compare with targets proposed by the Fed.

How Is It Used for Investment Decisions? The Fed affects money supply through its monetary policy such as open market operations. The following diagram summarizes its possible impact on the economy and the security market.

(1) Easy Money Policy
Fed buys securities → Bank reserves up → Bank lending up → Money supply up → Interest rates down → Loan demand up → Security market up

(2) Tight Money Policy
Fed sells securities → Bank reserves down → Bank lending down → Money supply down → Interest rates up → Loan demand down → Security market down

A Word of Caution: A rapid growth (excessively easy monetary policy) is viewed as inflationary and could impact the economy adversely; in contrast, a sharp drop in the money supply is considered to be recessionary and can hurt the economy and the security market. Moderate growth is thought to have a positive impact on the economy.

Also See: ECONOMIC INDICATORS AND BOND YIELDS, ECONOMIC INDICATORS: INTEREST RATES, ECONOMIC INDICATORS AND THE SECURITIES MARKET

39. ECONOMIC INDICATORS: PERSONAL INCOME AND CONFIDENCE INDEXES

What Are They? Personal income shows the before-tax income such as wages and salaries, rents, and interest and dividends, and other payments such as unemployment and Social Security received by individuals and unincorporated businesses.

There are two popular indexes that track the level of consumer confidence: One is the Conference Board of New York, an industry-sponsored, nonprofit economic research institute, and the other is the index compiled by the University of Michigan Survey Research Center, another research organization.

The Conference Board's Consumer Confidence Index measures consumer optimism and pessimism about general business conditions, jobs, and total family income.

The University of Michigan's index is called the Index of Consumer Sentiment. It measures consumers' personal financial circumstances and their outlook for the future. The index is used by the Commerce Department in its monthly Index of Leading Economic Indicators and is regularly charted in the department's *Business Conditions Digest*.

How Are They Computed? Personal income data are released monthly by the Commerce Department. The Conference Board's index is calculated on a 1985 basis of 100 and derived from a survey of 5,000 households nationwide, covering questions that range from home-buying plans to the outlook for jobs, both presently and during the next six months.

The University of Michigan's index is compiled through a telephone survey of 500 households.

Where Are They Found? Newspapers such as *Investor's Business Daily, USA Today*, and the *Wall Street Journal* report these indexes.

How Are They Applied? Personal income represents consumers' spending power. When personal income rises, it usually means that consumers will increase their purchases, which will in turn favorably affect the investment climate.

The Conference Board's index is considered a useful economic barometer because it provides insight into consumer spending, which is critical to any sustainable economic upswing. Many economists pay close attention to the index, for its insight into consumer attitudes toward spending and borrowing. Consumers account for two-thirds of the nation's economic activity (*i.e.*, national gross domestic product) and thus drive recovery and expansion.

How Are They Used for Investment Decisions? A low or decreased level of consumer confidence indicates concern about employment prospects and earnings in the months ahead. Uncertainty requires caution in investing.

On the other hand, an increased level of consumer confidence spells economic recovery and expansion, thus presenting an investment opportunity. In summary, an increase in personal income, coupled with substantial consumer confidence, is bullish for the economy and the security market.

A Word of Caution: To formulate the future prospects about the economy, investors must weigh various economic indicators such as inflation measures.

Also See: ECONOMIC INDICATORS AND BOND YIELDS, ECONOMIC INDICATORS AND THE SECURITIES MARKET

40. ECONOMIC INDICATORS: PRODUCTIVITY AND UNIT LABOR COSTS

What Are They? Productivity is defined as output per hour of work.

How Are They Computed? The data on productivity and unit labor costs is released by the Labor Department.

Where Are They Found? *Investor's Business Daily*, the *Wall Street Journal*, and *USA Today* report these figures when available.

How Are They Used for Investment Decisions? Increased productivity, or getting more worker output per hour on the job, is considered vital to increasing the nation's standard of living without inflation. Unit labor costs are a key gauge of future price inflation along with the Consumer Price Index (CPI), Producer Price Index (PPI), and Gross Domestic Product (GDP) Deflator.

A Word of Caution: These statistics cover only the manufacturing sector of the economy. They do not deal with the service sector, which is substantial in size.

Also See: ECONOMIC INDICATORS AND BOND YIELDS, ECONOMIC INDICATORS: INFLATION, ECONOMIC INDICATORS AND THE SECURITIES MARKET

41. ECONOMIC INDICATORS: RECESSION

What Is It? Recession means a sinking economy. Unfortunately, there is no consensus definition and measure of recession. In general, it means that the number of dollars moving through the economy is shrinking in size and the number of jobs being lost outnumbers the jobs being created.

How Is It Computed? The "official" keeper of economic downturns is the seven-member Dating Committee of the National Bureau of Economic Research, the nonprofit group tabbed by the government in the 1930s to be the official arbiter of recessions.

However, this committee doesn't issue its verdicts of the starts and ends of recessions until months, and sometimes years, after a recessionary trend has begun. As of August 1992, the committee had not yet deduced when the recession that began in July 1990 had ended although some estimates thought the downturn was completed by March 1991.

There are three primary ways economists define a recession.

1.   Three or more straight monthly drops of the Index of Leading Economic Indicators are generally considered a sign of recession.
2.   Two consecutive quarterly drops of GDP signal recession.
3.   Consecutive monthly drops of durable goods orders, which most likely result in less production and increasing layoffs in the factory sector, indicates a recession.

Where Is It Found? Newspapers such as *Investor's Business Daily, USA Today,* and the *Wall Street Journal* frequently report and chart recession-related indicators.

How Is It Used for Investment Decisions? Recession tends to dampen the spirits of consumers and investors and thus depress prices of various investment vehicles including securities and real estate.

A Word of Caution: Not all industries in the economy during recession go bad. Some industrial sectors (for example, consumer products industry) are recession-resistant or defensive. Investors need to analyze industry by industry.

Also See: ECONOMIC INDICATORS AND BOND YIELDS, ECONOMIC INDICATORS, GROSS DOMESTIC PRODUCT (GDP), ECONOMIC INDICATOR: INDEX OF LEADING INDICATORS, ECONOMIC INDICATORS AND THE SECURITIES MARKET, ECONOMIC INDICATORS: UNEMPLOYMENT AND INITIAL JOBLESS CLAIMS

42. ECONOMIC INDICATORS: RETAIL SALES

What Is It? This figure is the estimate of total sales at the retail level. It includes everything from bags of groceries to durable goods such as automobiles. It is used as a measure of future economic conditions: A long slowdown in sales could spell cuts in production.

How Is It Computed? The data are issued monthly by the Commerce Department.

Where Is It Found? *Investor's Business Daily, USA Today,* and the *Wall Street Journal* report this data when released.

How Is It Used for Investment Decisions? Retail sales are a major concern of analysts because they represent about half of overall consumer spending. Consumer spending, in turn, accounts for about two-thirds of the nation's GDP. The amount of retail sales depends heavily on consumer confidence about the economy.

A Word of Caution: Too strong retail sales could spurt inflation. It could hurt the stock market.

Also See: ECONOMIC INDICATOR: GROSS DOMESTIC PRODUCTS (GDP), ECONOMIC INDICATORS: PERSONAL INCOME AND CONFIDENCE INDEXES

43. ECONOMIC INDICATORS: UNEMPLOYMENT RATE AND INITIAL JOBLESS CLAIMS

What Are They? Unemployment, reported monthly, is the nonavailability of jobs for people able and willing to work at the prevailing wage rate. It is an important measure of economic health, since full employment is generally construed as a desired goal. When the various economic indicators are mixed, many analysts look to the unemployment rate as being the most important.

Weekly initial claims for unemployment benefits are another closely watched indicator along with the unemployment rate to judge the jobless situation in the economy. This is one of 11 components of the Index of Leading Indicators.

How Are They Computed? The unemployment rate is the number of unemployed workers divided by the total employed and unemployed who constitute the labor force. Both statistics are released by the Department of Labor.

Where Are They Found? They are frequently reported in daily newspapers and business dailies such as *Investor's Business Daily* and the *Wall Street Journal* (see Figure 42 on page 61).

How Are They Used for Investment Decisons? An increase in employment, a decrease in initial jobless claims, and a decrease in unemployment are favorable for the economy and the stock market; the opposite situation is unfavorable. The effect of unemployment on the economy is summarized in Figure 46.

Figure 46: Unemployment's Effects

1. **Less Tax Revenue:** Fewer jobs means less income tax to the state and nation, which means a bigger U.S. government deficit and forces states to make cuts in programs to balance their budgets.

2. **Higher Government Costs:** When people lose jobs they often must turn to the government for benefits.

3. **Less Consumer Spending:** Without a job, individuals can't afford to buy cars, computers, houses, or vacations.

4. **Empty Stores:** Retailers and homebuilders can't absorb lower sales for long. Soon they have to lay off workers and, and in more serious shortfalls, file for bankruptcy.

5. **Manufacturing Cuts:** The companies that make consumer products or housing materials are forced to cut jobs, too, as sales of their goods fall.

6. **Real Estate Pain:** As companies fail and as individuals struggle, mortgages and other bank loans go unpaid. That causes real estate values to go down and pummels lenders. One reason for the S&L crisis is the high number of defaulted loans.

A Word of Caution: No one economic indicator is able to point to the direction to which an economy is heading. It is common for many indicators to give mixed signals regarding, for example, the possibility of a recession.

Also See: ECONOMIC INDICATORS AND BOND YIELDS, ECONOMIC INDICATORS AND THE SECURITY MARKET, ECONOMIC INDICATOR: RECESSION

44. ECONOMIC INDICATORS: U.S. BALANCE OF PAYMENTS, VALUE OF THE DOLLAR

What Are They? A balance of payments is a systematic record of a country's receipts from, or payments to, other countries. In a way, it is like the balance sheets for businesses, only on a national level. Media references to the "balance of trade" usually refer to goods within the goods and services category of the current account. It also is known as merchandise or "visible" trade because it consists of tangibles such as foodstuffs, manufactured goods, and raw materials. "Services," the other part of the category, is known as "invisible" trade and consists of intangibles such as interest or dividends, technology transfers, services (such as insurance, transportation, financial), and so forth.

When the net result of both the current account and the capital account yields more credits than debits, the country is said to have a surplus in its balance of payments. When there are more debits than credits, the country has a deficit in the balance of payments.

How Are They Computed? Data is collected by the U.S. Customs Service. Figures are reported in seasonally adjusted volumes and dollar amounts. It is the only nonsurvey, nonjudgemental report produced by the Department of Commerce. The balance of payments appears in the *Survey of Current Business*.

Where Are They Found? Foreign exchange rates are quoted daily in the *Wall Street Journal* and *Investor's Business Daily* and on computer services such as Prodigy. Major currency rates are reported on television networks such as CNBC, The Business Channel, and Nightly Business Reports. Merchandise trade figures are reported periodically in such newspapers as *Investor's Business Daily*, *USA Today*, and the *Wall Street Journal*.

Figure 47 shows a sample from the *Orange County Register*.

Figure 47: Foreign Exchange Rate Report

CURRENCIES
Foreign exchange

	Fgn. currency in dollars		Dollar in fgn. currency	
	Tue.	Mon.	Tue.	Mon.
Germany	6051	6035	1 6527	1 6571
. . .	. . .	. . .	. . .	. . .
Japan	007514	007498	133 08	133 37

Source: *Orange County Register*, April 15, 1992.

How Are They Used for Investment Decisions? When deficits in the balance of payments persist, this generally depresses the value of the dollar and can boost inflation. The reason: A weak dollar makes foreign goods relatively expensive, often allowing U.S. makers of similar products to raise prices as well. It is necessary for an investor to know the condition of a country's balance of payments, since resulting inflation will affect the market.

What is better—a strong dollar or a weak dollar? The answer is, unfortunately, it depends. A strong dollar makes Americans' cash go further overseas and reduces import prices—generally positive for U.S. consumers and for foreign manufacturers. If the dollar is overvalued, U.S. products are harder to sell abroad and at home where they compete with low-cost imports. This adds to the U.S. its huge trade deficit.

A weak dollar can restore competitiveness to American products by making foreign goods comparatively more expensive. But too weak a dollar can spawn inflation, first through higher import prices and then through spiraling prices for all goods. Even worse, a falling dollar can drive foreign investors away from U.S. securities, which lose value along with the dollar. A strong dollar can be induced by interest rates. Relatively higher interest rates abroad will attract money dollar-denominated investments, which will raise the value of the dollar.

A Word of Caution: Unfortunately, it is difficult to establish a good correlation between the dollar's value and the stock market's performance. Attention should be focused on the domestic scene as well as on international economic developments.

Also See: ECONOMIC INDICATORS AND BOND YIELDS, ECONOMIC INDICATORS AND THE SECURITIES MARKET

45. EUROPEAN CURRENCY UNIT (ECU)

What Is It? This is the currency unit used by the European Monetary System (EMS). The objective is to keep a stable relationship in European currencies among members.

How Is It Computed? ECU is the grouping of the currencies of the members of the European Economic Community (EEC). This includes the Italian lira, Greek drachma, English pound, French franc, and West German deutsche mark. The weighting is based on the foreign currency in the ECU on a percentage relationship to the equivalent U.S. dollar. The current exchange rate for each European country's currency is considered in the weighting. A review of the makeup of the ECU is performed every five years.

Where Is It Found? ECU information may be obtained from the Federal Reserve System. It's published in *Barron's*.

How Is It Used for Investment Decisions? The ECU acts to stabilize exchange rates for currencies of European countries. The investor should examine the variation in exchange rates as a risk indicator. European bonds may be expressed in ECU terms. The ECU index may be used as a basis for cash settlement of foreign exchange futures contracts.

46. FOOTNOTES ON STOCK TABLES

What Are They? Due to the compressed nature of newspaper stock tables, footnotes are used to convey additional information about stocks. Footnotes are typically one- or two-letter abbreviations that appear on the line of type reporting a specific stock's results.

Footnotes can add greatly to the understanding of the quotations. Since the Associated Press supplies stock tables to the majority of newspapers, the footnotes tend to be consistent throughout the country.

How Are They Computed? The Associated Press gets its information directly from the major exchanges and trading houses that supply quotation data.

Where Are They Found? Most newspaper stock tables include small abbreviations that denote various bits of information about a company, its stock, and its price. The accompanying definitions for those footnotes typically run in a separate box near or within the stock tables.

Here are the translations for the footnote abbreviations used by many newspapers:

u - Stock traded at a new 52-week high during the day.

d - Stock traded at a new 52-week low during the day.

g - Dividend or earnings in U.S. dollars. No yield or P/E unless stated in U.S. money.

n - A new issue in the past 52 weeks. That means the high-low range begins with the start of trading and does not cover the entire 52-week period.

s - Split or stock dividend of 25% or more in the past 52 weeks. That means that the high-low range is adjusted from the old stock. Dividend begins with the date of split or stock dividend.

v - Trading halted on primary market.

x - Traded ex-dividend or ex-rights, that is, the first trading day when buyers will not get the previously declared dividend.

y - Ex-dividend and sales in full, rather than in 100s as is the rest of the table.

z - Sales figures in full, rather than in 100s as is the rest of the table.

pf - Preferred issue.

pp - Shareholders still owe installments of purchase price.

rt - Stock rights.

un - Units, typically containing common stock and rights or warrants.

wd - When distributed, shares traded in advance of a stock distribution.

wi - When issued, shares traded in advance of a stock issuance.

wt - Warrants.

ww - Stock trading with warrants attached.

xw - Stock trading without warrants.

vj - Company in bankruptcy or receivership or being reorganized or securities assumed by such companies.

The following are some footnotes specifically for dividends. Investors should note that, unless otherwise noted, the listed rates of dividends in stock tables are annual disbursements based on the last quarterly or semiannual declaration.

a - Regular dividend with extra dividends.

b - Annual rate plus stock dividend.

c - Liquidating dividend.

e - Declared or paid in preceding 12 months.

i - Declared or paid after stock dividend or split up.

j - Paid this year, dividend omitted, deferred or no action taken at last dividend meeting.

k - Declared or paid this year, an accumulative issue with dividends in arrears.

r - Declared or paid in preceding 12 months plus stock dividend.

t - Paid in stock in preceding 12 months, estimated cash value on ex-dividend or ex-distribution date.

These footnotes may appear with over-the-counter listings:

g - Dividend or earnings in Canadian money. Stock trades in U.S. dollars. No yield or P/E unless stated in U.S. money.

h - Temporary exception to NASDAQ qualifications.
These footnotes may appear with mutual fund tables:
e - Ex-capital gains distribution.
s - Share dividend or split.
x - Ex-cash dividend.
f - Previous day's quotation.
NL or n - No front-end load or contingent deferred sales load.
r - Redemption fee or contingent deferred sales load may apply.

How Are They Used for Investment Decisons? Footnotes give an investor information well beyond the typical high-low-and-closing price and trading volume data. The notes can alert an investor to news such as a bankruptcy or an omitted dividend; note the reaching of a peak or trough in share price in a year's time; or briefly help explain a company's dividend history.

A Word of Caution: Footnotes are not always up-to-date so investors are encouraged to double-check before acting on any information contained in these tables. In addition, the Associated Press is now offering new technologies to its client newspapers that will enable them to customize their stock tables. One feature will allow newspaper editors to create their own footnotes, thus likely ending over time the uniformity of tables.

Also See: YIELD ON AN INVESTMENT: CURRENT YIELD ON A BOND, CURRENT YIELD ON A STOCK, SHARE PRICE RATIOS: PRICE-EARNINGS RATIO (MULTIPLE)

47. FOREIGN STOCK INDEXES

DOW JONES WORLD STOCK INDEX

What Is It? In January 1993, Dow Jones & Co. introduced a new index, the Dow World, as the centerpiece of its expanded coverage of world markets. The index represents the collective performances of the world's major stock markets.

How Is It Calculated? The Index is an index of some 2,200 stocks from around the globe: the United States plus Australia, Belgium, Canada, France, Germany, Italy, Japan, Malaysia, Netherlands, New Zealand, Singapore, Spain, and the United Kingdom. The index's base of 100 equals December 31, 1991. The index tracks performance in U.S. dollars and is tabulated when U.S. markets close each business day.

Where Is It Found? The Index and its subindexes can be found in the *Wall Street Journal* and *Barron's*. Figure 48 shows the major classifications of the index, as reported in the *Wall Street Journal*.

How Is It Used for Investment Decisions? For investors with a global perspective, the index can be used to measure the relative performance of individual country's markets or a broad international portfolios's performances. The index can be also used as a way to measure the overall desirability of an international stock portfolio. A sinking index may be a buying opportunity for a broad basket of international shares while near-record heights in the index could be a selling signal.

A Word of Caution: The index is a newcomer and there could be problems with the index's ability to be a good measure of world stock performances. In addition, the smaller

Figure 48: Dow Jones World Stock Index Sample

REGION/ COUNTRY	EQUITY MARKET INDEX, LOCAL CURRENCY	PCT. CHG.	CLOSING INDEX	PCT. CHG.	PCT. CHG.	12-MO HIGH	12-MO LOW	12-MO CHG.	PCT. CHG.	FROM 12/31	PCT. CHG.
Americas			107.74	– 0.46	– 0.43	109.27	96.35	+ 6.44	+ 6.36	+ 3.47	+ 3.33
. . .											
Europe			98.34	+ 0.25	+ 0.26	101.85	88.80	– 1.55	– 1.55	+ 5.70	– 6.15
. . .											
Asia / Pacific			117.07	+ 1.85	+ 1.61	117.07	67.90	+44.55	+61.44	+ 37.82	+47.33
. . .											
Asia / Pacific (ex. Japan)			129.78	+ 1.57	+ 1.23	131.42	96.46	+17.10	+15.18	+ 24.78	+23.60
. . .											
World (ex. U.S.)			109.04	+ 1.18	+ 1.09	109.15	80.40	+25.57	+30.17	+ 24.51	+29.90
. . .											
DJ WORLD STOCK INDEX			108.56	+ 0.53	+ 0.49	108.64	88.03	+17.91	+19.75	+ 16.02	+17.31

Source: *Wall Street Journal*, August 2, 1993.

index does not yet include the performances of so-called emerging markets in smaller countries. Shares on these markets are very volatile but haver historically provided great returns when foreigners can get access to these markets.

Also See: DOW JONES INDUSTRIAL AVERAGE

FINANCIAL TIMES INDEXES

What Are They? The Financial Times 30 Index is a narrow index of 30 of the best United Kingdom industrial businesses. The Financial Times-Stock Exchange 100-Share Index is a capitalized market value index of 100 U.K. companies.

How Are They Computed? The Financial Times 30 Index is a geometric average, price-weighted index. Each security price is weighted the same, without regard to value or size. A base level of 100 was established in 1935. Many of the companies included in the below index are included in this one as well.

The Financial Times-Stock Exchange 100-Share Index (known as the "Footsie") is a narrow capitalized-weighted index of the market prices of the 100 most capitalized shares on the exchange. Some companies included in the index are Glaxo, Wellcome, Grand Metropolitan, British Steel, British Petroleum, Barclays Bank, Hanson, Rolls Royce, and Allied-Lyons. A 1,000 base was assigned in 1984.

Companies cannot be included in the index if they are treated as "resident overseas" for tax reporting, if dividends are not paid, or if they are a subsidiary of a company in the index.

Where Are They Found? Index information appears in *Barron's*, the *Financial Times* (London, England), *Investor's Business Daily*, the *New York Times*, and the *Wall Street Journal*. It is also found in the interactive on-line database Prodigy.

How Are They Used for Investment Decisions? The indexes reveal the price performance of United Kingdom stocks. The trend in the indexes should be examined. If prices are unrealistically depressed, a buying opportunity may exist.

These U.K. stock indexes reflect reflect worldwide business conditions and may be used as one indicator for predicting what lies ahead for the New York Stock Exchange. In this manner, it is a technical analysis tool. London is five hours ahead of New York so it also may be used to get a feeling of market sentiment before trading opens on the NYSE. London is the world's third largest stock market. Option contracts may be made in the index.

Also See: DOW JONES INDUSTRIAL AVERAGE

GERMAN SHARE INDEX (FRANKFURT DAX)

What Is It? This is an index of the market prices of shares of German companies traded on the Frankfurt Stock Exchange. It is Germany's version of the Dow Jones Industrial Average.

How Is It Computed? It is a narrowly determined capitalization-weighted index of 30 of the most active issues. The index is updated continuously on a daily basis. It comprises about 75% of German equity value. Some major stocks listed are Bayer, Deutsche Bank, Daimler-Benz, Volkswagen, and Schering. A base amount of 1,000 was assigned in 1987.

Where Is It Found? The index is found in brokerage research reports that follow German stocks. The CNBC, a major financial television network, reports this index on a daily basis. Reports may be found in *Barron's, Investor's Business Daily*, and the *Wall Street Journal*. The DAX is contained in the Prodigy on-line database.

Figure 49 shows how foreign market indicators including DAX appear in the *Wall Street Journal*.

Figure 49: Foreign Market Indicators

Exchange	5/1/91 Close	Net Chg	Pct. Chg
Tokyo Nikkei Average	26489.0	+ 377.75	+ 1.45
Tokyo Topix Index	1998.45	+ 35.03	+ 1.78
London FT 30-share	1966.7	+ 13.0	+ 0.67
London Gold Mines	139.9	- 2.2	- 1.55
London 100-share	2508.4	+ 22.2	+ 0.89
Frankfurt DAX	closed		
Zurich Credit Suisse	closed		

Source: *Wall Street Journal*, May 1, 1991.

How Is It Used for Investment Decisions? Index information can be used to determine if the index is overpriced or underpriced. If specific securities are undervalued, they may be purchased for capital gain potential.

GLOBAL STOCK MARKET INDEXES

What Are They? Overseas stock market indexes reflect the performance of the stocks in each foreign country. They reflect the closing price index and percentage of change.

How Are They Computed? The indexes are computed based upon a weighting of the stock prices of foreign companies included in the index.

Where Are They Found? The indexes of stock performance by foreign country is listed in newspapers such as *Barron's, Investor's Business Daily,* the *New York Times,* and the *Wall Street Journal.* Further, weekly magazines such as the *Economist* report market indexes. Examples of countries included in the global stock market listing are the United States, United Kingdom, Germany, France, Italy, and Japan. A sample listing of world stock market indexes from *Barron's* is shown in Figure 50.

Figure 50: World Stock Markets Indexes

	8/28/92 Close	Week's Change	-1992- High	Low
Australia				
All-Ord.	1553.90	- 5.40	1684.50	1545.30
Belgium				
Cash	1062.13	- 51.29	1235.40	1093.45
Canada				
Composite	3429.94	+ 12.62	3666.00	3318.10
France				
CAC	1687.53	- 51.29	2077.49	1667.72
Hong Kong				
Hang Seng	5628.60	- 119.21	6113.10	4301.78

Source: *Barron's,* August 31, 1992.

How Are They Used for Investment Decisons? The investor can examine the overseas market indexes to determine how the stocks in each foreign country are doing. Which countries are experiencing the best versus worst performances? If the investor believes the stock prices in a given foreign country are too high, he may either sell his holdings or not buy additional shares in companies in that country. On the other hand, if the investor concludes that the stock prices in a foreign country are overly depressed, a buying opportunity may be indicated for shares in companies in that foreign country.

A Word of Caution: Foreign exchange rates should be considered when investing in foreign stocks. There is currency risk associated with international investing.

MORGAN STANLEY CAPITAL INTERNATIONAL WORLD INDEX

What Is It? The index is a benchmark for comparing global investment funds. As of December 31, 1991, the approximate distribution of the market value of stock investments worldwide was U.S. 38%, Japan 28%, United Kingdom 11%, Other Europe 16%, and All Other Markets 7%.

How Is It Computed? The index is an arithmetical average weighted by market value of the performance of more than 1,500 securities listed on the stock exchanges of the U.S., Europe, Canada, Australia, New Zealand, South Africa, and the Far East. Nineteen of the world's stock exchanges are included. It represents about 60% of the capitalized value of each country's market. The index is unmanaged and includes net dividends reinvested.

Where Is It Found? The index is published by Morgan Stanley.

How Is It Used for Investment Decisions? If the investor concludes that the worldwide index is unrealistically depressed, a buying opportunity may exist in international markets. An international stock mutual fund may be attractive.

Also See: MORGAN STANLEY EAFE STOCK INDEX

MORGAN STANLEY EAFE INDEX

What Is It? The Morgan Stanley Europe, Asia, and Far East Index is considered the key "rest-of-the-world" index for U.S. investors, much as the Dow Jones Industrial Average is for the American market. The index is used as a guide to see how U.S. shares are faring against other markets around the globe. It also serves as a performance benchmark for international mutual funds that hold non-U.S. assets.

Morgan Stanley also compiles indexes for most of the world's major stock markets as well as for many smaller, so-called "emerging" markets. In addition, there are Morgan Stanley indexes for each continent and the entire globe.

How Is It Computed? First, Morgan Stanley has created its own indexes for 18 major foreign markets. To make the EAFE Index, those country indexes are weighted to reflect the total market capitalization of each country's markets as a share in the world market. The index's base of 100 equals January 1, 1970.

The index is quoted two ways: one in local currencies and a second in the U.S. dollar. This shows how American investors would fare addressing both share price and currency fluctuations.

Where Is It Found? The EAFE Index can be found in newspapers such as *Barron's*, and the *Wall Street Journal*.

How Is It Used for Investment Decisions? The EAFE index can be used by investors to gauge the proper exposure to foreign investments. Historically, foreign shares have produced slightly better results than U.S. issues, particularly in the past two decades as the American economy has matured and overseas industries are now the fastest growing.

When the EAFE Index is performing better than the U.S. markets, it may be time for investors to shift money overseas. Conversely, when U.S. market indexes are doing better than the EAFE Index, a shift away from foreign assets may be in order.

A Word of Caution: Currency fluctuations can play a major part of any overseas investment. A rising EAFE may be more a reflection of a weak U.S. dollar than improving foreign economies or strong opportunities in overseas stocks.

Also See: JAPANESE YEN, GERMAN DEUTSCHE MARK, BRITISH POUND, FINANCIAL TIMES INDEXES, NIKKEI STOCK INDEX

What Is It? It is the most widely watched barometer of Japan's stock market, the world's second largest behind the United States. The index, first published in May 1949, is to Japanese shares what the Dow Jones Industrial Average is to U.S. issues.

How Is It Calculated? The Nikkei is an average of prices of 225 stocks listed in the prestigious First Section of the Tokyo Stock Exchange. Companies included are Asahi Breweries, Fuji Film, Nippon Steel, and Yamaha. It is updated constantly throughout the trading day. The index is quoted in yen.

Where Is It Found? The index can be found in many daily newspapers and such newspapers as the *Wall Street Journal*, the *New York Times*, and *USA Today*.

How is It Used for Investment Decisions? The index tracks movement in Japansse share prices. Sharp gains in the Nikkei, especially in relationship to U.S. market indexes, may be a signal to move money across the Pacific to Tokyo. Conversely, a steep drop in the Nikkei, and it lost 40% of its value from 1989 through 1992, can be a warning sign that Japanese markets are quite volatile.

A Word of Caution: The Nikkei may be best known for its 5-digit numerology, which to the uninformed eye makes an already temperamental market seem very unnerving. Remember to keep that in perspective. So in August 1993, a 200-yen move in the Nikkei would equal about a 35-point move in the Dow Industrials.

Also, some experts feel that the Nikkei is too narrow a measure of Japanese stocks. The Tokyo Stock Exchange Index, or Topix, covers all of approximately 1,200 shares in the First Section and is viewed as a better barometer of Japanese market conditions.

48. (GERMAN) DEUTSCHE MARK

What Is It? As Germany has been Europe's economic powerhouse, the mark has become one of the world's most important currencies. Its relationship to the U.S. dollar is a key to the global marketplace and is seen as a barometer of Germany's economic strength versus that of the United States.

How Is It Computed? It is typically quoted in newspapers and financial reports on television and radio in terms of its relationship to the U.S. dollar. If the mark is at 1.4, that means that each U.S. dollar buys 1.4 marks. To figure out what 1 mark equals in U.S currency, investors use this formula:

$$1 \text{ mark} = \frac{\$1 \text{ U.S.}}{\text{Mark-to-dollar rate}}$$

Example: If $1 buys 1.4 mark, then 1 mark is equal to $1 divided by 1.4 or 71.4 cents.

Where Is It Found? Currency rates are listed daily in most major metropolitan newspapers as well as national publications like the *New York Times*, *USA Today*, and the *Wall Street Journal* and on computer services such as Prodigy.

How Is It Used for Investment Decisions? For American investors buying German securities, the mark's movement is a key part of the profit potential of the investment.

If the mark rises after an investment in German securities is made, the value of those stocks or bonds to a U.S. investor will get a boost from the currency. That's because when the investment is sold, the stronger mark will generate more dollars when the proceeds are converted to the U.S. currency. Conversely, a weak mark will be a negative to a German investment for a U.S. investor. In some cases, the movement of the mark also can be viewed as an indicator of German economic health. A strong mark can signal a buoyant economy, a possible indication to buy German stocks. The mark's strength, however, should be verified not only against the U.S. dollar but against other major currencies.

A Word of Caution: The mark's strength versus the dollar can be distorted by prevailing interest rates in each country. For example, a movement by the German central bank to slow down the economy by boosting German interest rates—two potential negatives for stock prices—could also increase the mark's price versus the dollar if U.S. rates are stagnant or falling. This scenario of a rising mark might give an incorrect reading on the potential for buying German securities.

Widely quoted currency rates are typically for transactions of $1 million or more. Consumers looking to use such figures to determine currency rates for foreign travel should expect to get somewhat less favorable exchange rates.

Also See: BRITISH POUND, JAPANESE YEN

49. GOLD SPOT PRICE

What Is It? The gold spot price is an indication of the market price for a troy ounce of gold purchased today. Gold is a major industrial commodity and a key jewelry component. It is viewed as the only measure of wealth universally recognized around the globe.

How Is It Computed? Gold is a global commodity, thus there is no one market price. Key spot prices watched by traders include: morning and afternoon fixings in Hong Kong and London and the most current month futures contract for gold on the New York Commodity Exchange.

The price is quoted in troy ounces that come 12 to the pound rather than those traditional ounces for food and liquids that are 16 to the pound.

Where Is It Found? Gold's spot price is listed in commodity roundups in most metropolitan newspapers as well as *Barron's*, the *New York Times*, and the *Wall Street Journal*. Also, it can be found on computerized databases such as Prodigy.

How Is It Used for Investment Decisions? Gold usually does the opposite of common stock: As common stock returns move down, returns on gold move up. In other words, gold compensates for a declining stock market. Transaction costs for gold vary with the type of gold, but the higher the quantity purchased, the lower the percentage commission.

The investor can acquire indirect ownership by purchasing shares in a gold mine. However, the prices of shares do not always move in the same manner as the price of the gold itself. Securities of gold mines do enhance portfolio diversificaiton, though, in the same way that the metal itself does. Mining company stocks are traded on organized exchanges and the over-the-counter market.

The investor also can acquire shares of mutual funds that maintain a strong position in gold stocks or gold bullion. Mutual fund investment offers diversification. Gold futures can be bought on some commodities exchanges. The investor need give only about 10% in cash of the contract's value to buy. This low margin requirement provides a leveraging opportunity. Commissions typically are less than 1% of the contract's value. Gold futures are traded in several U.S. and foreign exchanges.

Gold ownership has several disadvantages, including:

- Storage costs are high.
- High transaction costs are common.
- Dividend revenue is not received on gold.
- Capital gain or loss potential is significant.
- Wide price volatility means high risk. It is a speculative investment.
- Certain gold investments are in bearer form. If they are lost or stolen, the owner loses the entire investment. Two examples are bullion and coins.

Gold has been long viewed as a defensive investment for times of financial or political upheaval. It was a poor performer in the decade following its 1980-81 peak of more than $800 an ounce.

Rising gold prices, however, are still viewed as a signal that investor skittishness is rising. Higher gold prices, also, are bullish signals for mining company stocks whose profits are greatly bolstered when the price is up.

A Word of Caution: There are major risks associated with investing in commodity futures and options. These securities provide substantial leverage—that is, the chance to control a huge amount of product for a fraction of the cost. But the wrong bet can be financially devastating. Option players can only lose their entire investment while futures specutors can be liable for more than they originally invested if they're way off on their hunches.

50. GREED INDEX

What Is It? This index is a contrary opinion rule. Prepared by Lee H. Idleman, the index measures how greedy investors are. Greed, as measured by the index, is synonymous with bullish sentiment or optimism. The more greedy or optimistic investors are, the more likely the market is to fall under this contrary opinion rule.

How Is It Computed? The Greed Index comprises ten different factors that are assigned a value from one to ten. Among these factors are portfolio aggressiveness (high technology versus defensive stocks), acceptance of new ideas, ratio of positive to negative comments by investment analysts, willingness to invest in untested issues, and the like.

Where Is It Found? It appears in *Barron's*.

How Is It Used for Investment Decisions? When the Greed Index exceeds 60, it is considered to be bearish. It rose to 69 in March 1983 before a market selloff began. It hit its all-time high of 89 in December 1968 during the go-go days of a bull market. When the Greed Index drops below 30, this is interpreted as a buy signal. For example, the index was at 28 before the great market upturn of June 1982.

A Word of Caution: While the Greed Index may provide some market clues, it is less than exacting. For example, the investor who began to go short when the index hit 60 in 1968 would have suffered large losses before the index rose to 89.

51. GROSS INCOME MULTIPLIER (GIM)

What Is It? The Gross Income Multiplier (GIM) is a method to compute the price of income-producing property.

How Is It Computed? The multiplier equals the asking price (or market value) of the commercial property divided by the current gross rental income.

If current gross rental income is $25,000 and the asking price is $300,000, the GIM equals:

$$\frac{\$300,000}{\$25,000} = 12$$

If similar income-producing properties in the area are selling for "15 times annual gross," this property is undervalued and should be bought. The property would be worth $375,000 (15 × $25,000) in the market.

Where Is It Found? The GIM for commercial property in an area may be determined by asking real estate brokers and by referring to published real estate data. The investor also should get a feel for the real estate market in the locality by asking around and finding out what similar property has been sold for or is being offered at.

How Is It Used for Investment Decisions? The GIM approach should be used with caution. Different properties have different operating expenses that must be considered in determining the value of a property.

The GIM is used by the investor to determine an approximate market value of property. A property may be bought if it is undervalued (the multiplier on the property is less than the "going market" multiplier). On the other hand, a property that is overvalued should not be purchased. If the investor currently owns the property and it has a higher multiplier than the "going market" multiplier, the property is overvalued and can be sold before a decline in market price materializes.

Also See: REAL ESTATE RETURNS: CAPITALIZATION RATE (CAP RATE, INCOME YIELD), REAL ESTATE RETURNS: NET INCOME MULTIPLIER (NIM)

52. HERZFELD CLOSED-END AVERAGE

What Is It? Tracks 20 closed-end mutual funds traded on the stock exchange.

How Is It Computed? The average is the capitalized market value of closed-end funds emphasizing investment in U.S. companies. It equals about 50% of the value of all the funds. It is assumed that the same amount is invested in each of the funds with capital gains reinvested in new shares. There is no assumed dividend reinvestment. The component funds making up the average are seen in Figure 51.

Where Is It Found? The average may be obtained from Thomas J. Herzfeld Advisors, Inc., The Herzfeld Building, P.O. Box 161465, Miami, Florida 33116. Telephone number (315) 271-1900. It is published in *Barron's*.

How Is It Used for Investment Decisions? The investor can follow the performance of closed-end mutual funds by examining the trend in the average. An upward trend is a positive sign in a bullish market.

A Word of Caution: The price of a closed-end fund is based on a demand/supply relationship because the shares are traded on the stock exchange. New shares are not issued. Therefore, the net asset value of the fund may be more or less than its current market price of stock.

Also See: MUTUAL FUNDS: EXPENSE RATIOS

Figure 51: Herzfeld Closed-End Average Components

1.	Adams Express Corporation	11.	Lehman Corporation
2.	Baker, Fentress & Company	12.	Liberty All-Start Equity Fund
3.	Blue Chip Value Fund	13.	Morgan Grenfell SMALLCap Fund
4.	Central Securities	14.	Nicholas Applegate Growth Equity
5.	Claremont Capital Corporation	15.	Niagara Share Corporation
6.	Cypress Fund	16.	Royce Value Trust
7.	Financial News Composite Fund	17.	Schafer Value Trust
8.	Gabelli Equity Fund	18.	Source Capital
9.	General American Investors	19.	Tri-Continental Corporation
10.	Growth Stock Outlook Trust	20.	Zweig Fund

53. INDEX NUMBER TREND

What Is It? An index is assigned in order to compare a financial statement account or item covering at least three years. In computing a series of index numbers, a base year is selected and all other years are compared to it.

How Is It Computed? A base year that is most representative (typical) of the company's operations is selected and assigned an index of 100. All index numbers are computed by reference to the base year.

$$\text{Index} = \frac{\text{Current year amount}}{\text{Base year amount}}$$

Where Is It Found? The investor should determine index numbers for financial statement items important to him that are found in the company's annual report. The investor may look at the trend in sales, net income, total assets, and so on.

Example: The base year is 19X1 and net income was $6,000,000. Thus, an index of 100 is assigned for 19X1. Net income for 19X2 and 19X3 were $6,600,00 and $5,000,000, respectively. The index numbers are:

19X2 $6,600,000/$6,000,000 = 110
19X3 $5,000,000/$6,000,000 = 83

The sharp decline in net income should be of concern to the investor. A declining profitability spells financial troubles for the company. In such a case, an investment in the company may not be warranted.

How Is It Used for Investment Decisions? When a comparison of accounts covering three years or more is made, the year-to-year method of comparison may become too cumbersome. The best way to look at a long-term trend for comparison purposes is through the use of index numbers. The investor can identify any financial statement accounts or items that appear out of line.

If sales and profitability of the company are significantly increasing, growth is indicated. This may be a time to buy the stock. However, the investor who owns a stock in a company that has a drastically falling revenue base should consider selling it.

A Word of Caution: As in the case with the computation of year-to-year percentage changes, certain changes, such as those from negative to positive amounts, *cannot* be expressed by means of index numbers. Further, the base year selected as most typical may not in retrospect be.

Also See: PROFITABILITY: (TREND) HORIZONTAL ANALYSIS

54. INITIAL PUBLIC OFFERINGS

What Are They? Initial public offerings are companies issuing stock to the public for the first time.

How Are They Computed? Lists of companies "going public" through initial public offerings are compiled from information filed at the Securities and Exchange Commission and from brokerages underwriting these new issues. Investment Data Corp. tallies data on the number of companies going public and the lead underwriter that handled the deals, as well as the value and number of shares sold.

Where Are They Found? Publications such as *Barron's*, the *New York Times*, and the *Wall Street Journal* publish weekly listings of recent SEC new-issue filings and issues in the SEC review process expected to be sold in the coming week. Data of new issue volume are reported in the *Wall Street Journal* as part of a quarterly wrap-up of how the major brokerages fared in this lucrative business of taking companies public.

How Are They Used for Investment Decisions? Lists of upcoming new issues can provide an investor two potential insights: One, a chance to learn the name of companies that offer the chance to get in on the ground floor. Two, a contrarian view; it can be viewed as a signal of what industries—or equities in general—to shun when initial public offerings soar. A surge in initial public offerings is often viewed as a signal that the market as a whole, or a sector having a flurry of new issues, has peaked in its current cycle.

A Word of Caution: Initial public offerings have great investment sex appeal. However, they are filled with risks. Studies have shown that investors lose money more than half the time when buying new shares.

55. INSIDERS' TRADING ACTIVITY

What Is It? Insiders are corporate directors, officers, other executives of the company, and stockholders who own 5% or more of the company's voting shares. Insiders know important information that is not publicly available. Insiders' trading activity refers to the number of shares bought or sold by insiders.

How Is It Computed? Net insider share volume = Insider shares bought less insider shares sold

$$\text{Insider buy/sell ratio} = \frac{\text{Insider shares bought}}{\text{Insider shares sold}}$$

A higher ratio is more bullish while a lower ratio is more bearish.

Where Is It Found? Insiders' trading activity is published in the SEC monthly *Official Summary of Security Transactions and Holdings*. Insider information is also available in newsletters and financial publications such as *Invest Net*, *Consensus of Insiders* (COI) published by Perry Wysong, *The Insider Indicator* (Portland, Oregon), *The Insiders* (the Institute for Econometric Research at Fort Lauderdale, Florida) and *Vickers Weekly Insider Report* (Vickers Stock Research Corporation, Brookside, New Jersey). For example, the COI provides a listing of the 20 most attractive stocks. These private services analyze the insiders buying and selling and, based on such analysis, make recommendations. *The Insider Chronicle* (editorial section of the *Commercial and Financial Chronicle*) publishes a selected listing of insiders' transactions for about 400 companies. Other sources include

Barron's, Insider Trading Monitor, and the *Wall Street Journal. Insider Trading Monitor* (North Miami, Florida) is a database service that reports SEC filings.

While the published information of insider transactions is after the fact, it is still a strong indicator. The SEC requires insiders to report transactions in their companies stocks by the tenth day of the month following the transactions. Further, the SEC prohibits insiders from selling the stock at a gain within six months of purchase.

How Is It Used for Investment Decisions? When officers or directors of a company are purchasing significantly more shares than they are selling, this is a bullish sign—perhaps earnings will be growing. On the other hand, if officers and directors are selling their shares rather than buying, something unfavorable may be on the horizon. In bear markets these signs may not be as accurate because the insiders may be selling for tax or personal reasons. Some executives may be selling shares to obtain cash to exercise stock options.

The most knowledgeable investors are company insiders because they are familiar with the current and prospective financial happenings of the business. Insiders typically earn unusually high returns after considering any risks involved. After all, they have information not yet publicly released. If insiders are buying, the investor *may* do likewise. If insiders are selling, so should the investor.

According to Vickers Stock Research Corporation, the investor should purchase securities when the buy/sell ratio is below 1.5. The investor should sell when the ratio goes above 2.0 and the stock market has declined by 5% from the buy level.

A Word of Caution: There is a timeliness problem because insider information may be several months old by the time it is released. Therefore, the investor's timing is crucial or else there will be little benefit to knowing insider transactions.

Insiders may be trading the stock for other reasons than inside information to profit on. For example, an officer may sell shares to obtain extra funds to buy a new home. Although the insider has sold shares, the price of the stock may in fact increase. In 1992, for example, even though key officers of Toys R Us sold stock, the market price actually went up because of investor interest in the company.

56. INTEREST RATES: DISCOUNT, FED FUNDS, AND PRIME

What Are They? These are three key interest rates closely tied to the banking system. The discount rate is the rate the Federal Reserve Board charges on loans to banks that belong to the Fed system. The federal or fed funds rate is the rate that bankers charge one another for very short-term loans, although the Fed can manage this rate as well. The prime rate is the much discussed benchmark rate that bankers charge their better corporate customers.

How Are They Computed? The three rates, at times, work in tandem.

The discount rate is the major tool that the nation's central bank, the Federal Reserve, has to manage interest rates. Discount rate changes are made by the Fed when it wants to use monetary policy to alter economic patterns.

The discount rate can instantly impact the fed funds rate. This rate is more market-driven and changes throughout each business day. Although it can at times be managed by the Federal Reserve, it also can move as bankers and traders anticipate Federal Reserve activity.

The prime rate is a heavily tracked rate although it isn't as widely used as a loan benchmark as it has been in the past. The prime is set by bankers to vary loan rates to smaller businesses and on consumers' home equity loans and credit cards.

Where Are They Found? Changes in the discount rate and prime rate are often front-page news, particularly in times of economic troubles. Many major newspapers such as the *Baltimore Sun*, the *Miami Herald*, and the *Los Angeles Times* carry a daily rate tally that includes the discount, fed funds, and the prime rates.

How Are They Used for Investment Decisions? A watcher of these three interest rates will see a reflection of the banking system's view of the strength of the U.S. economy.

These rates tend to rise when the Federal Reserve is in a tight money posture, when it tries to keep an expanding economy from overheating and creating too much inflation. This is often viewed as a negative signal for both stock and bond investments as a cooled economy and higher rates can hurt many securities prices.

Conversely, the rates tend to fall when the Federal Reserve is in an easy money mode, when it wants available credit and low interest rates to stimulate a moribund U.S. economy. For the risk-taking investor, this can be a signal to boost stock and bond holdings. An expected economic recovery may boost equity issues while falling rates should be a boon to bond prices.

At times, these rates may send contradictory signals, as bankers and the Federal Reserve may disagree on the economy's direction.

Also See: CASH INVESTMENTS: MONEY MARKET FUND YIELDS, ECONOMIC INDICATORS AND BOND YIELDS, INTEREST RATES: THREE-MONTH TREASURY BILLS

57. INTEREST RATES: 30-YEAR TREASURY BONDS

What Is It? The most widely watched interest rate in the world, the security known as the "T-bond" is seen as the daily barometer of how the bond market is performing. The 30-year Treasury bond is a fixed-rate direct obligation of the U.S. government. There are no call provisions on Treasury bonds.

How Is It Computed? Traders watch the price of the U.S. Treasury's most recently issued 30-year bond, often called the "bellwether." The price is decided by a series of dealers who own the exclusive right to make markets in the bonds in U.S. markets. (The bond trades around the clock in foreign markets. Bond yields are derived from the current trading price and its fixed coupon rate.

Where Is It Found? The T-bond price and yield can be found in the credit market wrap-up in newspapers such as the *Boston Globe*, *Investor's Business Daily*, the *New York Times*, and the *Wall Street Journal*, plus computer databases such as Prodigy.

How Is It Used for Investment Decisions? Traders who hold T-bonds are exposed to a great deal of risk. Their willingness or unwillingness to take on that risk—and the resulting changes which that brings to 30-year bond prices and yields—is often viewed as a proxy on the long-term outlook for the U.S. economy.

Because of its long-term nature, the T-bond is extra sensitive to inflation that could ravage the buying power of its fixed-rate payouts. Thus, the T-bond market also is watched as an indicator of where inflation may be headed.

Also, T-bond rates directly impact fixed-rate mortgages. Consequently, they also are seen as a barometer for the housing industry, a key leading indicator for the economy.

Also See: INTEREST RATES: THREE-MONTH TREASURY BILLS, MORTGAGE RATES

58. INTEREST RATES: THREE-MONTH TREASURY BILLS

What Is It? The Treasury bill rate is a widely watched rate for secure, cash investments. In turbulent times the rate can be volatile and can be viewed as a signal of the economy's health.

How Is It Computed? T-bills, both three-month and six-month issues, are auctioned every Monday by the U.S. Treasury through the Federal Reserve.

Rather than pay interest, the securities are sold at a varying discount depending on the prevailing interest rate. The investors get their interest by redeeming the T-bill at full face value when it matures.

The government reports the average effective interest rate it paid each week.

Where Is It Found? Results of the Monday auctions can be found in most major daily newspapers' business sections such as the *New York Times* and the *Wall Street Journal*. Trading in the secondary markets for T-bills also is reported in these papers as well as in most major daily newspapers and on business TV channels such as CNBC. *Barron's* reports it this way (see Figure 52).

How Is It Used for Investment Decisions? The T-bill rate shows what can be expected to be earned on no-risk investments. Historically, T-bills have returned little more than the inflation rate. Many conservative investors buy T-bills directly from the government. T-bill rates approximate rates on money market mutual funds or statement savings accounts, also popular savings tools for the small investor.

When these low-risk rates are high or rising, it can be a negative signal for stocks and bonds because in such situations individual investors tend to shy from riskier investments. Ironically, T-bill rates often rise in anticipation of an economic strengthening—a bullish sign for stocks.

Figure 52: Money Rates Report

	Latest Week	Previous Week	Year Ago Week
Discount Rate (NY Fed charge to member banks)	3.50	3.50	6
Prime Rate (base rate)	6½	6½	8¾-9
Federal Funds-a (Rate on interbank overnight loans; benchmark for other money market rates)			
Average effective	3 5/8	4 1/16	5½
Average weekly auction-c	4.09	3.94	6.00
Treasury Bills (Discount short-term government securities)			
13 weeks, Coupon Equivalent Yield Apr. 9:	4.04	4.18	5.78
13 weeks, Average Discount Rate Apr. 9:	3.95	4.08	5.60
26 weeks, Coupon Equivalent Yield Apr. 9:	4.16	4.34	5.95
26 weeks, Average Discount Rate Apr. 9:	4.02	4.19	5.68
52 weeks, Coupon Equivalent Yield Apr. 9:	4.55	4.55	6.16
52 weeks, Average Discount Rate Apr. 9:	4.34	4.34	6.05
Average weekly auction-c:	4.01	4.03	5.75
Call Money (Charge for brokers loans)	6	6	7½-8½

Source: *Barron's.*

Conversely, when T-bill rates are low or falling, small savers tend to look to markets like stocks, real estate, or bonds to beef up their returns. However, experts contend that falling T-bill rates may show economic weakness, which is not a healthy situation for the stock market.

A Word of Caution: Short-term rates can fluctuate greatly in times of economic uncertainty. Thus, their ability to indicate longer-term trends can be impacted by very short-term events.

Also See: CASH INVESTMENTS: CERTIFICATE OF DEPOSIT YIELDS, CASH INVESTMENTS: MONEY MARKET FUND YIELDS, INTEREST RATES: 30-YEAR TREASURY BONDS

59. INVESTING STYLES

GROWTH INVESTING

What Is It? This strategy used by many well-known money managers, such as Fidelity Magellan Fund's former boss Peter Lynch and Twentieth Century Investors, is associated with stocks of fast-growing companies. "Growth" issues are often considered risky because their share prices trade at high price-earnings ratios compared to other shares in the market.

How Is It Computed? Growth-oriented portfolios traditionally contain stocks that have higher-than-average sales and growth rates. An investor seeking growth investments must obtain these or other ratios of growth for the investment he is reviewing as well as key market benchmarks or peer securities.

Example:

Security	5-year sales growth rate	5-year profit growth rate
MSL Technology	45%	33%
Old Line Manufacturing	10%	9%
GeeWhiz Growth Fund	33%*	40%*
S&P 500	18%*	20%*

*Average

In this example, MSL Technology and the GeeWhiz Growth Fund are the growth selections. The company, and the companies in the fund, are seeing sales and profits grow faster than, for example, the averages for the Standard & Poor's 500-stock index.

Where Is It Found? Many brokerage reports or computerized investment databases can be used to locate a company's key ratios and then compare them to market or industry averages. Another way to find lists of growth stocks is to get copies of semiannual reports from growth mutual funds. A growth investor "screens" out stocks with below-average sales and/or profit growth. For mutual funds, Morningstar's fund reports clearly detail average earnings growth ratios for each fund as well as describe what funds have a growth bias.

How Is It Used for Investment Decisions? Growth investing is a strategy that calls for the investor to try to buy the "best" companies, often regardless of share prices. This strategy appeals to many investors because they feel comfortable buying expanding, profitable companies. In fact, most of the best performing equity mutual funds, for example, have practiced growth investing.

Fast-growing companies typically see their share prices grow through a constant price multiple being applied to their expanding profits—or in the best case, and increased multiple given by the market to the growing profits.

A Word of Caution: Growth stocks are considered risky because they tend to trade at above-market price-to-book and price-earnings ratios. This makes them very susceptible to wide price swings when earnings or sales start to slow down. Like many other investment disciplines, growth stocks have their cycles of investor popularity and disfavor. When growth stocks are out of favor, investors tend to buy up "value" or "cyclical" shares that can have below-average price-to-book and/or price-earnings ratios.

But investors must carefully check the sales and earnings of fast-growing companies. Is the increase sustainable? Or is it coming from short-lived events such as the sale of assets or accounting gimmickry? Thus, ratios alone cannot be the only guide to an investment decision. Only fundamentals, such as management's abilities, overall profitability, industry positioning, should be checked before investing.

Also See: MORNINGSTAR MUTUAL FUND RANKINGS, SHARE PRICE RATIOS: PRICE-EARNINGS RATIO (MULTIPLE)

VALUE INVESTING

What Is It? This strategy, used by some well-known money managers such as Wellington Investments' John Neff, is associated with buying out-of-favor stocks. "Value" issues often are perceived to have lower risks because their share prices already have been discounted compared to other shares in the market.

How Is It Computed? Value-styled portfolios traditionally contain stocks that have lower-than-average price-to-book ratios and/or price-earnings ratios. An investor seeking value investments must obtain these or other ratios of value for the investment he is reviewing as well as key market benchmarks or peer securities.

Example:

Security	Price-to-book ratio	Price-earnings ratio
XYZ Corp.	2.2	19
Widget Growth Fund	3*	32*
Manufacturing Co. of Iowa	0.8	6
S&P 500	1.9*	16*

*Average

In this example, Manufacturing Company of Iowa's stock is the value selection. Its shares are trading not only at a discount to the other choices but it is also at a discount to averages for the Standard & Poor's 500-stock index.

Where Is It Found? Many brokerage reports, *Barron's*, and computerized investment databases can be used to locate a company's key ratios and then compare them to market or industry averages. A value investor "screens" out above-average or overpriced issues before making his selections. For mutual funds, Morningstar's fund reports clearly detail average price-to-book and price-earnings ratios for each fund as well as describe what funds have a value bias.

How Is It Used for Investment Decisions? Value investing is a somewhat contrarian art where the investor truly tries to buy low and sell high. In theory, the purchase of value stocks at these lower multiples should reduce the risk of major losses.

However, there may be good reasons for a company's stock to be valued lower than its peers'. Factors such as stiff competition, poor management, and heavy debts could be scaring off investors. These are problems that could eventually severely damage the company and create large investment losses.

And, value investing has its cycle like other investment disciplines. In the late 1980s, value investors were left way behind the pack when growth-oriented stocks—issues that tend to trade at high multiples—were investor favorites.

A Word of Caution: Like many other investment disciplines, value stocks have their cycles of investor popularity and disfavor. When value stocks are out of favor, investors tend to buy up "growth" shares regardless of their steep, premium price-to-book, and/or price-earnings ratios.

There are also reasons beyond simple ratios that certain stock prices are depressed. In some cases, these below-average figures are tipping off investors that such potential "value" shares are poor investments and that the share price will go only lower.

Thus, ratios alone cannot be the only guide to an investment decision. Only fundamentals, such as management's abilities, overall profitability, and industry positioning, should be checked before investing.

Also See : SHARE PRICE RATIOS: PRICE BOOK VALUE RATIO, SHARE PRICE RATIOS: PRICE-EARNINGS RATIO MULTIPLE, MORNINGSTAR MUTUAL FUND RANKINGS

60. *INVESTOR'S BUSINESS DAILY* FUND INDEX

What Is It? This is an index used to track the performance of 20 mutual funds.

How Is It Computed? This is a narrow index of mutual funds whose investment makeup is capital appreciation, growth, multinational, and natural resources. It is a total return index made up of net asset value and capital gain reinvestment into more shares. It does not assume dividend reinvestment. A base level of 100 was set in 1984. Some of the specific mutual funds listed are Twentieth Century Vista (capital appreciation), Fidelity Magellan (growth), Merrill Lynch Pacific (multinational), and T. Rowe Price New Era (natural resources).

Where Is It Found? The index appears in *Investor's Business Daily*.

How Is It Used for Investment Decisions? The investor can use this index to determine how well a broad portfolio of mutual funds is doing. The investor should determine whether the rate of return earned by the mutual fund is adequate for the risk assumed. The investor can select those mutual funds that satisfy his objectives.

61. *INVESTOR'S BUSINESS DAILY'S* "INTELLIGENT" TABLES

What Is It? *Investor's Business Daily's* "intelligent" tables contain three "intelligent" numbers: earnings per share rankings, relative price strength, and changes in trading volume. According to *Investor's Business Daily* who has developed these numbers, to profit in today's stock market, investors must look well beyond P/E ratios, dividend yields, and a company's last earnings report.

How Is It Computed? (1) Earnings per share rankings (EPS Rank) A major study suggests that a percentage increase in a company's earnings per share is a better barometer of stock price performance than P/E ratios or dividends. *Investor's Business Daily* tracks a company's per-share earnings growth over the last 5 years and ranks that earnings performance against all other publicly traded issues. The percentage change in the last two quarters' earnings vs. the same quarters a year earlier is combined and averaged with the 5-year record. The result is compared to all companies in the tables and ranked on a scale of 1 to 99, with 99 being the highest. It gives EPS Rank for more than 6,000 publicly traded companies in its daily stock tables: NYSE, AMEX, and OTC/NASDAQ. A ranking of 80, for example, means that the company produced earnings results in the top 20%.

(2) Relative price strength (Rel Str)

Ranked on a scale of 1 to 99, the Rel Str column measures each stock's price movement over the last year and compares its performance against 6,000 other stocks. A Rel Str ranking of 80, for example, means that the stock performed in the top 20% of all publicly traded issues.

(3) Changes in trading volume (Vol. % Change)

The daily change in a stock's "normal" trading volume is a critical measurement tracked by intelligent investors. Investors are interested in not just how many shares were traded that day, but how that day's volume compares to the stock's average trading volume during the last 50 days—up or down. For example, a listing of +120 means that the stock traded 120% above its normal trading volume for the day.

Where Is It Found? The intelligent numbers are found exclusively in *Investor's Business Daily*. A sample is presented below in Figure 53.

How Is It Used for Investment Decisions? Investors can use the rankings given by *Investor's Business Daily's* "intelligent" tables to pick profitable stocks and formulate their own portfolio. EPS Rank measures a company's earnings per share in the last five years and the stability of that growth. Companies with superior earnings records rank 80 or higher.

As for Rel Str Rank, stocks that rank below 70 indicate weaker or more laggard relative price performance. Vol % Chg reveals whether a stock's price change occurs on an abnormal volume increase or decrease. Not just how many shares were traded that day, but how that day's volume compares with the stock's average trading volume during the last 50 days—up or down—is a critical decision variable.

A Word of Caution: Investors must look at P/E ratios, dividend yields, and a company's last earnings report.

Also See: PERFORMANCE AND RISK: BETA FOR A SECURITY, SHARE PRICE RATIOS: PRICE-EARNINGS (P/E) RATIO (MULTIPLE), YIELD ON AN INVESTMENT: DIVIDEND YIELD PAYOUT RATIO, EARNINGS GROWTH

Figure 53: Sample of "Intelligent Tables"

52-week				EPS	Rel	Vol.	Vol.				
High	Low	Stock	PE*	Rnk	Str	100's	% Chg	Hi	Lo	Close	Chg
N H	15 1/2	ABCCorp	18	74	90	244	+201	29 3/4	29 1/2	29 5/8	+1 1/2
18	5	XYZCo	22	49	7	228	-69	7 1/4	7	7 1/4	+ 1/8
44¾	28 3/4	ANYCo	31	88	71	130	-37	42 3/4	41 1/2	41 1/2	-1 1/4

* % Yield is shown on Fridays.

62. JAPANESE CANDLESTICK CHARTS

What Is It? Candlestick charts use the same type of data as bar charts but construct each day's "candlestick" to emphasize the relationship between the day's open and close. They resemble a candlestick with wicks on each end. The thick bar of the candlestick is referred to as the real body and is determined by the day's open and close.

Traditionally in Japan, if the close is higher than the open, the body is colored red. However, this does not photocopy well so it is common to leave it open (white) and is called Yang. When the close is below the open, the body is filled (black) and is called Yin.

The lines that extend from the top and bottom of the real body are called the shadow and represent the day's high and low trading range.

The close is also a period of great activity as day traders and "weak hands" unwind their positions. Weak hands refer to those traders who do not have great confidence in their positions and will easily reverse them. During periods of uncertainty, this will be done before the market closes, as these traders are afraid to suffer losses while the markets are closed and they cannot trade out of a position.

Patterns and signals from Japanese candlesticks tend to focus on determining trend reversal points without forecasting the magnitude or price objectives of these new trends. Some of these signals can be generated from a single day's candle, while most require two to three days to develop.

How Is It Computed? Each candlestick unit represents the trading activity for one time period. The body of the candlestick is defined by the opening and closing prices of the trading period. The close is above the open if it was higher than the open and the body of the candlestick is colored white (left empty). The close defines the bottom of the body if the closing price was below that of the open and the body is colored black (filled). The small vertical lines that extend above and below the body are called shadows. They represent the high and low trading range for the trading period.

Example: The basic candle patterns are presented in Figure 54, along with their interpretations. Some patterns change in meaning and name depending upon whether they occur in an up or down market. A hanging man in a market top closely resembles the market bottom signal of a hammer. Other chart patterns closely resemble Western patterns. The three Buddha's chart (not shown) looks like the familiar head and shoulders pattern.

Where Is It Found? The following software provides Japanese candlestick charts:
- CandlePower (N-Squared Computing, 5318 Forest Ridge Rd., Silverton, OR 97381; (503) 873-4420)
- MetaStock-Professional (EQUIS International, P.O. Box 26743, Salt Lake City, UT 84126; (800) 882-3040)
- Compu Trac (Compu Trac Inc., 1017 Pleasant St., New Orleans, LA 70115; (800) 535-7990)

How Is It Used for Investment Decisions? The futures market is well-suited to candlestick charting since the open and close are periods of great activity. Overnight news and rumors help to determine opening price and often result in an opening price noticeably different from that of the close. In equity markets, the opening price tends to closely match the close unless a dramatic event occurred while the markets were closed.

A Word of Caution: Candlestick charts can, however, be used for equities. In fact, the Japanese use the chart to trade Japanese equities. Some individuals also recommend candlestick charts to help trade options. There are certain patterns that forecast increases and decreases in market volatility. Such changes in volatility would impact upon an option's premium and options traders could establish positions to benefit from such changes.

Also See: CHARTING

Figure 54: Basic Candle Lines and Patterns

Long Black Line/Major Yin
Opening at or near the top
Closing at or near the bottom
Wide price range during the day
Large real body
Interpretation: bearish

Long White Line/Major Yang
Opening at or near the bottom
Closing at or near the top
Wide price range during the day
Large real body
Interpretation: bullish

Spinning Top
Small real body in middle of trading range
Interpretation: provides no indications of direction independently. May play role when part of pattern

Hammer/Umbrella Line
Small real body at top of day's range
Little or no upper shadow
Lower shadow at least twice the length of real body
Interpretation: Bullish when appears in trend down

Hanging Man/Umbrella Line
Small real body at top of day's range
Little or no upper shadow
Lower shadow at least twice the length of the real body
Interpretation: bearish when appears in trend up

Long-Legged Doji
Open and close are the same price
Upper and lower shadow same length
Interpretation: turning point in trend. Takes on additional significance if two develop within a short period (double doji)

Dragonfly Doji
Open and close are the same price
Upper shadow shorter than lower shadow
Interpretation: turning point in trend. Takes on additional significance if two develop within a short period (double doji)

Gravestone Doji
Open and close are the same price and at the day's low
Upper shadow, but no lower shadow
Interpretation: turning point in trend. Takes on additional significance if two develop within a short period (double doji)

Dark Cloud Cover
Long white line followed by a long black line. Opens above previous day's high. Greater significance if closes below midpoint of the open real body
Interpretation: bearish

Piercing Line
Long black line followed by a long white line that opens lower than the previous day's low but closes above midpoint of the real body
Interpretation: bullish

Engulfing Line
Small black line followed by long white line in which the open is below the previous day's close and the close is above the previous day's open
Interpretation: bearish when occurs after noticeable trend up

Engulfing Line
Small white line followed by long black line in which the open is above the previous day's close and the close is below the previous day's open
Interpretation: bullish when occurs after noticeable trend down

Evening Star
Long white line followed by a shorter white line in which there is no overlapping of the real bodies. This is followed by a long black body in which the real body does not overlap with short white line, yet drops below midpoint of first long white line
Interpretation: bearish

Morning Star
Long black line followed by a short white line below it. The real bodies of the two lines should not overlap. The short white line is followed by a long white line which opens above the close of the previous day and closes above the midpoint of the long black body
Interpretation: bullish

Doji Star
A doji after a gap from the previous day. A gap occurs when the doji's open and close (which are the same) fall outside the range of the previous day's real body.
Interpretation: turning point in trend

Shooting Star
White line followed by black line that gaps the previous day, has a small body near the low, and a long upper shadow
Interpretation: mildly bearish

Harami
Small real body within the previous day's real body
Interpretation: slowing of trend (momentum)

Harami Cross
Doji within the previous day's real body
Interpretation: trend reversal

63. JAPANESE YEN

What Is It? As Japan's export business has soared, the yen has become one of the world's most important currencies. Its relationship to the U.S. dollar is a key to the global marketplace and is seen as a barometer of Japan's economic strength versus that of the U.S.

How Is It Computed? It is typically quoted in newspapers and financial reports on television and radio in terms of its relationship to the U.S. dollar. If the yen is at 135, that means that each U.S. dollar buys 135 yen. To figure out what 1 yen equals in U.S. currency, investors use this formula:

$$1 \text{ yen} = \frac{\$1 \text{ U.S.}}{\text{Yen-to-dollar rate}}$$

Example: If $1 buys 135 yen, then 1 yen is equal to $1 divided by 135 or $.00741.

Where Is It Found? Currency rates are listed daily in most major metropolitan newspapers as well as national publications like the *New York Times, USA Today,* and the *Wall Street Journal* and on computer services such as Prodigy.

How Is It Used for Investment Decisions? For American investors buying Japanese securities, the yen's movement is a key part of the profit potential in the investment. F he yen rises after an investment in Japanese securities is made, the value of those stocks or bonds to a U.S. investor will get a boost from the currency. That's because when the investment is sold, the stronger yen will generate more dollars when the proceeds are converted to the U.S. currency. Conversely, a weak yen will be a negative to a Japanese investment for a U.S. investor.

In some cases, the movement of the yen also can be viewed as an indicator of Japanese economic health. A strong yen can signal a buoyant economy, a possible indication to buy Japanese stocks. The yen's strength, however, should be verified not only against the U.S. dollar but against other major currencies.

A Word of Caution: The yen's strength versus the dollar can be distorted by prevailing interest rates in each country. For example, a movement by Japan's central bank to slow down the economy by boosting Japanese interest rates—two potential negatives for stock prices—could also increase the yen's price versus the dollar if U.S. rates are stagnant or falling. This scenario of a rising yen might give an incorrect reading on the potential for buying Japanese securities.

Widely quoted currency rates are typically for transactions of $1 million or more. Consumers looking to use such figures to determine currency rates for foreign travel should expect to get somewhat less favorable exchange rates.

Also See: BRITISH POUND, GERMAN DEUTSCHE MARK

64. JENSEN'S PERFORMANCE MEASURE (ALPHA)

What Is It? The Jensen measure called alpha, involves an ordinary least-squares regression to calculate risk-premium for an asset's return and the market return. A positive alpha means that the asset performed better than the market (e.g., Standard & Poor's 500) in risk-adjusted terms. A negative alpha means the opposite. If alpha is zero there is equality of return between the asset and the market on a risk-adjusted basis.

How Is It Computed? Jensen's formula is: $(r_i - r_f) = a + b (r_m - r_f)$ where
$(r_i - r_f)$ = risk premium for portfolio i or asset i
r_f = risk-free rate
r_m = market return
b = beta coefficent
a = Jensen's performance measure (also termed alpha)
r_i = return on portfolio i or asset i

The alpha is computed with the ordinary least-squares regression subject to a sampling error. The alpha may or may not be statistically significant.

The Jensen's alpha may be used to rank the performance of a portfolio when it is appropriately adjusted. The adjustment involves dividing each asset's alpha by the beta coefficient. For example, if assets X and Y are being ranked, use the ratio of a_x/b_x.

Example: The ABC Fund, T-bills, and the Standard & Poor's 500 had the following returns over the previous five years:

Year	ABC Fund % Return	T-Bills % Return	S&P 500 % Return
19X5	9	4	7
19X6	-4	8	-3
19X7	12	6	10
19X8	10	5	8
19X9	16	9	15

The alpha and beta coefficients for ABC Fund over the five-year period can be computed as follows:

The following model of the ordinary least-squares regression is used:
$$(r_i - r_f) = a + b \ (r_m - r_f)$$
The variables for the regression in risk-premium terms are:
$$Y \text{ variable} = (r_i - r_f)$$
$$X \text{ variable} = (r_m - r_f)$$
The following equation should be computed: $Y = a + bx$

$$a = \bar{Y} - b\bar{x} \text{ when } \bar{Y} = \frac{\Sigma Y}{N} \quad \bar{x} = \frac{\Sigma x}{N}$$

$$b = \frac{N\Sigma XY - \Sigma X \Sigma Y}{N\Sigma X^2 - (\Sigma X)^2}$$

Year	r_m S&P 500 Returns	r_i ABC Fund Returns	r_f T-Bill Returns	$(r_m - r_f)$ X	$(r_i - r_f)$ Y	XY	X^2
19X5	7%	9%	4%	3%	6%	18	9%
19X6	-3	-4	8	-11	-12	132	121
19X7	10	12	6	4	8	28	16
19X8	8	10	5	3	7	21	9
19X9	15	16	9	6	10	60	36
				$\Sigma X = 5$	$\Sigma Y = 19$	$\Sigma XY = 259$	$\Sigma X^2 = 191$

$$\bar{Y} = \frac{19}{5} = 3.8 \qquad \bar{X} = \frac{5}{5} = 1$$

$$a = \bar{Y} - b\bar{x} \qquad a = 3.8 - (1.29)(1) = 2.51$$

$$b = \frac{5(259) - (5)(19)}{5(191) - (5)^2} = \frac{1,295 - 95}{955 - 25} = \frac{1,200}{930} = 1.29$$

Because of the positive alpha (a = 2.51), the ABC Fund performed better than the market in risk-adjusted terms for the time period involved.

Example: An investor invests in the following stocks whose alpha and beta coefficients follow:

Stocks	a (Alpha)	b (Beta)
DEF Company	1.10%	.80
LMN Company	1.30	1.20
PQR Company	1.05	.90

The stocks would be ranked in performance by the Jensen measure as follows:

a/b

DEF = 1.10%/.8 = 1.375% (second)

LMN = 1.30%/1.20 = 1.083% (third)

PQR = 1.05%/.90 = 1.676 (first)

The positive values for Jensen's alpha reflect an underpricing of the security and thus an investment is financially attractive on a risk-adjusted basis.

Where Is It Found? The measure is found in Morning Star Mutual Fund Values. Investors may compute it themselves based on information extracted from financial publications including *Barron's* and the *Wall Street Journal*.

How Is It Used for Investment Decisions? The Jensen formula can be used to appraise the performance of a portfolio or asset.

Funds with positive and statistically significant alpha values can be said to outperform the market. On the other hand, funds with negative and statistically significant alpha values can be said to underperform the market. Funds with alphas not significantly different from zero perform equal to the market.

A Word of Caution: Measure is restricted to investors with some mathematical abilities.

Also See: MUTUAL FUNDS: ALPHA FOR A MUTUAL FUND

65. LIPPER MUTUAL FUND INDEXES

What Are They? These are daily benchmarks for stock mutual funds compiled by Lipper Analytical Services of New Jersey. These indexes show the value of (or lack thereof) various mutual fund portfolios.

How Are They Computed? Each member fund contributes an equal weighting to its respective index. Lipper compiles the following daily fund indexes:

- Growth—The first Lipper fund index, it uses the performance of the 30 largest growth funds, the most widely watched type of stock fund. At year-end 1992, these 30 funds represented 59% of all growth fund assets and 21% of all stock fund assets. The index's base of 100 is from December 31, 1968.
- Growth & Income—Uses the performance of the 30 largest growth and income funds, a popular conservative type of stock fund. At year-end 1992, these 30 funds represented 72% of all growth and income fund assets and 26% of all stock fund assets. The index's base of 100 is from December 31, 1968.
- Balanced—Uses the performance of the 30 largest balanced funds that combine stock and bond holdings. At year-end 1992, these 30 funds represented 96% of all balanced fund assets and 3% of all stock fund assets. The index's base of 100 is from December 31, 1960.
- Equity Income—Uses the performance of the 30 largest equity income funds that tend to hold income-producing stocks. At year-end 1992, these 30 funds

represented 76% of all equity income fund assets and 8% of all stock fund assets. The index's base of 100 is from December 31, 1978.

- Capital Appreciation—Uses the performance of the 30 largest capital appreciation funds, the most aggressive stock funds. At year-end 1992, these 30 funds represented 87% of all capital appreciation fund assets and 9% of all stock fund assets. The index's base of 100 is from December 31, 1980.
- Small Company Growth—Uses the performance of the 30 largest small company growth funds. At year-end 1992, these 30 funds represented 71% of all small company growth fund assets and 5% of all stock fund assets. The index's base of 100 is from December 31, 1980.
- International—Uses the performance of the 30 largest international funds that buy stocks from around the globe. At year-end 1992, these 30 funds represented 85% of all growth and income fund assets and 3% of all stock fund assets. The index's base of 100 is from December 31, 1984.
- Science & Technology—Uses the performance of the ten largest funds specializing in science and technology issues. At year-end 1991, these ten funds represented 0.6% of all stock fund assets. The index's base of 100 is from December 31, 1984.
- Gold—Uses the performance of the ten argest gold funds. At year-end 1991, these ten funds represented 0.4% of all stock fund assets. The index's base of 100 is from December 31, 1984.

Where Are They Found? Daily readings of these indexes are in newspapers such as *USA Today* and the *Wall Street Journal* and on computer database Prodigy. (See Figure 55.)

How Are They Used for Investment Decisions? The indexes give investors a reading of how mutual fund managers are faring, especially when their results are compared to broad market indexes. Using the indexes, an investor also can gauge how his mutual fund, or his own portfolio, is faring against a "batting average" of top-paid professionals.

The index also can be used as a benchmark for growth-oriented stocks, issues of companies that display above-average potential for rising sales and profits. When this index is outpacing a more cyclical index like the Dow Jones Industrial Average, it can be viewed as a signal that investor sentiment is turning toward growth issues.

A Word of Caution: Many mutual fund managers use various management styles even within a single portfolio or turn to cash in particularly rough markets. In some cases,

Figure 55: Lipper Indexes

Indexes	Prelim. Close	Percentage chg. Prev.	Wk age	since Dec. 31
Capital appreciation	336.93	+ 0.42	- 1.17	- 4.94
Growth Fund	617.78	+ 0.32	- 0.57	- 1.02
Small Co. Growth	324.41	+ 0.25	- 1.57	- 5.75
Growth & Income Fd	951.98	+ 0.24	+ 0.20	+ 4.54
Equity Income Fd	619.34	+ 0.15	+ 0.19	+ 4.27
Science & Tech Fd	227.26	+ 0.65	- 0.82	- 5.88
International Fund	342.29	+ 0.60	+ 0.18	- 2.48
Gold Fund	131.53	- 0.41	- 1.84	- 6.52
Balanced Fund	743.23	+ 0.09	+ 0.19	+ 3.22

Source: Lipper Analytical Services, Inc., *Wall Street Journal*, September 29, 1992.

the fact that a Lipper index outperforms the Dow Industrials may not be a sign of a certain style's strength. For example, it could be that skittish managers are holding large amounts of money out of a falling market.

Also See: LIPPER MUTUAL FUND RANKINGS

66. LIPPER MUTUAL FUND RANKINGS

What Are They? These are widely watched measures of how mutual funds perform against each other both on an industrywide and peer-group basis, as compiled by Lipper Analytical Services of New Jersey. Lipper issues reports weekly, monthly, and quarterly. Its long-term rankings—with track records of 1 to 15 years—are the most quoted.

How Are They Computed? Lipper tracks more than 3,000 funds—stock, bond, and money markets. The Lipper rankings are based strictly on total return, which is price appreciation or depreciation plus dividends paid out. No further analysis is done. That's unlike rankings by Morningstar of Chicago that consider funds for both return, consistency of that return, and risk-taking. Lipper then splits funds into various categories that range from broad ones (stocks, bonds, money funds) to extremely narrow ones (international stock funds by specific country).

Where Are They Found? Lipper results are the basis for many newspapers' weekly and quarterly coverage of the fund industry. Every business day, the *Wall Street Journal* uses Lipper data to highlight the best and worst funds in a specific fund category. Lipper's report on the quarterly performance of stock funds is issued within a week of a quarter's end and gets nationwide media coverage. The *Wall Street Journal* and the *Orange County Register* prints Lipper's total return data for more than 2,500 funds each quarter as does *Barron's* (see Figure 56). The Lipper performance numbers also frequently appear in mutual fund advertising.

How Are They Used for Investment Decisions? The Lipper numbers often are used to rate one mutual fund against another. Investors can compare their funds to its peers for total return performance.

There are also the often discussed Lipper industrywide rankings which, for example, propelled Peter Lynch of Fidelity Investments into prominence. During his 15-year tenure on the Fidelity Magellan Fund, no fund manager beat Lynch's total return figures as compiled by Lipper.

Lipper's fund category rankings can help investors who want to invest in narrow sector funds that limit assets to one industry or country. Groups with rising performance figures could be an investment while a category taking on losses could be ripe for selling.

A Word of Caution: Experts suggest that investors look at long-term track records of 5 years or more when choosing among funds. They also advise that past performance figures like Lipper's are no indication of what the future may bring.

Also See: MORNINGSTAR MUTUAL FUND RANKINGS

67. MISERY INDEX

What is it? This is an index that tracks economic conditions including inflation and unemployment. It was particularly referred to in the economically depressed period of 1977 through 1981 in the United States. The inflation rate was in the double digits at that time.

How Is It Computed? Misery Index = inflation rate + unemployment rate + prime rate

Where Is It Found? It may be found in the Bureau of Labor Statistics publications and the *Wall Street Journal*.

How Is It Used for Investment Decisions? The index typically is negatively correlated tothe current condition of the stock market.

A Word of Caution: The misery index is not useful in predicting future stock prices.

Figure 56: Sample of Lipper Mutual Fund Rankings

LIPPER MUTUAL FUND PERFORMANCE AVERAGES

Weekly Summary Report: May 27, 1993
Cumulative Performances With Dividends Reinvested

NAV Mil. $	No. Funds		10/11/90- 5/27/93	7/12/90- 5/27/93	5/28/92- 5/27/93	12/31/92- 5/27/93	5/20/93- 5/27/93
General Equity Funds:							
45,892.1	139	Capital Appreciation	+ 79.97%	+ 38.04%	+ 15.73%	+ 5.60%	+ 1.00%
149,999.8	409	Growth Funds	+ 72.46%	+ 35.19%	+ 13.26%	+ 3.35%	+ 0.64%
31,236.2	170	Small Company Growth	+102.26%	+ 46.71%	+ 20.92%	+ 4.46%	+ 1.03%
156,333.3	309	Growth and Income	+ 64.92%	+ 35.74%	+ 12.37%	+ 5.24%	+ 0.57%
47,363.3	89	Equity Income	+ 62.20%	+ 37.72%	+ 13.63%	+ 6.91%	+ 0.71%
430,824.7	1116	Gen. Equity Funds Avg.	+ 74.51%	+ 37.46%	+ 14.52%	+ 4.60%	+ 0.73%
Other Equity Funds:							
3,906.2	14	Health/Biotechnology	+ 66.23%	+ 40.09%	− 1.81%	− 8.42%	+ 0.40%
2,202.9	24	Natural Resources	+ 23.54%	+ 15.21%	+ 18.70%	+ 21.65%	+ 1.58%
238.7	10	Environmental	+ 18.13%	− 10.27%	− 2.24%	− 1.16%	+ 0.77%
2,737.7	20	Science & Technol.	+127.15%	+ 54.42%	+ 30.20%	+ 10.70%	+ 0.95%
1,811.4	29	Specialty/Misc.	+ 88.84%	+ 42.92%	+ 19.23%	+ 10.36%	+ 1.16%
20,912.7	45	Utility Funds	+ 56.94%	+ 49.54%	+ 17.19%	+ 7.79%	+ 1.12%
2,620.3	14	Financial Services	+168.38%	+100.53%	+ 29.62%	+ 7.14%	+ 1.20%
777.3	6	Real Estate	+ 71.04%	+ 37.77%	+ 21.53%	+ 11.04%	− 0.61%
104.7	3	Option Income	+ 43.41%	+ 23.90%	+ 8.93%	+ 4.76%	+ 0.21%
3,019.4	32	Gold Oriented Funds	+ 24.71%	+ 17.75%	+ 38.08%	+ 55.65%	+ 4.28%
19,106.3	67	Global Funds	+ 34.74%	+ 13.78%	+ 9.03%	+ 11.32%	+ 1.62%
2,959.7	13	Global Small Co. Funds	+ 58.14%	+ 25.71%	+ 16.10%	+ 16.29%	+ 1.02%
20,197.5	118	International Funds	+ 24.95%	+ 5.93%	+ 8.38%	+ 16.65%	+ 2.11%
3,432.5	29	European Region Fds	+ 4.25%	− 10.19%	− 4.91%	+ 9.14%	+ 1.19%
2,810.3	27	Pacific Region Funds	+ 42.04%	+ 17.82%	+ 20.69%	+ 24.09%	+ 2.70%
839.6	6	Japanese Funds	+ 4.50%	− 15.76%	+ 30.65%	+ 40.17%	+ 4.43%
393.8	7	Latin American Funds	N/A	N/A	− 12.58%	+ 2.54%	+ 0.16%
67.0	3	Canadian Funds	+ 19.07%	+ 7.51%	+ 19.19%	+ 22.43%	+ 1.36%
52,826.1	302	World Equity Funds Avg.	+ 26.73%	+ 8.78%	+ 12.50%	+ 20.02%	+ 2.14%
518,962.7	1583	All Equity Funds Avg.	+ 66.96%	+ 33.40%	+ 14.51%	+ 7.98%	+ 1.03%
Other Funds:							
14,126.8	81	Flexible Portfolio	+ 54.26%	+ 36.45%	+ 12.19%	+ 5.11%	+ 0.52%
3,256.8	16	Global Flex Port.	+ 36.51%	+ 26.15%	+ 11.02%	+ 9.63%	+ 1.01%
35,026.8	102	Balanced Funds	+ 54.57%	+ 37.10%	+ 11.72%	+ 4.76%	+ 0.43%
930.5	9	Balanced Target	+ 60.56%	+ 43.32%	+ 14.93%	+ 5.71%	+ 0.29%
3,166.3	26	Conv. Securities	+ 69.57%	+ 43.96%	+ 17.96%	+ 7.54%	+ 0.64%
10,033.4	17	Income Funds	+ 54.88%	+ 42.25%	+ 13.01%	+ 6.79%	+ 0.56%
27,601.4	114	World Income Funds	+ 22.86%	+ 31.72%	+ 6.04%	+ 5.65%	+ 0.26%
304,337.2	886	Fixed Income Funds	+ 40.47%	+ 37.85%	+ 10.96%	+ 4.61%	+ 0.02%
917,441.9	2834	Long-Term Average	+ 57.21%	+ 35.06%	+ 12.95%	+ 6.65%	+ 0.64%
		Long-Term Median	+ 52.20%	+ 35.00%	+ 11.80%	+ 5.10%	+ 0.40%
		Funds with % Change	1691	1643	2249	2660	2781

Source: *Barron's*, May 27, 1993. Reprinted by permission of *Barron's*, ©1993 Dow Jones & Company, Inc., All Rights Reserved Worldwide.

68. MOMENTUM GAUGES

DOW JONES INDUSTRIAL AVERAGE MOMENTUM RATIO

What Is It? The ratio measures the percentage difference between the DJIA and its average price for the prior 30 days.

How Is It Computed?

$$\frac{\text{DJIA closing price}}{\text{DJIA price for preceding 30 days}}$$

Where Is It Found? The ratio is found in *Barron's*.

How Is It Used for Investment Decisions? If the ratio exceeds 3% above its 10-day moving average, it indicates a market peak. An investor using a contrarian philosophy would believe that it is time to sell securities at a market top. If the ratio is more than 3% below the 10-day moving average, a market trough is indicated. Again, a contrarian would buy at this time, with the expectation of increasing prices.

A Word of Caution: The contrarian assumption that is the basis for this ratio may not always hold.

Also See: DOW JONES INDUSTRIAL AVERAGE

OSCILLATORS

What Are They? Oscillators are an internal measure (strength) of momentum. They are used to measure a price index by looking at the rate of change (ROC). They are a short-term to intermediate-term breadth indicator. This technical analysis method is used to obtain historical comparative information. Oscillators reflect movements of similar proportion in the same way. An example of a momentum oscillator is the advance/decline line.

How Are They Computed? Momentum is measured by computing the rate of change in a market average or index over a prescribed time period. It is calculated by subtracting a 39-day exponential moving average of the net difference between the number of advancing issues and the number of declining issues from a 19-day exponential moving average of the net difference between the number of advancing issues and the number of declining issues. New York Stock Exchange data is used in the calculation.

Example: To construct an index measuring a 26-week rate of change, the current price is divided by the price 25 weeks ago. If the current price is 150 and the price 25 weeks ago was 160, the rate of change (momentum index) is 93.8 (150/160). The next reading in the index would be determined by dividing next week's price by the price 24 weeks ago.

Where Are They Found? Oscillators are found in brokerage research reports prepared by technical analysts. They appear in the monthly and weekly editions of Merrill Lynch's *Investment Strategy*.

How Are They Used for Investment Decisions? Oscillators can show the rhythm in price movement, which could aid the investor in determining the degree of momentum associated with stocks. Are stocks in a down or up cycle? Strength in stock price is a bullish indication while weakness in stock prices is a bearish sign.

The oscillator signals when the market is overbought or oversold. The oscillator typically reaches an extreme reading prior to a change in the trend of stock prices.

The bear market selling climax is indicated by an oscillator reading of approximately -150. A surge of buying activity, implying an overbought condition, is signaled by an oscillator reading above 100.

The oscillator normally passes through zero near market tops and bottoms. When the oscillator goes below to above zero, it is considered bullish for stock prices. On the other hand, when it goes from above to below zero, it is interpreted as bearish for the stock market.

Numerous chart patterns in the indicator are supposed to signal various market conditions. A detailed explanation of these chart formations are beyond the scope of this book. However, a full description of how to interpret the McClellan Oscillator is included in *Patterns for Profit: The McClellan Oscillator and Summation Index* (Trade Levels, Inc., 22801 Ventura Boulevard, Suite 210, Woodland Hills, CA 91364).

Also See: MOMENTUM GUAGES: SUMMATION INDEX

RELATIVE STRENGTH ANALYSIS

What Is It? Relative strength is the price performance of a company's stock compared to the price performance of an overall market and/or industry index. In addition, the investor can compare how the performance of the stocks within an industry has done relative to the overall market. Market indexes that might be used are the Dow Jones Industrial Average, Standard & Poor's 500, and New York Stock Exchange Composite. Relative strength is an approach used in technical investment analysis by chartists.

How Is It Computed? Relative strength for a company's stock may be computed using one or both of the following ratios:

$$\frac{\text{Monthly average stock price}}{\text{Monthly average market index}}$$

$$\frac{\text{Monthly average stock price}}{\text{Monthly average industry group index}}$$

An increase in these ratios means that the company's stock is performing better than the overall market or industry. This is a positive sign. A relative strength index (RSI) also may be computed for a security as follows:

$$RSI = 100 - \frac{100}{1 + RS}$$

where

$$RS = \frac{\text{14-day average of up closing prices}}{\text{14-day average of down closing prices}}$$

Relative strength for an industry also may be determined as follows:

$$\frac{\text{Specific industry group price index}}{\text{Total market index}}$$

An increasing ratio indicates that the industry is outperforming the market.

Where Is It Found? Brokerage research reports and *Value Line Investment Survey* may provide relative strength information on companies and industries. Relative strength charts and interpretation may be obtained from Securities Research. The investor also may compute the monthly average price of a company's stock and that of a market index by referring to price quotations in newspapers.

How Is It Used and Applied? Relative strength is an approach that helps the investor determine the quality of a price trend of an index by comparing it with the trend in another index. If there is an improvement in relative strength after a drastic decline, this is an indicator of strength. If there is a deterioration in relative strength after a prolonged increase in price, weakness exists.

An industry index (*e.g.*, utilities) may historically lead an overall market index (*e.g.*, Dow Jones Industrial Average) so that a change in that industry index may infer a future change in the overall market index. A graph may be prepared charting these indexes relative to one another.

How Is It Used for Investment Decisions? The investor can evaluate relative strength to predict individual stock prices. If a stock or industry group outperforms the market as a whole, the investor should view that stock or industry positively. The presumption is that strong stocks or groups will become even stronger.

A high relative strength index for a security (stock or bond) or commodity indicates an overbought situation while a low RSI indicates an oversold environment.

A Word of Caution: A distinction must be made between relative strength in a contracting market and relative strength in an expanding market. When a stock outperforms a major stock average in an advance, it possibly may soon turn around. But when the stock outperforms the rest of the market in a decline, the stock will likely remain strong.

SUMMATION INDEX

What Is It? The McClellan Summation Index is simply a cumulative total of the McClellan Oscillator. It is used for interpreting intermediate to long-term moves in the stock market.

How Is It Computed? This is simply a cumulative total of the McClellan Oscillator.

Where Is It Found? It is frequently reported on the cable TV network *CNBC*.

How Is It Used for Investment Decisions? Similar to the McClellan Oscillator, the McClellan Summation Index gives buy and sell signals. When it crosses zero, it is considered bullish for stock prices. When it crosses from above to below zero, it is interpreted as a bearish sign for the stock market.

A Word of Caution: This index reading is far from an exact science.

Also See: MOMENTUM GUAGES: OSCILLATORS

"WALL STREET WEEK" TECHNICAL MARKET INDEX

What Is It? This index is based on a survey of ten technical investment analysis methods. These technical indicators include financial conditions, market activity, investor behavior, insider purchases, calls and puts, and monetary policy. The index is used to substantiate an upward or downward trend in the stock market. Fundamental analysis is not taken into account.

How Is It Computed? This measure is based on assigning +1 for a bullish characteristic, -1 for a bearish situation, and 0 for no effect for each of the ten technical indicators. The ratings are then added to obtain a total. The ten indicators in the index are:

1. *Market Breadth*—A moving average for ten days for the net effect of advancing issues relative to declining issues.
2. *Put/Call Options Premium*—A ratio of premium on put options to premium on call options.

3. *Arms Short-Term Trading Index*—An advance/decline ratio of "Big Board" stocks divided by the ratio of volume increasing to volume decreasing.
4. *Insider Buy/Sell Ratio*—A ratio of insider buys to insider sells.
5. *Low-Price Activity percentage*—The volume of low-priced "risky" securities to the volume of high-quality stocks.
6. *Bearish Sentiment Index*—An indicator of how investment newsletters perceive as the future condition of the stock market. It is determined by Investor's Intelligence.
7. *DJIA Momentum Ratio*—The difference between the closing DJIA and the average DJIA for 30 days.
8. *NYSE High-Low Index*—The number of stocks accomplishing new highs relative to those reaching new lows over the previous 10 trading days applied on a daily basis.
9. *NYSE Securities at Market Prices Above 10-Week and 30-Week Moving Averages*—The percentage of stocks selling above their 10-week and 30-week highs.
10. *Ratio of Ending Prices on Fed Funds to the Discount Rate.* When the Federal Reserve Board tightens the money supply the rate of Fed increases relative to the discount rate. This is because the Federal Reserve Board is charging a higher rate between member banks and a lower rate (discount rate) is being charged by the Federal Reserve for member banks to borrow from the Federal Reserve.

The upper and lower limits for the Wall Street Week Technical Market Index is +10 to -10. A reading of +1 to -1 is neutral. A reading of +5 or more is a buy signal while a reading of -5 is a sell signal.

Where Is It Found? The index is found in *Futures* and *Investor's Analysis* (published by Robert Nurock) magazine.

How Is It Used for Investment Decisions? The index indicates from a technical standpoint whether the bottom or top is indicated. At market bottom there is a buy indicator while at market top there is a sell indicator. For example, at the market bottom stock prices are expected to increase.

69. *MONEY'S* SMALL INVESTOR INDEX

What Is It? *Small Investor Index*, developed by *Money* magazine, is an index that measures gains and losses of the average investor relative to a base of 100 set on December 27, 1991. It is based on a portfolio that includes the types of investments held by average small investors.

How Is It Computed? This index can be used to measure the average investor's gains and losses. It is based on a portfolio that includes ten types of investments held in proportions consistent with Federal Reserve data on what the average household owns.

Where Is It Found? The index is reported weekly each Monday in daily papers such as the *Orange County Register* and *USA Today* and monthly as part of *Money's* "Investor's Scorecard."

Example: The value of the index on August 22, 1992, was 103.98, which reflected a 0.03% gain for the week and an 8.08% gain over a year earlier.

How Is It Used for Investment Decisions? Although this index is not widely used on Wall Street, it provides the individual investor with a standard against which he can assess both the composition and performance of his portfolio.

A Word of Caution: *Money*'s Small Investor Index is by no means an optimal allocation for every investor. Incidentally, the *American Association of Individual Investors (AAII)* periodically surveys where individuals commit their assets, as shown in Figure 57.

Also See: ASSET ALLOCATION

Figure 57: Asset Commitments

AAII Allocation Survey:
Where Individuals Commit their Assets

The percentage of individual investors' portfolios committed to stocks and bonds rose during June. Stocks are currently 30% of assets, up 5%; and bonds are 12%, up 2% from May. During the same period, the portion allocated to cash and stock funds declined. Cash currently represents 26% of assets, down from 29%; and stock funds represent 21% of assets, down from 25% in May. The percentage committed to bond funds remained unchanged during June at 11% of assets.

Each month, AAII members are asked to calculate the percentage of their portfolio invested in cash, bonds, bond funds, stock and stock funds.

The dashed lines indicate the average allocation of each category over the duration of the survey. The graph indicates where individuals commit their assets over time. It is an average; individual portfolios should vary according to personal circumstances and risk tolerances.

It is interesting to note that while investor sentiment varies widely over time, individual investors' actual allocation of their assets remains remarkably stable, indicating that investors on average do not tend to make major portfolio changes based on short-term impulses.

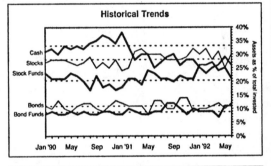

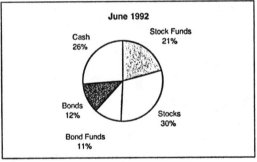

Source: *AAII Journal*, August, 1992.

70. MORNINGSTAR MUTUAL FUND RANKINGS

What Are They? A risk measurement system for comparing more than 2,000 mutual funds' long-term performance is available from Chicago-based Morningstar. The system rates stock and bond funds from 5 stars (the best) to no stars (the worst or unrated).

How Are They Computed? Morningstar uses a proprietary system that measures a mutual fund's price and dividend performance as well as the risks taken by the fund management to get those results.

The rankings are then made from comparing a fund both in its own category and against the industry as a whole. Thus the best performing fund in a category that has been a weak market sector might get only 2 or 3 stars.

Where Are They Found? Morningstar sells it rating service, *Morningstar Mutual Funds*, to the public in a print or computerized compact disc version. The printed version is sold in a loose-leaf book style much like Value Line's well-known rankings of individual stocks. (See Figure 10, pages 16-17.) The service updates each of its 10 parts every six months by issuing new reports on a rotating basis approximately twice a month. Morningstar rankings are also often discussed in the newspaper and magazine accounts of the fund industry. They are the basis for the *New York Times'* quarterly fund report.

How Are They Used for Investment Decisions? When choosing among mutual funds, investors can use Morningstar rankings to find potentially better-performing investments. Many brokerages and financial planning firms limit their clients' investments to 5-star and 4-star funds.

But choosing a 5-star fund over a 3-star fund is not always the correct choice. For one, Morningstar's rankings reflect past performance and that often slants the reviews toward funds with recently successful investment styles.

In addition, within each category—notably a poorly performing sector—the highest rated fund may have succeeded by limiting its exposure to certain risks. If an investor believed that an out-of-favor market sector was ready to return, he might want to buy a fund with a lower rating that was more fully invested in that sector.

A Word of Caution: Before buying or selling a fund, investors should consult other fund-watching sources. *Business Week*, *Forbes*, and *Money* magazines all print periodic analyses of individual funds as do many newsletters and newspapers.

Also See: LIPPER MUTUAL FUND RANKINGS

71. MORTGAGE RATES

WEEKLY AVERAGE

What Are They? These are a national average of interest rates offered on mortgages—both 30-year fixed and starting rates for 30-year adjustable loans that vary once a year—from surveys by the Federal National Mortgage Association, also known as Fannie Mae, and the Federal Home Mortgage Corp., or Freddie Mac.

How Are They Computed? Fannie Mae and Freddie Mac poll major lenders nationwide and compile an average for these two key mortgage products.

Where Are They Found? The two agencies release the information every Thursday and Friday, and short stories about it appear in major daily newspapers such as the *Los Angeles Times* and the *Wall Street Journal*. It is also found in the statistical tables of *Barron's* as seen in Figure 58.

How Are They Used for Investment Decisions? For those shopping for a mortgage, the averages can be reviewed to see how available loans compare. Movements in the weekly average can help loan shoppers decide when to lock in a rate on a new mortgage.

Figure 58: Mortgage Rates Report

	Latest Week	Previous Week	Year Ago Week
Other Money Rates			
Eurodollar average weekly auction-c	4.21	4.26	6.24
Freddie Mac Home Loan Mtg Rates-b:			
30-Year Conventional fixed mortgage	8.47	8.62	9.42
1-Year Adjustable mortgage	5.625	5.625	6.50
Fannie Mae Home Loan Mtg Rates-b:			
30-Year Conventional fixed mortgage	8.47	8.61	9.36
1-Year Adjustable mortgage	5.85	6.15	7.20
Merrill Lynch Ready Assets Trust	3.63	3.63	5.94
Bank money market accounts-z	3.55	3.57	5.34
Super NOW accounts-z	2.92	2.94	4.78
6-Month Certificates-z	3.88	3.87	6.04
12-Month Certificates-z	4.11	4.10	6.26
30-Month accounts-z	4.97	4.91	6.61
5-Year Certificates-z	6.03	5.98	7.04
U.S. Savings Bonds	6.38	6.38	7.19

Source: *Barron's*. Sources: a-Prebon Yamanp (USA) Inc. b-Telerate Systems. c-Annualized yields, adjusted for constant maturity reported by the Federal Reserve on a weekly average basis. z-Bank Rate Monitor.

In the big picture, mortgage rates are often seen as a good indicator of the housing industry. Falling rates can be a boost to home building, a key element of any economic recovery. However, low mortgage rates do not guarantee a pickup in home sales or building activity. One group that clearly will benefit from falling rates is lenders, who also can profit from mortgage refinancings.

Also See: INTEREST RATES: 30-YEAR TREASURY BONDS

ADJUSTABLE LOAN BENCHMARKS

What Are They? Various indexes serve as the base rate for variable mortgages. Indexes are selected by the borrower when the loan is made. Typically, lenders determine monthly payments by charging between 2 percentage points and 4 percentage points above the indexes.

How Are They Computed? The indexes come from a variety of sources. The most widely used is an odd average known as the 11th District Cost of Funds Index. This monthly index, compiled by the Federal Home Loan Bank of San Francisco, tracks monthly costs of deposits at savings and loans in California, Nevada, and Arizona.

Other popular benchmarks are figures compiled by the Federal Reserve known as constant maturity averages for various U.S. Treasury issue maturities. They are reported weekly. Another benchmark is the London Interbank Offered Rate or LIBOR. It is reported daily and reflects what the world's bankers charge one another for money.

Where Are They Found? Many newspapers' business or real estate sections such as the *Dallas Morning News*, the *Los Angeles Times*, the *New York Times*, and the *Orange County*

Register, now track the more widely used benchmarks weekly. Major adjustable loan lenders can also be contacted directly for periodic updates on the indexes. Figure 59 is a *Wall Street Journal* sample.

Figure 59: Federal Home Loan Arm Indexes

Cost of funds indexes supplied by the Office of Thrift Supervision. These indexes may be used by federally chartered institutions in establishing rates on adjustable rate mortgages (ARMs) for previously occupied homes.

Contract rate for major lenders-a	7.58%
Cost-of-funds July natl mnthly median-b	5.13%
Apr.-Jun. national average-b	5.35%
Jan.-Jun. national average-b	5.57%
11th OTS district average for August	4.874%

a-National average supplied by the Federal Housing Finance Board for August. b-To Savings Association Insurance Fund (SAIF) insured institutions.

Source: *Wall Street Journal.*

How Are They Used for Investment Decisions? A borrower considering an adjustable loan must juggle several factors, notably which index to choose.

History shows that no one index stands out as best for the consumer. The 11th District index is known for its slow change while Treasury or Libor benchmarks can be more volatile. Movements of these benchmarks can show how fat—or stretched—the homeowner's wallet is. That's not a bad economic indicator.

Also, new mutual funds that concentrate on buying securities backed by adjustable rate mortgages have become popular, low-risk alternatives to money market mutual funds and savings accounts. Trends in these benchmarks would show up in the yields of such funds just a few months in the future.

72. MOST ACTIVE ISSUES

What Is It? The most active issues are the stocks that have the largest share volume for the trading period, usually daily. They are listed in the order of shares traded. Active stocks reflect the activity of institutional investors, and account for about 20% of total NYSE volume.

How Is It Determined? A tabulation is made of the stocks of each exchange and over-the-counter market in terms of trading volume.

Where Is It Found? Statistics on the most active stocks are published in the financial press on both a daily and weekly basis. For example, the *New York Times* lists the 15 most active issues for the trading day on the NYSE, AMEX, and NASDAQ markets. It lists the volume, last price, and change. *Barron's* lists the high/low/last prices and change. Prodigy on-line database service lists the most active issues on the NYSE, AMEX, and NASDAQ.

Summaries of the most active stocks are prepared by technical services. For example, *Indicator Digest* publishes biweekly the trend in up stocks and down stocks.

How Is It Used and Applied? The quality of the volume leaders will be a key indicator. If they are blue chip companies, the future might be bright. If they are secondary issues, investors should be somewhat cautious.

How Is It Used for Investment Decisions? The most active issues are those involving the greatest share volume because of their interest to institutional buyers and sellers of stock. Such issues are highly marketable. In addition to looking at share volume, the investor must consider price movement. If the number of shares traded on a company's stock is very high but its market price is constant, the security is fairly stable in price. However, increasing price on heavy volume is significant. The security may be making a significant upward movement. On the other hand, decreasing price on heavy volume might be alarming as it may signal a significant downward movement—the "Big Boys" are unloading. The investor must look out for substantial price changes coupled with heavy trading activity.

The investor should determine the reason and significance of the heavy trading. Is it due to an announcement of superior earnings, heavy buying by institutions, or a takeover attempt? Can the volume and price movement be sustained?

Some company stocks such as General Electric, American Telephone and Telegraph, and Philip Morris are listed frequently because of their wide ownership and institutional backing. The listing of a stock for the first or second time is quite significant and must be thoroughly studied.

The investor should be alert to repetition. If an industry or one company appears regularly within a short period of time, there is something happening as evidenced by institutional interest.

A Word of Caution: A stock may be very active one day for a special reason such as a possible acquisition. However, that rumored acquisition may not materialize. Further, after that one day spurt in activity, the stock may become dormant.

Also See: TRADING VOLUME

73. MOVING AVERAGES

What Is It? A moving average (MA) is an average that is updated as new investment information is received. The investor uses the most recent stock price and/or volume to calculate an average, which is used to predict future market prices and/or volume.

A moving average also can be used to evaluate intermediate and long-term stock movements. The moving average shows the underlying direction and magnitude of change of very volatile numbers.

How Is It Computed? The most recent observation is used to calculate a moving average. Moving averages are constantly updated. It is determined by averaging a portion of the series and then adding the subsequent number to the numbers already averaged, omitting the first number, and obtaining a new average.

For instance: A 30-week MA records the average closing price of a stock for the 30 most recent Fridays. Each week, the total changes because of the addition of the latest week's closing figures and the subtraction of those of 30 weeks ago. Then, the new total is divided by 30 to obtain the MA.

Example 1:

Month-end stock prices for the following months:

January	$20
February	23
March	20
April	21
May	16

(February–May) } 4 months

Using a 4-month moving average, the predicted stock price for June is computed as follows:

$$\frac{23 + 20 + 21 + 16}{4} = \frac{80}{4} = 20$$

Example 2:

Day	Index	Three-Day Moving Total	Three-Day Moving Average
1	121		
2	130		
3	106	357 (Days 1-3)	119 (357/3)
4	112	348 (Days 2-4)	116 (348/3)

Where Is It Found? Moving average information and charts may be found in brokerage research reports. Many technical analysts prepare and chart 200-day moving averages in their reports. Otherwise, the investor can determine the moving average from stock price quotations and volume figures on a stock published in financial newspapers, brokerage reports, and such. Typically, daily or weekly price changes are graphed. Market indexes are also published in financial publications such as the *Wall Street Journal*.

How Is It Used and Applied? Many analysts are of the opinion that a reversal in a significant uptrend in the price of a stock and/or overall market may be identified beforehand or at least confirmed by examining the movement of current prices compared to the long-term moving average of prices. A moving average shows the direction and degree of change of a fluctuating series of prices.

How Is It Used for Investment Decisions? Moving average is used as a prediction model to determine the future expected market price of stock. The investor can choose the number of periods to use on the basis of the relative importance he attaches to old versus current data. For example, an investor might compare two possibilities, a five-month and three-month period. In terms of the relative importance of new versus old data, the old data received a weight of 4/5 and current data 1/5. In the second possibility, the old data received a weight of 2/3, while current observation received 1/3 weight.

By examining the movement of present prices compared to the long-term moving average of prices, the investor can foresee a reversal in a major uptrend in price of a particular security or the general market.

A 200-day moving average of daily ending prices is usually used. The investor can graph the average on stock price charts to see directions. The investor should buy when the 200-day average line becomes constant or rises after a decline and when the daily price of stock moves up above the average line. A buy also is indicated when the stock price rises above the 200-day line, then goes down toward it but not through it, and then goes up again. The investor should consider selling when the average line becomes constant or slides down after a rise and when the daily stock price goes down through the average line. A sell also is indicated when the stock price is below the average line, then rises toward it, but instead of going through it the price slips down again.

74. MUNI-BOND INDEXES

DOW JONES MUNICIPAL BOND YIELD AVERAGE

What Is It? The index shows the weighted-average yield on tax-free municipal bonds.

How Is It Computed? This is an average of the yields of low-coupon bonds in five states and 15 major cities.

Where Is It Found? The index is available from Dow Jones. It appears in financial publications such as *Barron's*.

How Is It Used for Investment Decisions? The investor can compare the yield on a tax-free municipal bond to the yield on a taxable corporate bond to determine whether it is worth buying on a before-tax basis. For example, a 6% tax-free bond for an investor in the 40% tax bracket has an equivalent taxable yield of 10% (6%/1-.4). The investor can use the index of average yield to determine the financial attractiveness of a particular municipal bond. For example, if the average yield is 5.5% and a particular municipal yields 6.5% assuming similar risk, it is an atrractive investment.

Also See: BOND MARKET INDEXES: BOND BUYER INDEXES, YIELD ON AN INVESTMENT: TAX-EQUIVALENT YIELD

STANDARD & POOR'S MUNICIPAL BOND INDEXES

What Are They? The indexes reveal price and effective rate of return data on municipal bonds. The two indexes are Municipal Bond Price Index and Municipal Bond Yield Index.

How Are They Computed? The Municipal Bond Price Index is based on high quality (AAA to A) municipal bonds having a maturity of about 20 years. Yield to maturity is translated to an equivalent selling price to a 20-year, 4% bond. An average yield is then determined for the bonds.

The Municipal Bond Yield Index is determined from 15 highly rated (AAA to A) municipal bonds. The index is an arithmetic average of the effective interest rate.

Data for these indexes are obtained from dealers in municipal bonds.

Where Are They found? Index information is obtained from *Barron's* and Standard & Poor's.

How Are They Used for Investment Decisions? The municipal bond index information can be used by investors in high tax brackets to determine whether the tax-free yield is more attractive than the rates of return on other investments.

75. MUTUAL FUND CASH-TO-ASSETS RATIO

What Is It? This ratio refers to the level of cash investments held by stock mutual funds, as compiled by Investment Company Institute, a trade group also called ICI. This is seen as an indicator of how much money leading money managers are willing to commit to the stock market.

How Is It Computed? Each month the ICI surveys fund companies about the assets they hold. This ratio is determined by totaling the cash holdings of stock mutual funds and dividing it by the total assets in those funds. A report is issued typically near the end of the month with statistics on the previous month's fund activity.

Where Is It Found? The monthly ICI report is covered in such publications as the *New York Times* and the *Wall Street Journal*. *Barron's* runs a chart weekly on the most recent monthly data.

How Is It Used for Investment Decisions? The ratio is seen as a measure of the stock fund manager's outlook for stocks.

At its simplest, when the level of cash is falling, it is often seen as a signal of market strength. Mutual funds represent one of the biggest stock buyers today. Conversely, when the ratio is rising, it may show that stock fund managers are getting nervous about holding stocks and that an investor may want to do likewise and lighten his exposure to equities.

Conversely, market conditions also can be brought into the analysis.

For example, when stock fund managers' exuberance for stocks brings the ratios to less than 5% and the market is still rising, some analysts believe that this is a signal to sell. Such analysts fear that there will be little support left for the stock market as mutual funds become fully invested.

On the other hand, when fund managers are aggressively adding to cash in a down market, some may consider such activity a signal that the market bottom may be approaching. Indeed, in such a situation the turnaround could be dramatic as the funds, heavy with cash, rush to buy shares once they start an upswing.

A Word of Caution: The data are often dated, by at least one month, which can make analysis difficult.

Also See: ECONOMIC INDICATORS AND THE SECURITIES MARKET

76. MUTUAL FUNDS: EVALUATION TECHNIQUES

ALPHA FOR A MUTUAL FUND

What Is It? Alpha is the excess return that the portfolio manager is able to earn above an unmanaged portfolio (or market portfolio) that has the same risk. In the context of a mutual fund, an alpha value is the value representing the difference between the return on a fund and a point on the market line, where the market line describes the relationship between excess returns and the portfolio beta.

How Is It Computed? Alpha is beta x (market return - risk-free return)

Example 1: If the market return is 8% and the risk-free rate (such as a rate on a T-bill) is 5%, the market excess return equals 3%. A portfolio with a beta of 1 should expect to earn the market rate of excess returns equal to 3% (1 x 3%).

A fund with a beta of 1.5 should provide excess returns of 4.5% (1.5 x 3%).

Where Is It Found? Morningstar (53 West Jackson Blvd., Chicago, IL 60604, (800) 876-5005 offers two publications—*Morningstar Mutual Funds* and *Mutual Fund Source Book*—that show alpha values of more than 1,000 funds. (See Figure 10 on pages 16-17.)

How Is It Used and Applied? Alpha value is used to evaluate the performance of mutual funds. Generally, a positive alpha (excess return) indicates superior performance while a negative value leads to the opposite conclusion.

Example 2: The fund in Example 1 has a beta of 1.5, which indicates an expected excess return of 4.5% along the market line. Assume that the fund had an actual excess return of only 4.1%. That means the fund has a negative alpha of .4% (4.1% - 4.5%). The fund's performance is therefore inferior to that of the market.

How Is It Used for Investment Decisions? "Keep your alpha high and your beta low" is a basic strategy for those who wish to invest in a mutual fund.

This measure should cover at least three years of data to give the most accurate picture about the performance of the fund. The key question for investors is: Can a fund consistently perform at positive alpha levels?

A Word of Caution: Alpha should be analyzed together with risk measures such as beta, R-squared, and standard deviation and other fund selection criteria, such as fees, investment objectives, shareholder services, and the fund manager's experience.

Also See: JENSEN'S PERFORMANCE MEASURE, BETA FOR A MUTUAL FUND, MUTUAL FUNDS: R-SQUARED, MUTUAL FUNDS: STANDARD DEVIATION, SHARPE'S RISK-ADJUSTED RETURN

EXPENSE RATIOS

What Are They? An expense ratio is a measure of how much it costs to own a mutual fund. Other than commissions or other sales fees, these costs are not directly billed to the investors. That makes them hard to follow. These expenses, from the fund's legal bills to the manager's profit, are taken out of the fund's net asset value.

How Are They Computed? The ratio reflects the various expenses charged against the value of the assets in a fund. These expenses include management fees paid to the fund company, the cost of running the fund, and added charges for marketing the fund, which are called 12b-1 fees. They are totaled and then divided by the total assets in the fund. The ratio equates to the amount the fund's total return is reduced in comparison to directly owning the same securities.

The expense ratio does not include sales commissions or the fund's costs of trading securities.

Where Are They Found? Investors can track these expenses in two places. Every mutual fund prospectus details these expenses both as a percentage of the fund's assets and expressed in terms of how much a saver is charged to own the fund over five years. Figure 60 shows one fund's expense ratio summary.

In addition, many fund-watching services, most notably Morningstar of Chicago, track such charges. See Figure 10, pages 16-17.

How Are They Used for Investment Decisions? Experts say that while no investment should be made solely because of a fund's level of expenses, it is something to watch closely. It is particularly important for bond funds where expenses, rather than management expertise, can be crucial.

To evaluate a fund, an investor would look at his fund's total annual expenses and then compare his costs with the following industrywide averages as of June 1992:

Equity funds, 0.93%.
Taxable bond funds, 1.03%.
Tax-exempt bonds, 0.69%.
Money-market funds, 0.60%.

Also See: LIPPER MUTUAL FUND RANKINGS, MORNINGSTAR MUTUAL FUND RANKINGS

The Fund

SUMMARY OF FUND EXPENSES

The expense summary format below was developed for use by all mutual funds to help you make your investment decisions. Of course, you should consider this expense information along with other important information in this Prospectus, including the Fund's investment objective and its past performance.

A. Shareholder Transaction Expenses

Maximum Sales Load Imposed on Purchases	None
Maximum Sales Load Imposed on Reinvested Dividends	None
Deferred Sales Load Imposed on Redemptions	None
Exchange Fee	None

B. Annual Fund Operating Expenses (as a percentage of average net assets)

Management Fee	0.75%
12b-1 Fee	None
Other Expenses	0.42%
Total Fund Operating Expenses	1.17%

C. Example:

You would pay the following expenses on a $1,000 investment in the Fund, assuming (1) a 5% annual return and (2) full redemption at the end of each time period:

1 Year	$ 12
3 Years	37
5 Years	64
10 Years	142

Source: Fidelity Asset Manager Prospectus.

NET ASSET VALUE

What Is It? The value of a mutual fund share is measured by net asset value (NAV), which describes what each share of a mutual fund is worth.

How Is It Computed? NAV equals

$$\frac{\text{Fund's total assets} - \text{liabilities}}{\text{Number of shares outstanding in the fund}}$$

Example: Assume that a fund owns 100 shares each of General Motors (GM), Xerox, and International Business Machines (IBM). Assume also that on a particular day, the market values below existed. The NAV of the fund is calculated as follows (assume the fund has no liabilities or cash):

(a) GM—$90 per share x 100 shares =	$ 9,000
(b) Xerox—$100 per share x 100 shares =	10,000
(c) IBM—$160 per share x 100 shares =	16,000
(d) Value of the fund's portfolio =	$35,000

(e) Number of shares outstanding in the fund =   1,000
(f) Net asset value (NAV) per share =(d)/(e) = $35

If an investor owns 5% of the fund's outstanding shares, or 50 shares (5% x 1,000 shares), then the value of the investment is $1,750 ($35 x 50).

Where Is It Found? NAV is reported in the mutual fund section of the financial pages of every daily newspaper. NAVs on some selected funds are listed on computer services such as Prodigy.

How Is It Used for Investment Decisions? There are two ways to make money in mutual funds. NAV represents one component of the return on mutual fund investments—the current market value of the underlying portfolio. An investor also receives capital gains and dividends. Therefore, the performance of a mutual fund must be judged on the basis of these two returns.

An investor should monitor the closing daily change in the NAV of a fund. Such information provides an indicator of the return he's earned on his money. Of course, fund managers make every effort to increase the NAV, since their performance is partly evaluated on its change.

A Word of Caution: It is important to remember that there are other measures of the quality of a fund such as beta, alpha, R-squared, standard deviation, and Sharpe's risk-adjusted return.

Also See: MUTUAL FUNDS: ALPHA FOR A MUTUAL FUND, BETA FOR A MUTUAL FUND, RISK-ADJUSTED RETURN, MUTUAL FUNDS: STANDARD DEVIATION, SHARPE'S R-SQUARED

R-SQUARED

What Is It? R-squared (R^2) is the percentage of a fund's movement that can be explained by changes in the S&P 500. In statistics, it is called the coefficient of determination, designated R^2 (read as R-squared).

Simply put, R^2 tells us how the overall relationship is between the dependent variable y and the explanatory variable x. More specifically, the coefficient of determination represents the proportion of the total variation in y that is explained by x. It has the range of values between 0 and 1.

How Is It Computed? The coefficient of determination is computed as

$$R^2 = 1 - \frac{\Sigma(y-y')^2}{\Sigma(y-y)^2}$$

However, there is a short-cut method available:

$$R^2 = \frac{[n\Sigma xy - (\Sigma x)(\Sigma y)]^2}{[n\Sigma x^2 - (\Sigma x)^2][n\Sigma y^2 - (\Sigma y)^2]}$$

Example: To illustrate the computation of R-squared, we will refer to the following data.

| S&P Returns | XYZ Fund Returns | | | |
x	y	xy	x^2	y^2
9%	15%	135	81	22
19%	20%	380	361	40
11%	14%	154	121	19
14%	16%	224	196	25
23%	25%	575	529	62
12%	20%	240	144	40
12%	20%	240	144	40
22%	23%	506	484	52
7%	14%	98	49	19
13%	22%	286	169	484
15%	18%	270	225	32
17%	18%	306	289	32
174%	225%	3,414	2,792	4,359

From the table above:

$\Sigma x = 174$ $\Sigma y = 225$ $\Sigma xy = 3,414$ $\Sigma x^2 = 2,792$

$x = \Sigma x/n = 174/12 = 14.5$ $y = \Sigma y/n = 225/12 = 18.75$

Using the short-cut method for r^2,

$$r^2 = \frac{(1,818)^2}{(3,228)\,[(12)\,(4,359) - (225)^2\,]} = \frac{3,305,124}{(3,228)\,(52,308-50,625)}$$

$$= \frac{3,305,124}{(3,228)\,(1,683)} = \frac{3,305,124}{5,432,724} = 0.6084 = 60.84\%$$

This means that about 60.84% of the total variation in XYZ Fund returns is explained by the market (represented in this example by the S&P 500 index). A relatively low R^2 indicates that there is little correlation between XYZ Fund and the market.

Where Is It Found? Morningstar (53 West Jackson Blvd., Chicago, IL 60604, (800) 876-5005) sells two publications, *Morningstar Mutual Funds* and *Mutual Fund Source Book*, that show R-squared values of more than 1,000 funds. See Figure 10, pages 16-17.

How Is It Used for Investment Decisions? If the R^2 of a mutual fund is close to 100, the fund is well diversified. The further a mutual fund is from 100, the less the fund is diversified.

A Word of Caution: This measure should cover at least three years of data to give the most accurate picture about the performance of the fund. Further, R-squared should be analyzed together with risk measures such as beta and standard deviation and other fund selection criteria, such as fees, investment objectives, shareholder services, and the fund manager's experience.

Also See: MUTUAL FUNDS: ALPHA FOR A MUTUAL FUND, BETA FOR A MUTUAL FUND, MUTUAL FUNDS: STANDARD DEVIATION, SHARPE'S RISK-ADJUSTED RETURN,

STANDARD DEVIATION

What Are They? The standard deviation is the measure of tightness of the probability distribution. In other words, it measures the tendency of data to be spread out. Investors can make important inferences from past data with this measure. The standard deviation, denoted with the Greek letter σ, read as sigma, is defined as follows:

$$\sigma = \sqrt{\frac{(x - \bar{x})^2}{n}}$$

where $\bar{x}$ is the mean (arithmetic average).

How Are They Computed? More specifically, the standard deviation can be calculated, step-by-step, as follows:

1. Subtract the mean from each element of the data.
2. Square each of the differences obtained in step 1.
3. Add together all the squared differences.
4. Divide the sum of all the squared differences by the number of values minus one.
5. Take the square root of the quotient obtained in step 4.

Example:
One and one-half years of quarterly returns are listed below for ABC Mutual Fund.

Time period	x	$(x - \bar{x})$	$(x - \bar{x})^2$
1	10%	0	0
2	15	5	25
3	20	10	100
4	5	-5	25
5	-10	-20	400
6	20	10	100
	60		650

From the above table, note that

$$\bar{x} = 60/6 = 10\%$$

$$\sigma = \sqrt{\frac{(x-\bar{x})^2}{n}} = \sqrt{\frac{650}{6}} = \sqrt{108} = 10.41\%$$

ABC Fund has returned on the average 10% over the last six quarters and the variability in its average return was 10.41%. The high standard deviation (10.41%) relative to the average return of 10% indicates that the fund is very risky.

Where Is It Found? Morningstar (53 West Jackson Blvd., Chicago, IL 60604, (800) 876-5005) sells two publications, *Morningstar Mutual Funds* and *Mutual Fund Source Book*, that show standard deviations of more than 1,000 funds. See Figure 10, pages 16-17.

How Is It Used and Applied? The calculation of the standard deviation may not seem simple, but the calculation can be done easily with a calculator with a square root key, a financial calculator with the standard deviation key, or spreadsheet programs such as Lotus 1-2-3, Quatro Pro, and Microsoft Excel that have a built-in standard deviation function (for example, @STD).

The standard deviation can be used to measure the variation of such items as the expected return. It also can be used to assess the risk associated with investments.

It is used to measure risk for a security. The smaller the standard deviation, the tighter the probability distribution and, accordingly, the lower the riskiness of the security.

How Is It Used for Investment Decisions? If the expected rate of return of XYZ Fund is 15% and the standard deviation is 10%, the actual return of the fund will be in the range as follows:

1. 68% of probability:
   The actual return = 15% + 10% (or -10%), from 5% to 25%
2. 95% of probability:
   The actual return = 15% + 20% (or -20%), from -5% to 35%

It is assumed that the probability distribution of returns is normal.

A Word of Caution: In calculating the standard deviation, there are a number of related issues, such as the divisor used or the minimum number of data points necessary for the calculation to function properly. Generally, the fewer data points used, the less useful the calculation of volatility. To properly measure the volatility (variability) of the investment's return, an investor must also consider other measures such as beta.

Also See: MUTUAL FUNDS: ALPHA FOR A MUTUAL FUND, BETA FOR A MUTUAL FUND, MUTUAL FUNDS: R-SQUARED, SHARPE'S RISK-ADJUSTED RETURN, R-SQUARED

77. MUTUAL FUNDS: MONTHLY SALES

What Is It? The fund industry's trade group issues a monthly report on sales and redemption of stock, bond, and money market funds. The report is usually out four weeks after a month ends. The report is seen as a reflection of small investors' opinion on the climate for buying stocks or bonds or for holding cash.

How Is It Computed? The Investment Company Institute (ICI) polls its members on their cash inflows and outflows. ICI then tabulates industrywide figures, excluding such items as dividend payments. The report includes figures on new sales, redemptions, and the most closely watched net sales figure.

Where Is It Found? In recent years, the monthly sales figure has become grist for stories in daily newspapers such as the *Wall Street Journal* and the *New York Times*. The figures have been reported each week for years in *Barron's*.

How Is It Used for Investment Decisions? With the growing popularity of mutual funds among small savers, the monthly reports are seen as good indicators of the individual investor's appetite for stocks and/or bonds. There is some debate, though, over the meaning of small investors' buying habits. Some experts feel these savers tend to be bad investors and should be considered a contra-indicator. Others, however, say the small investor has again become a powerful market force, one that could lead stock or bond advances in the future.

In addition, the monthly ICI report contains a reading on the cash position of stock funds. This figure is watched as an indicator of the bullish or bearish nature of mutual fund managers.

A Word of Caution: Fund investors, much like the consuming public, can have buying habits altered by marketing campaigns. In some cases, fund purchases or redemptions may reflect fund companies' marketing strategies, altering the industrywide numbers' ability to reflect investor sentiment.

Also See: MUTUAL FUND CASH-TO-ASSETS RATIO

78. NASDAQ INDEXES

What Are They? The NASDAQ indexes follow the price performance of over-the-counter securities. The indexes include:

- Industrial Index, tracks about 3,000 industrial companies such as Microsoft, Intel, Apple, and Liz Claiborne.
- Bank Index, a broad index covering about 250 stocks of commercial and savings banks along with ancillary companies (*e.g.*, trust, currency, check-cashing). The index tends to follow smaller institutions and was initiated in 1971.
- Finance Index, shows the performance of about 100 insurance companies and banks.
- Other Finance Index, a broad-based index of the stocks of about 750 financial service companies other than banks. Some companies included in the index are Midlantic, Shawmut National, and First Union Corp.
- Insurance Index, a capitalized weighted-average market value index of 133 stocks including insurance brokers and agents. Some companies included in the index are St. Paul and Hanover.
- Transportation Index, a narrow index of about 80 transportation businesses. Some companies included in the index are Laidlaw Transportation Roadway Services, and Alexander and Baldwin.
- Utilities Index, a broad-based index of about 175 utilities, natural gas companies, communications and cable TV companies, and broadcasters. Companies included in the index are MCI Communications, LIN Broadcasting, and Cellular Communications.

How Are They Computed? The indexes are based on a capitalized weighted market value.

Where Are They Found? The indexes are published by the National Association of Securities Dealers. They appear in *Barron's*. Some brokerage research reports track these indexes.

How Are They Used for Investment Decisions? If an index is very low, an investor may expect an increase to more normal levels. A low index may represent a buying opportunity in selected stocks.

An overbought situation is when the index is at its peak and the investor believes that a correction is imminent. In this case, the investor may sell overpriced stocks he owns or sell short in expectation of a downturn in price.

The Bank and Finance indexes could signal interest rate changes.

A Word of Caution: An index represents an average—some companies may be doing well while others are doing poorly. An index usually does not include the performance of all companies in a given sector.

A major risk affecting the performance of insurance companies included in the Insurance Index is natural disasters.

Also See: MUTUAL FUND CASH-TO-ASSETS RATIO

79. NEW HIGHS AND LOWS

NEW HIGHS/NEW LOWS RATIO

What Is It? The new highs/new lows ratio is the number of new issues that traded at their highest 52-week price divided by the number of issues that traded at their lowest 52-week price.

How Is It Computed? New Highs/New Lows Ratio equals:

$$\frac{\text{Number of issues at 52–week highest price}}{\text{Number of issues at 52–week lowest price}}$$

A graph might be prepared as shown in Figure 61.

Example: The number of issues with new 52-week highs and lows are 2 and 10, respectively. The ratio is therefore .20, which is low. This is a bearish situation.

Where Is It Found? Listings of new highs and new lows for the trading day are published in the financial pages of newspapers and magazines such as *Barron's*, *Investor's Business Daily*, the *New York Times*, and the *Wall Street Journal*.

How Is It Used for Investment Decisions? An uptrend in the ratio of new highs to new lows is a bullish indicator of the stock market while a downtrend is a bearish sign.

The investor may look at specific companies having new highs as the basis to make an investment decision. If the investor feels the stock is overvalued, he should not buy it or, if it is currently held, sell it. Of course, if the investor believes the company will do even better, the stock should be retained. On the other hand, a company listed as a new low might be bought if the investor feels the price is overly depressed and the company has potential.

A Word of Caution: The number of new highs to new lows is just one measure of performance. Other indicators of stock performance must be examined as well. For example, there might be more new lows than new highs but the Standard & Poor's 500 index may have increased.

Also See: BREADTH (ADVANCE/DECLINE) INDEX, NEW HIGHS AND LOWS: NEW YORK STOCK EXCHANGE HIGH-LOW INDEX

Figure 61: New Highs to New Lows

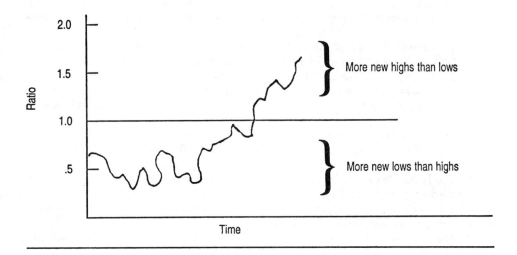

NEW YORK STOCK EXCHANGE HIGH-LOW INDEX

What Is It? The index compares stocks accomplishing new highs relative to those reaching new lows.

How Is It Computed?

$$\frac{\text{Number of stocks reaching new highs in a day}}{\text{Number of stocks reaching new lows in a day}}$$

The index is computed over a 10-day period.

Where Is It Found? The index may be determined from information provided in *Barron's* and the *Wall Street Journal*.

How Is It Used for Investment Decisions? The index may be used as a momentum indicator. There are few securities that reach new lows at market ceilings. On the other hand, few securities reach their highs at the market's trough.

According to the contrary theory of investments, when everyone is buying the stock, it is time to sell because the stock has reached a high.

A Word of Caution: A security may in fact be at its all-time low even at the top of the bull market.

Also See: NEW HIGHS AND LOWS: NEW HIGHS/NEW LOWS RATIO

80. NEW YORK STOCK EXCHANGE INDEXES

What Are They? The New York Stock Exchange Indexes consist of the Composite Index and its four subindexes which are the Industrial Index, Transportation Index, Utilities Index, and Financial Index.

How Are They Computed? The Composite Index is a capitalized market value weighted index of all NYSE issues. There are 46 industry groups represented. The index is adjusted for new issues, mergers, and bankruptcies. The index is computed as follows:

1. Multiply the market value of each common share by the number of shares.
2. Add the results for all issues to derive the total market value.
3. The index is a number showing the relationship between total current market value and a base market value (established in 1966). Any needed adjustments are made. Fifty is the base value for the index. Point changes are in terms of dollars.

The total market value is not affected by stocks splits.

The Industrial Index is comprised of more than 1,000 industrial companies in about 30 industrial sectors.

The Transportation Index is a broad one of about 175 transportation companies such as air carriers, truckers, and railroads.

The Utilities Index is a narrow one of about 40 utilities including the areas of electric power, gas, water, and telecommunications.

The Financial Index is a broad base of about 400 financial companies including the areas of banking, insurance, credit, brokerage, and investment.

Where Are They Found? The NYSE indexes are reported in *Barron's*, the *New York Times*, and the *Wall Street Journal*. The indexes also may be accessed through an on-line computerized investment database such as Prodigy.

Figure 62 shows the index information as it appears in the *New York Times*.

How Are They Used for Investment Decisions? The New York Stock Exchange Composite Index is a measure of the performance of New York Stock Exchange issues. It is a barometer of market conditions. If the index consistently increases, a bull market exists. However, if the index consistently decreases, there is a bear market. Therefore, investors

Figure 62: New York Stock Exchange Index

	NYSE INDEX			
	High	Low	Close	Chg.
Index	228.43	227.72	228.43	+.70
Industrial	282.69	281.62	282.69	+.10
Transport	186.13	185.16	186.13	+.82
Utility	103.26	103.14	103.23	-0.02
Finance	177.73	172.40	177.76	+.30

Source: *New York Times*, August 31, 1992.

can use the index as one indicator of whether to buy stocks or avoid them. A healthy, expanding stock market with future upward potential provides a buying opportunity.

The New York Stock Exchange Composite Index may be looked at as confirmation of a change in other indexes such as the Dow Jones Industrial Average and Standard & Poor's 500. If all three indexes move in the same direction with similar magnitude, there is consistency. Thus, the investor can be more confident of the degree of market strength or weakness when several indexes confirm each other.

The NYSE Composite Index also provides the base for options written on the index and for futures contracts.

81. OPTIONS

CBOE PUT-CALL RATIO

What Is It? The Chicago Board Options Exchange (CBOE) ratio compares put volume to call volume on option contracts. In a put, the investor bets the market will go down. In a call, the investor bets that the market will go up.

How Is It Computed?

$$\text{CBOE Put-Call Ratio} = \frac{\text{Put volume}}{\text{Call volume}}$$

Example: The following option volume information is presented for the week:

	Puts	Calls
S&P 100	600,000	500,000
CBOE Equity	200,000	600,000

The ratios are:

S&P 100 = 600,000/500,000 = 120/100
CBOE Equity = 200,000/600,000 = 133.3/100

Where Is It Found? The CBOE ratio appears in *Barron's*.

How Is It Used for Investment Decisions? Investors must examine the trend in the ratio over time (*e.g.*, weekly). A put-call ratio of 70 puts to every 100 calls on the S&P's 100 and 65 puts to every 100 calls on the CBOE Equity ratio is a positive sign. However, a put-call ratio of only 40 puts to 100 calls on the S&P 100 and on the CBOE Equity ratio is a negative indicator. The CBOE put-call ratio is a contrarian tool. For example, a low put volume reflects bullishness.

A Word of Caution: Although the put-call ratio is expected to be a contrary indicator, this may not always be the case.

Also See: CBOE OPTIONS: PUT/CALL OPTIONS PREMIUM RATIO

PUT/CALL OPTIONS PREMIUM RATIO

What Is It? This is a short-term contrarian method to predict future movement in stock prices. A premium is the cost to the investor of buying a call or put option.

How Is It Computed? The Put/Call Options Premium Ratio equals:

$$\frac{\text{Average premium on listed put options}}{\text{Average premium on listed call options}}$$

A put option is the right to sell a company's shares at a given price by a certain date while a call option is the right to buy those shares. With a put option an investor makes money if the stock price decreases; with a call option an investor makes money if the stock price increases.

Example: Assume an average premium on listed put and call options of 110 and 130, respectively. The put/call options premium ratio is 84.6%.

Where Is It Found? The ratio is published in *Barron's*.

How Is It Used for Investment Decisions? The investor should use this ratio as a technical investment analysis contrary approach. Put premiums are usually high when investors feel bearish. However, from a contrarian frame of reference, the time to buy is when investors are negative because a bullish stock market is deemed to occur. On the other hand, a low ratio means that investors are positive, which is a bearish indicator. For example, a ratio above 90% may indicate a stock market bottom and therefore a buying opportunity. A ratio below 40% may indicate a stock market peak and therefore the time to sell.

A Word of Caution: The contrarian approach does not always work.

Also See: OPTIONS: VALUATION OF OPTIONS (CALLS AND PUTS)

SPREAD STRATEGY

What Is It? A spread is the purchase of an option (long position) and the writing of an option (short position) in the same security, using call options. A sophisticated investor may write many spreads to gain from the differences in option premiums. The return potential is significant, but the risk is very high. There are different types of spreads:

- A vertical spread is the purchase and writing of two contracts at different striking prices with the same expiration date.
- A horizontal spread is the purchase and writing of two options with the same strike price but for different periods.
- A diagonal spread combines the horizontal and vertical.

How Is It Computed? Spreads require the investor to buy one call and sell another call. The gain or loss from a spread position depends on the change between two option prices as the price of the stock increases or decreases. The difference between two option prices is the price spread.

Where Is It Found? A spread may be bought through brokerage houses and members of the Put and Call Brokers and Dealers Association. Put and call traders devise many spread situations involving different maturities or different strike prices.

How Is It Used for Investment Decisions? The speculator who uses a vertical bull spread anticipates an increase in the price of stock, but this strategy reduces the risk. There is a ceiling on the gain or loss.

The speculator using a vertical bear spread expects the stock price to decline. This investor sells short the call with the lower strike price and places a cap on upside risk by buying a call with a higher strike price.

Also See: OPTIONS: PUT/CALL OPTIONS PREMIUM RATIO, OPTIONS: STRADDLING STRATEGY, OPTIONS: VALUATION OF OPTIONS (CALLS AND PUTS)

STRADDLING STRATEGY

What Is It? Straddling integrates a put and call on the same stock with the identical exercise (strike) price and exercise date. It is employed to take advantage of significant variability in stock price. High beta stocks might be most suited for this. A straddle may be bought either to maximize return or to minimize risk. This investment approach should be left to sophisticated investors.

How Is It Computed?
   Profit on call or put
   Less: cost of call
   Less: cost of put
   Net gain

Where Is It Found? A straddle is not traded on listed exchanges but rather must be acquired through brokerage houses and members of the Put and Call Brokers and Dealers Association.

Example: An investor buys a call and put for $4 each on September 30 when the stock price is $42. The expiration period is four months. The investment is $8, or $800 in total. Assume the stock increases to $60 at expiration of the options. The call earns a profit of $14 ($18 - $4) and the loss on the put is $4. The net gain is $10, or $1,000 altogether.

How Is It Used for Investment Decisions? A straddle is used by a speculative investor trading on both sides of the market. The speculative investor hopes for significant movement in stock price in one direction so as to make a gain that exceeds the cost of options. If the price movement does not go as expected, however, loss will equal the cost of the options. The straddle holder may widen risk and profit potential by closing one option before closing the other.

Investors using straddles often use extensive computer analysis.

Also See: OPTIONS: PUT/CALL OPTIONS PREMIUM RATIO, OPTIONS: SPREAD STRATEGY, OPTIONS: VALUATION OF OPTIONS (CALLS AND PUTS)

VALUATION OF OPTIONS (CALLS AND PUTS)

What Is It? Calls and puts are a type of stock options that may be bought or sold in round lots, usually 100 shares. They come in bearer negotiable form and have a life of one month to nine months.

The investor who purchases a call is buying the right to buy 100 shares of a stock at a fixed exercise price for a predetermined period. He does this when he expects the price of that stock to rise. In buying a call, the investor stands a chance of making a significant gain from a small investment, but he also risks losing his full investment if the stock does not rise in price.

Purchasing a put gives an investor the right to sell 100 shares of a stock at a fixed exercise price for a predetermined period. An investor might buy a put when he expects a stock price to fall. By purchasing a put he gets an opportunity to make a considerable gain from a small investment, but he will lose the entire investment if the stock price does not fall.

The purchase of calls and puts gives the investor tremendous financial leverage with limited downside risk. The buying of puts can be used as a strategy for protecting unrealized capital gains.

How Is It Computed? The cost of an option is referred to as a premium. It is the price the purchaser of the call or put has to pay the writer. (With other securities, the premium is the excess of the purchase price over a determined theoretical value.)

The premium for a call depends on:

- The dividend trend of the related security.
- The volume of trading in the option.
- The exchange on which the option is listed.
- The variability in price of the related security. (A higher variability means a higher premium because of the greater speculative appeal of the option.)
- Prevailing interest rates.
- The market price of the stock it relates to.
- The width of the spread in price of the stock relative to the option's exercise price. (A wider spread means a higher price).
- The amount of time remaining before the option's expiration date. (The longer the period the greater the premium's value.)

When the market price exceeds the strike price, the call is said to be in the money. But when the market price is less than the strike price, the call is out of the money. Call options in the money have an intrinsic value equal to the difference between the market price and the strike price.

Value of call = (Market price of stock - exercise price of call) x 100

Assume that the market price of a stock is $45, with a strike price of $40. The call has a value of $500.

Out-of-the-money call options have no intrinsic value.

If the total premium (option price) of an option is $7 and the intrinsic value is $3, there is an additional premium of $4 arising from other considerations. In effect, the total premium consists of the intrinsic value plus speculative premium (time value) based on factors such as risk, variability, forecasted future prices, expiration date, leverage, and dividend.

Total premium = Intrinsic value + speculative premium

The definition of in the money and out of the money are different for puts because puts permit the owner to sell stock at the strike price. When the strike price exceeds market price of the stock, the investor has an in-the-money put option. Its value is determined as follows:

Value of put = (Exercise price of put - market price of stock) x 100

Assume the market price of a stock is $53 and the strike price of the put is $60. The value of the put is $700.

When the market price of the stock exceeds strike price, there is an out-of-the-money put. Because a stock owner can sell it for a greater amount in the market than he could get by exercising the put, there is no intrinsic value of the out-of-the-money put.

	XYZ calls at 50 strike price	XYZ puts at 50 strike price
	Stock price	Stock price
In the money	Over 50	Under 50
At the money	50	50
Out of the money	Under 50	Over 50

The theoretical value for calls and puts indicates the price at which the options should be traded. But typically they are traded at prices higher than true value when options have a long period to go. This difference is referred to as investment premium.

$$\text{Investment premium} = \frac{\text{Option premium} - \text{option value}}{\text{Option value}}$$

Assume a put has a theoretical value of $1,500 and a price of $1,750. It is therefore traded at an investment premium of 16.67%.

Example 1: A two-month call option allows an investor to acquire 500 shares of XYZ Co. at $20 per share. Within that time period, he exercises the option when the market price is $38. He makes a gain of $9,000 before paying the brokerage commission. If the market price had declined from $20, he would not have exercised the call option, and he would have lost the cost of the option.

Example 2: Significant percentage gains on call options are possible from the low investment compared to the price of the related common stock. Assume a stock has a present market price of $35. A call can be purchased for $300 allowing the acquisition of 100 shares at $35 each. If the price of the stock increases, the call will also be worth more. Assume that the stock is at $55 at the call's expiration date. The profit is $20 on each of the 100 shares of stock in the call, or a total of $2,000 on an investment of $300. A return of 667% is thus earned. In effect, when the holder exercises the call for 100 shares at $35 each, he can sell them immediately at $55 per share. Note that the investor could have earned the same amount by investing directly in the common stock, but the investment would have been $3,500, so the rate of return would have been significantly lower.

Example 3: An investor can buy a call giving him the right to acquire 100 shares of $30 stock at $27. The call will trade at a price of about $3 a share. Call options also may be used when an investor believes the stock price will increase in the future but has a cash flow problem and is unable to buy the stock. He will, however, have sufficient cash to do so later. In this situation, he can buy a call so as not to lose a good investment opportunity.

Example 4: On February 6 an investor purchases a $32 June call option for $3 a share. If the stock has a market price of $34½, the speculative premium is $½. In June, he exercises the call option when the stock price is $37. The cost of the 100 shares of stock for tax reporting is the strike price ($32) plus the option premium ($3), or $35.

Example 5: A stock has a market price of $35. An investor acquires a put to sell 100 shares of stock at $35 per share. The cost of the put is $300. At the exercise date of the put, the price of the stock goes to $15 a share. He therefore realizes a profit of $20 per share, or $2,000. As the holder of the put, the investor simply buys on the market 100 shares at $15 each and then sells them to the writer of the put for $35 each. The net gain is $1,700.

Example 6: Assume that TUV Co. stock's price was $55 on March 2. An investor buys a $56 June put for $4. The speculative premium is therefore $3. On June 7, the stock price falls to $47 and the price of the June $56 put to $8. The intrinsic value is $9 and the speculative premium is $1. As the put holder, the investor now has a gain of $4.

Example 7: As an example of a hedge, an investor buys 100 shares of JJJ Corp. at $26 each and a put for $200 on the 100 shares at an exercise price of $26. If the stock remains static, he will lose $200 on the put. If the price decreases, his loss on the stock will be offset by his gain on the put. If the stock price rises, he'll earn a capital gain on the stock and lose his investment in the put. In other words, to get the benefit of a hedge, an investor must incur a loss on the put. (Also note that at the expiration of the put, he incurs a loss with no further hedge.)

Example 8: An investor buys a put to hedge his position on a stock. He holds 100 shares of BBC Corp. stock purchased at $60 a share. That stock increases to $80, earning a profit of $20 a share. To guarantee his profit he buys a put with an $80 exercise price at a cost of $300. No matter what happens later, he will have a minimum gain of $1,700. If the stock price falls, he'll realize an additional profit.

Example 9: An investor might buy a call to protect a short sale from the risk of increasing stock price. By doing this, he hedges his position as follows: when he uses a call, he as a short seller will not suffer a loss in excess of a given amount. However, he has lowered his profit by the cost of the call.

Example 10: A speculator purchases an option contract to buy 100 shares at $25 a share. The option costs $150. Assume a rise in stock price to $33 a share. The speculator exercises the option and sells the shares in the market, realizing a gain of $650 ($33 - $25 - $1.50 = $6.50 x 100 shares). Now the speculator can sell the option in the market and make a profit because of its increased value. However, if there is a decline in stock price, the loss to the holder is limited to $150 (the option's cost). Of course, brokerage fees are also involved. In effect, this call option permitted the speculator to purchase 100 shares worth $2,500 for $150 for a short period.

Where Is It Found? Calls, puts, and index options are listed in financial publications such as *Barron's*, *Investor's Business Daily*, the *New York Times*, and the *Wall Street Journal*.

Calls and puts are typically written for widely held and actively traded stock on organized exchanges. Calls and puts are traded on the NYSE and on listed option exchanges, which are secondary markets like the Chicago Board Options Exchange, AMEX, Philadelphia Stock Exchange, and Pacific Stock Exchange. They also are traded in the over-the-counter market. Option exchanges deal only in the purchase and sale of call and put options. Listed options are options traded on organized exchanges. Conventional options are those options traded in the over-the-counter market.

How Is It Used and Applied? Options can be traded for speculative or conservative purposes. Commissions and transaction costs are involved when a call or put is purchased or sold or written. Brokerage fees depend on the amount and value of the option contract. For instance, a contract with a value ranging from $100 to $800 has a fee of about $35.

With calls there are no voting rights, ownership interest, or dividend income. However, option contracts are adjusted for stock splits and stock dividends.

Calls and puts are not issued by the company with the common stock but rather by option writers. The maker of the option receives the price paid for the call or put minus commission costs. Calls and puts are written by and can be acquired through brokers and dealers. The writer is required to purchase or deliver the stock when requested.

Holders of calls and puts do not necessarily have to exercise them to earn a return. They can sell them in the secondary market for their current value. The value of a call increases as the underlying common stock goes up in price. The value of a put decreases as the underlying common stock goes down in price.

Owners of call and put options can hedge by holding on to two or more securities to lower risk and at the same time make some profit. It may involve buying a stock and later purchasing an option on it. For example, a stock may be bought along with writing a call on it. Also, a holder of a stock that has risen in price may buy a put to furnish downside risk protection.

The writer of a call agrees to sell shares at the strike price for the price paid for the call option. Call option writers do the opposite of what buyers do. Investors write options because they believe that a price increase in the stock will be less than what the call purchaser expects. They may even expect the price of the stock to remain static or to decrease. Option writers receive the option premium minus related transaction costs. If the option is not exercised, the writer earns the price paid for it. However, when an option is exercised, the writer suffers a loss, sometimes a quite significant one.

When the writer of an option decides to sell shares, he must come up with stock at the agreed upon price if the option is exercised. In either case, the option writer receives income from the premium. (shares are sold in denominations of 100). An investor usually sells an option when he expects it not to be exercised. The risk of option writing is that the writer, if uncovered, must buy stock or, if covered, loses the gain.

A writer can buy back an option to terminate his exposure. For example, assume the strike price is $40 and the premium for the call option is $5. If the stock is at less than $40, the call would not be exercised, and the investor must provide 100 shares at $40. However, the call writer would lose money only if the stock price exceeded $45.

Options may be naked (uncovered) or covered. Naked options are options on stocks that the writer does not own. The investor writes the call or put for the premium and will keep it if the price change is in his favor or is immaterial in amount. But the writer's loss exposure is unlimited. Covered options are written against stocks the writer owns and are not quite as risky. For example, a call can be written for stock the writer owns or a put can be written for stock sold short. This is a conservative mechanism to obtain positive returns. The goal is to write an out-of-the-money option, keep the premium paid, and have the market price of the stock equal but not exceed the option exercise price. Writing a covered call option is similar to hedging a position since if the stock price falls, the writer's loss on the stock is partly netted against the option premium.

How Is It Used for Investment Decisions? The major factors affecting the price of an option are the exercise price, the time premium, and the price of the underlying security.

An investor who feels that a stock may rise in value can buy a call option at a substantially lower price than the price of the stock with substantially higher leverage, risking only the cost of the call. Conversely, if the investor believes the stock will fall in price, a put option can be purchased for a fraction of the cost of the stock and profit when the stock declines in value with similar leverage.

Option strategies can be used for the purposes of increasing leverage, hedging risk, and improving the rate of return. This is accomplished by utilizing a call option writing strategy.

Call option writing strategies are also a very conservative method of investing since the premium from the call options provides a substantial hedge for a portfolio for downward price movements.

VALUATION OF STOCK WARRANTS

What Is It? A warrant is an option to purchase a certain number of securities at a stated price for a given time period at an exercise (subscription) price that is higher than the current market price. A warrant may or may not come in a one-to-one ratio with stock owned. Unlike an option, a warrant is usually good for several years; some, in fact, have no maturity date.

A warrant may be received as a sweetener when buying a bond or preferred stock.

How Is It Computed? When warrants are issued, the exercise price is greater than the market price. Assume a warrant of PPP Co. stock enables an investor to buy one share at $25. If the stock exceeds $25 before the expiration date, the warrant increases in value. If the stock goes below $25, the warrant loses its value.

The exercise price for a warrant is usually constant over the warrant's life. However, the price of some warrants may rise as the expiration date approaches. Exercise price is adjusted for stock splits and large stock dividends.

The return on a warrant for a holding period of no more than one year equals:

$$\frac{\text{Selling price} - \text{acquisition price}}{\text{Acquisition price}}$$

Assume that an investor sells a warrant at $21. That same warrant cost him only $12. The return is:

$$\frac{\$21 - \$12}{\$12} = \frac{\$9}{\$12} = 75\%$$

The return on a warrant for a holding period in excess of one year equals:

$$\frac{\dfrac{\text{Selling price} - \text{acquisition price}}{\text{Years}}}{\text{Average investment}}$$

Assume that there is a holding period of four years on the warrant the investor just sold for $21. The return is:

$$\frac{\dfrac{\$21 - \$12}{4}}{\dfrac{\$21 + \$12}{2}} = \frac{\$2.25}{\$16.50} = 13.6\%$$

The value of a warrant is greatest when the market price of the related stock is equal to or greater than the exercise price of the warrant. The value of a warrant thus equals:

(Market price of common stock - exercise price of warrant) × number of common stock shares bought for one warrant

For example, suppose that a warrant has an exercise price of $25. Two warrant equal one share. The market price of the stock is $30. The warrant has a value of:

($30 - $25) × .5 = $2.50

Usually the market value of a warrant is greater than its intrinsic value, or premium, because of the speculative nature of warrants. Premium equals the market price of the warrant minus its intrinsic value. For example, if the warrant referred to above has a market price of $4, the premium is $1.50.

Example 1: An investor holds eight warrants. Each warrant permits the investor to purchase one share of stock at $12 for one year. The warrant will have no value at the issue date if the stock is selling below $12. If the stock increases in value to $25 a share, the warrant should be worth about $13. The eight warrants will thus be worth approximately $104.

Example 2: Assume DDD Co. common stock is $40 per share. One warrant can be used to buy one share at $34 in the next three years. The intrinsic (minimum) value per warrant is $6 - ($40 - $34) x 1. Because the warrant has three years left and can be used for speculation, it may be traded at an amount higher than $6. Assuming the warrant was selling at $8, it has a premium of $2. The premium is the $2 difference between warrant price and intrinsic value.

Even when the stock is selling for less than $34 a share, there might be a market value for the warrant because speculators may wish to buy it on the expectation of an attractive increase in common stock price in the future. For instance, if the common stock was at $30, the warrant has a negative intrinsic (minimum) value of $4, but the warrant might have a dollar value of, for example, $1 because of an expected rise in common stock value.

Example 3: An investor may use the leveraging effect to boost dollar returns. Assume he has $7,000 to invest. If he buys common stock when the market price is $35 a share, he can buy 200 shares. If the price increases to $41 a share, he will have a capital gain of $1,200. But if he invests the $7,000 in warrants priced at only $7 a share, he can acquire 1,000 of them. (One warrant equals one share.) If the price of the warrants increases by $6, his profit will be $6,000. In this instance, he earns a return of only 17.1% on the common stock investment whereas on the warrants he would get a return of 85.7%.

On the other hand, assume that the price of the stock drops by $6. If he invests in the common stock, he will lose $1,200 for a remaining equity of $5,800. However, if he invests in the warrant, he will lose everything (assuming no warrant premium exists).

Example 4: Assume that an investor sells short 100 shares at $15 each. Then he buys warrants for 100 shares at $13 a share. The cost of the option is $3, or 3 points a share, a total of $300. In effect, he is buying the stock at $16 a share. Thus, if the stock rises above $15, his loss is limited to $1 a share.

Where Is It Found? The prices of warrants may be found in financial publications such as *Barron's*. The exact terms of the warrants, however, often must be obtained from the company, brokers, and financial publications such as Value Line.

Figure 63 shows stock warrant information as it appears in *Investor's Business Daily*.

How Is It Used and Applied? Warrants are not available for all securities. They pay no dividends and carry no voting privileges. The warrant enables the holder to take part indirectly in price appreciation of common stock and to obtain a capital gain. One warrant usually equals one share, but in some cases more than one warrant is needed to get one share.

Warrants can be bought from a broker. The price of a warrant is usually listed along with that of the common stock of the company.

Warrants can be used to protect a speculative transaction. For example, assume an investor sells a stock short and the price rises. The speculator cannot keep the short posi-

Figure 63: Stock Warrants and Rights

EPS Rel Rnk Str.		52-Week High	Low	Stock Name	Closing Price	Chg.	Vol. % Chg.	Vol. 100s	PE	Day's High	Price Low
39	71	39 1/2	24 1/2	BritishAirway	35 7/8	1/8	-7	1044	..	36 1/4	35 3/4 o
57	34	51 3/8	39	British Gas	43 1/8 +	3/8	+6	346	9	43 3/8	43
		9 3/8	1 7/8	BritP wt	2 1/4 -	1/4		1825	..	2 1/2	2 1/8

Source: *Investor's Business Daily*, December 5, 1991.

tion continually open, and it may be too costly to wait until the stock goes down. To protect the short sale, the investor may purchase a warrant fixing the purchase price and limiting the potential loss on the trade.

Advantages of warrants are:

- The price change in a warrant follows that of the related common stock, making a capital gain possible.
- The low unit cost allows a leverage opportunity in the form of lowering the capital investment without damaging the investment's capital appreciation. This increases the potential return.
- Lower downside risk potential exists because of the lower unit price.

Disadvantages of warrants are:

- If no price appreciation occurs before the expiration date, the warrant loses it value.
- The warrant holder receives no dividends.
- Investment in warrants requires sophistication.

How Is It Used for Investment Decisions? When the price per common share goes up, the holder of the warrant may either sell it (since the warrant also increases in value) or exercise the warrant and get the stock. Trading in warrants is speculative. There is potential for high return, but high risk exists because of the possibility of variability in return.

If an investor is to get maximum price potential from a warrant, the market price of the common stock must equal or exceed the warrant's exercise price. Also, lower-priced issues offer greater leverage opportunity. Furthermore, a warrant with a low unit price generates higher price volatility and less downside risk, and thus is preferable to a warrant with a high unit price.

Warrants are speculative because their value depends on the price of the common stock for which they can be exchanged. If stock prices fluctuate widely, the value of warrants will sharply vacillate.

VALUE OF STOCK RIGHTS

What Is It? Some common stock owners have the preemptive right, which allows them to maintain their proportionate share in the company. Thus, they can buy new shares issued before they go on sale to the general public. This way they can maintain their percentage of ownership. One right is issued for each share of stock owned.

Rights typically have a life of no more than three months, with several weeks being customary.

How Is It Computed? Since a stock right gives the holder the right to purchase a stock at a fixed price below the current market price by a certain period of time, it has its own market value. The value of a right depends on whether the stock is traded rights-on or rights-off. In a rights-on trade, the stock is traded with rights attached so the investor who purchases a share receives the attached stock right. In a rights-off or ex-rights trade, the stock and its rights are separate from each other and are traded in different markets.

The formula to determine the value of one right needed to buy a share of stock has to be adjusted for the rights-on and ex-rights conditions.

Rights-on condition

$$\text{Value of one right} = \frac{\text{Market value of stock, rights-on} - \text{subscription price}}{\text{Number of rights required to purchase 1 share} + 1}$$

Ex-rights condition

$$\text{Value of one right} = \frac{\text{Market value of stock, ex-rights} - \text{subscription price}}{\text{Number of rights required to purchase 1 share}}$$

Where Is It Found? The information needed to determine the value of a stock right and its attractiveness is found in the rights offering announcement distributed by the company to its stockholders. The rights offering includes the subscription price, number of rights to be received, expiration date, and other relevant terms. The current market price of the stock may be found in the stock pages of newspapers.

Example 1: An investor owns 3% of MNO Co. If the company issues 5,000 additional shares, he may receive a stock rights offering—a chance to buy 3%, of 150 shares, of the new issue. This right enables him to purchase new common stock at a subscription price (sometimes called an exercise price) for a short time. This subscription price, or exercise price, is lower than the current market price of the stock.

Example 2: Assume the current market price of stock is $30 a share. The new share has an exercise price of $26. An investor needs two rights to obtain one new share. One ex-right equals:

$$\frac{\$30 - \$26}{2} = \frac{\$4}{2} = \$2$$

Provided the stock price holds at around $30 a share, the right has a value of $2.

How Is It Used for Investment Decisions? A rights offering is important to current stockholders because it confers on them the right of maintaining equivalent financial control over a company despite a new stock offering, as well as offering them the ability to protect against dilution of the value of the shares during a new stock offering. Further, the rights offering may allow the purchase of stock at a discount below the current market price per share. Additionally, brokerage commissions may be saved.

A secondary market exists for those stockholders who do not wish to exercise their right to purchase additional stock and wish, instead, to sell the stock right. Normally the market price of a right exceeds its theoretical value as it is not unusual for investors to "bid up" the price of the stock in anticipation of future performance. Since rights do offer excellent leverage, investors can earn higher returns by purchasing rights rather than the stock. As the expiration date of the stock right is approached, its premium market value corresponds more closely to its theoretical value.

An interesting aspect of stock rights issues is that a small percentage of stockholders, normally about 1.5%, will not exercise or sell their rights. The net result is that these stockholders lose substantial sums of money by not exercising or selling their stock rights.

A Word of Caution: A stock right should not be exercised in a financially troubled company that is expected to decrease in market price per share.

82. PROFITABILITY

EARNINGS SURPRISES

What Is It? An "earnings surprise" occurs when a company reports profits or losses that differ from brokerage house analysts' expectations. A surprise can be either positive (higher than expected) or negative (lower than expected).

How Is It Computed? Zacks of New York is the leading tracker of analysts' earnings projections. The firm constantly polls brokerages for their earnings estimates. From that survey, Zacks publishes a compilation that includes the high, low, and mean prediction for a company's upcoming quarterly and fiscal year results.

When earnings are announced by the companies, Zacks then rates the "surprise" factor of the reported earnings as a percentage of the expected mean earnings. Zacks also ranks companies by the percentage size of the surprises.

Where Is It Found? Zacks' earnings expectations are available on many electronic quotation services such as Bloomberg Business News. The *Wall Street Journal* publishes a short list on notable surprises each day along with its daily listings of quarterly corporate results. Three other services also track such data, IBES, Nelson's, and First Call. Many brokerage houses have information from these two services available.

How Is It Used for Investment Decisions? From a macro viewpoint, earnings surprises can be used as a way to view the potential strength of the economy. A series of disappointing results from well-known companies could be a sign of overall weakness. Conversely, a string of profit news besting Wall Street's expectation is a signal that the national financial fortunes may have turned up.

On a microeconomic view, negative earnings surprises can have a devastating impact on stock prices, especially when they involve issues of fast-growing companies. Many institutional investors are known to dump shares soon after downside earnings surprises because they see it as a sign of potential trouble or because the traders may have lost confidence in their own abilities to project the company's future.

On the other hand, upward surprises can be beneficial for a company's stock because it reflects a positive earnings picture for the company.

HORIZONTAL (TREND) ANALYSIS

What Is It? Horizontal analysis is a time series analysis of financial statement items covering more than one year. It looks at the percentage change in an account over time.

How Is It Computed? The percentage change equals the dollar change divided by the base year amount.

$$\text{Percentage change} = \frac{(\text{Year 2} - \text{Year 1})}{\text{Year 1}}$$

Example: If a company's sales in 19X1 and 19X2 were $5,000,000 and $4,000,000, respectively, there is a 20% decrease ($1,000,000/$5,000,000). The significant deteriorating sales position of the company appears to make it unattractive for investment.

Where Is It Found? Most companies report horizontal percentage changes in their annual reports. Figure 64 shows the percentage changes in the financial highlights section of Procter & Gamble's 1992 annual report. If not, the investor finds a company's financial

Figure 64: Percentage Changes in Procter & Gamble's Annual Report

(Dollars in millions except per share amounts)

	1991	1992	% Chg.
Net Sales	27,026	29,362	+9%
Net Earnings	1,773	1,872	+6%
Per Common Share*			
Net Earnings	2.46	2.62	+7%
Net Earnings Assuming Full Dilution	2.31	2.45	+6%
Dividends	.975	1.025	+5%
Capital Expenditures	1,979	1,911	-3%
Research and Development Costs	786	861	+10%

*Adjusted for two-for-one stock split effective May 15, 1992.

statement numbers in its annual report. He then computes the percentage change for what are considered to be important items such as net income and sales.

The percentage change in market price of stock may be obtained by using the year-end market price per share, published in the stock quotations section in financial newspapers.

How Is It Used for Investment Decisions? By examining the magnitude of the direction of a financial statement item, the investor can evaluate whether the company's financial position is getting better or worse. For example, if there is a significant growth trend in earnings, the investor may be advised to buy the stock.

A Word of Caution: Past trends in price may not necessarily predict the trend in future prices. The environment may have changed.

Also See: PROFITABILITY: VERTICAL (COMMON-SIZE) ANALYSIS

PROFITABILITY RATIOS

What Are They? Profitability ratios look at the company's earnings relative to sales and assets employed. They are important operating performance measures.

How Are They Computed? Net profit margin is a ratio that reveals the profitability generated from sales. The higher the profit margin from each sales dollar generated, the better the company is doing financially.

$$\text{Net profit margin} = \frac{\text{Net income}}{\text{Net sales}}$$

The gross profit margin ratio is helpful in appraising a company's ability to effectively use its asset base to generate revenue.

$$\text{Gross profit margin} = \frac{\text{Gross profit}}{\text{Net sales}}$$

$$\text{Gross profit} = \text{Sales} - \text{Cost of sales}$$

$$\text{Net sales to total assets} = \frac{\text{Net sales}}{\text{Average total sales}}$$

Return on investment or ROI measures the effectiveness of the company's assets to create profits. Are assets being used productively?

$$\text{Return on investment (ROI)} = \frac{\text{Net income}}{\text{Average total assets}}$$

where

$$\text{Average total assets} = \frac{\text{Total assets (beginning)} + \text{Total assets (ending)}}{2}$$

ROI is the product of two important factors, net profit margin and total asset turnover as follows:

$$\text{ROI} = \frac{\text{Net income}}{\text{Average total assets}} = \frac{\text{Net income}}{\text{sales}} \times \frac{\text{Sales}}{\text{Average total assets}}$$

= Net profit margin × Total asset turnover

The return on stockholders' equity or ROE ratio reveals the earnings earned by stockholders in the business.

$$\text{Return on stockholders equity (ROE)} = \frac{\text{Net income}}{\text{Average stockholders' equity}}$$

Where Are They Found? The profitability and rate of return ratios appear in brokerage research reports, such as *Value Line Investment Survey*, prepared by fundamental analysts. They are sometimes mentioned in management's discussion within the annual report. In any event, the investor may easily calculate these ratios from the financial information contained in the balance sheet and income statement published in the company's annual report.

Example 1: A company reports the following information:

	19X2	19X3
Gross profit	$15,000	$20,000
Net income	8,000	9,600
Sales	65,000	80,000
Relevant ratios follow:		
Net profit margin	.12	.12
Gross profit margin	.23	.25

The net profit margin was constant, indicating that the earning power of the business remained static. However, there was an improvement in gross profit probably due to increased sales and/or control of costs of sales. The reason the gross profit margin is up but net profit margin is constant, even though sales increased, is probably due to a lack of control in operating expenses.

Example 2:

	19X5	19X6
Net income	$259,358	$384,346
Average total assets		
Beginning of year	1,548,234	1,575,982
End of year	1,575,982	1,614,932
Average total assets	1,562,108	1,595,457
Return on total assets	16.50%	24.09%

There has been growth in the return on assets over the year, indicating the assets' greater productivity in generating earnings.

How Are They Used for Investment Decisions? An indication of good financial health is a company's ability to earn a satisfactory profit and return on investment. The investor should be reluctant to associate himself with an entity that has poor earnings potential because the market price of stock and future dividends will be adversely affected.

By examining a company's profit margin relative to previous years and to industry norms, the investor can evaluate the company's operating efficiency and pricing strategy as well as its competitive status within the industry. The profit margin may vary greatly within an industry since it is subject to sales, cost controls, and pricing.

ROI and ROE are used to measure a company's success, and to rank companies in the same industry.

A Word of Caution: Profitability ratios may appear attractive but they may be overstated because the company has manipulated its earnings, reduced discretionary costs needed for future growth, or obtain one-time earnings boosts.

Also See: PROFITABILITY: QUALITY OF EARNINGS, SHARE PRICE RATIOS: CASH PER SHARE, SHARE PRICE RATIOS: EARNINGS PER SHARE

QUALITY OF EARNINGS

What Is It? Quality of earnings are the realistic earnings of a company that conform to economic reality. Quality of earnings is a multifaceted concept that embraces many accounting and financial considerations and involves qualitative and quantitative elements. Qualitative elements such as cash flow are subject to measurement. Quantitative elements such as the quality of management cannot be measured objectively. This discussion will look only at the quantitative aspect since that is subject to computation. Quality of earnings can be analyzed only by a sophisticated investor.

How Is It Computed?

Reported net income
Add: Items unrealistically deducted from earnings
Less: Items unrealistically added to earnings
Quality of earnings

There is no absolute "true" (real) earnings figure. However, the "quality of earnings" figure (adjusted earnings) should be more representative of the company's operational activity than reported net income.

$$\text{Salomon Brothers' Earnings Quality Index} = \frac{\text{Economic profits}}{\text{Net income}}$$

Salomon Brothers defines economic profits as reported profits adjusted to remove inventory profits and inadequate depreciation. A high ratio indicates better quality of earnings.

Example 1: A company reports sales of $1,000,000 and net income of $400,000. Included in the net income figure is research and development expense of $50,000, or 5% of sales. However, in past years the company's research and development relative to sales was 8%. Competing companies are showing 8% this year as well. Thus, the investor can conclude that research and development should be realistically $80,000 (8% x $1,000,000). Hence, R&D is understated by $30,000 ($80,000 - $50,000). The adjusted earnings follows:

Reported net income	$400,000
Less: Understatement of R&D	30,000
Quality of earnings	$370,000

In this example, there was only one adjustment. Of course, many adjustments would typically be required.

Example 2: Assume a company's earnings per share (EPS) of $6.00 includes some low quality components. These items are listed below as deductions from reported EPS. In order to arrive at an "acceptable" quality EPS certain items must be deducted. These were chosen with a view toward developing an approach that allows for a clearer understanding of the adjustment process. In reality, of course, reported EPS would be adjusted upward or downward for various reconciling items. An example of an upward adjustment would be the adding back to EPS of the effect of an unjustified accounting cushion arising from overestimated warranty provisions or bad debt provisions.

Reported EPS	$6.00
Deductions from reported EPS in order to arrive at an "acceptable quality" EPS	
Unjustified cutbacks in discretionary costs (*e.g.*, advertising, repairs) as a percentage of sales	.03
Extraordinary gains (*e.g.*, sales of real estate)	.04
A decline in the warranty provision that is not consistent with previous experience	.02
Increase in deferred expenditures that do not have future economic benefit	.01
"Acceptable quality" EPS	$5.90

Where Is It Found? Some investment advisory research reports are solely devoted to the analysis and computation of a company's quality of earnings. An example is Thorton O'Glove's *Quality of Earnings Report* published by Reporting Research Corporation (New York). In addition, David Hawkins (Harvard University) prepares a quality of earnings analysis for brokerage houses.

The knowledgeable, sophisticated investor also may determine for himself a company's quality of earnings by analyzing financial information released by the company in its annual report and SEC filings (*e.g.*, Form 10-K). There are books devoted to evaluating and determining a company's quality of earnings that the investor may refer to. Examples are *Quality of Earnings: The Investor's Guide to How Much Money A Company Is Really Making* by Thorton O'Glove (New York: Macmillan 1987), *How to Analyze Businesses, Financial Statements, and the Quality of Earnings* by Joel Siegel (New Jersey: Prentice-Hall, 1991, second edition), and *Financial Statement Analysis* by Leopold Bernstein (Illinois: Richard D. Irwin, 1989, fourth edition).

How Is It Used and Applied? Quality of earnings is the result of many factors including accounting policies used, adequacy of repairs and maintenance, stability in operations and earnings, accounting changes, income manipulation, appropriateness of deferring costs, underaccrued or overaccrued expenses, revenue recognition methods, adequacy of discretionary costs, degree of accounting estimates, inflationary profits, business risk, cash earnings, residual income (net income less minimum return on total assets), sales returns, and extent of diversification.

How Is It Used for Investment Decisions? Earnings quality is relative rather than absolute; it applies to comparing the characteristics of net incomes among companies in the same industry. The investor should note the following:

- The "quality of earnings" encompasses much more than the mere understatement or overstatement of net income; it refers also to such factors as the stability of income statement components, the realization risk of assets, and the maintenance of capital.
- Quality of earnings affects the market price of stocks and bonds, dividends, and credit rating.
- Identical earnings of competing companies may possess different degrees of quality. The key to evaluating a company's earnings quality is to compare its earnings profile (the mixture and the degree of favorable and unfavorable characteristics associated with reported results) with the earnings profile of other companies in the same industry. Investors attempt to assess earnings quality in order to render the earnings comparable, and ascertain the value to be placed on such profits.

"Poor earnings quality" occurs when the company's accounting policies are not realistic.

A Word of Caution: The analysis of the quality of earnings should be performed only by investment professionals.

Also See: PROFITABILITY: PROFITABILITY RATIOS, SHARE PRICE RATIOS: CASH PER SHARE, SHARE PRICE RATIOS: EARNINGS PER SHARE

VERTICAL (COMMON-SIZE) ANALYSIS

What Is It? In vertical analysis, a financial statement item is used as a base value. All other accounts in the financial statements are compared to it.

How Is It Computed? In the balance sheet, total assets equal 100%. Each asset is stated as a percentage of total assets. Similarly, total liabilities and stockholders' equity are assigned 100% with a given liability or equity account stated as a percentage of the total liabilities and stockholders' equity.

In the income statement, 100% is assigned to net sales with all revenue and expense accounts related to it.

Where Is It Found? Most companies report common-size percentages in their annual reports. If not, the investor finds a company's financial statement figures in its annual report, and then computes the vertical percentages.

Example 1:

Net sales	$300,000	100%
Less: cost of sales	60,000	20%
Gross profit	$240,000	80%
Less: operating expenses	150,000	50%
Net income	$ 90,000	30%

Example 2:

Current assets	$200,000	25%
Noncurrent assets	600,000	75%
Total assets	$800,000	100%

How Is It Used for Investment Decisions? Common size analysis can be compared from one period to another to see how the company is doing.

Vertical analysis tends to exhibit the internal structure of the enterprise. It indicates the relative amount of each income statement account to revenue. It shows the mix of assets that produces the income and the mix of the sources of capital, whether provided by current or long-term liabilities, or by equity funding.

The vertical percentages of a company should be compared to its competitors or to industry percentages so that the investor may ascertain the firm's relative position.

If vertical analysis indicates improved financial condition, such as increasing profit relative to sales, the investor may consider buying the stock.

A Word of Caution: The percentage relationship of an item to sales in one year may drastically change in another year. For example, a company's profit margin (net income to sales) may go from 30% in one year to 2% in the next year. One cause might be a recession.

Also See: PROFITABILITY: HORIZONTAL (TREND) ANALYSIS

83. REAL ESTATE RETURNS

CAPITALIZATION RATE (CAP RATE, INCOME YIELD)

What Is It? The capitalization rate is a method used to determine the rate of return on a real estate investment.

How Is It Computed? The capitalization rate equals net operating income (NOI) divided by the purchase price.

Assume NOI is $25,000 and the investment was $200,000. The capitalization rate equals:

$$\frac{\$\ 25,000}{\$200,000} = 12.5\%$$

If the market rate is 10%, the fair market value of similar property is $250,000 ($25,000/10%). The property may be underpriced.

Where Is It Found? The capitalization rate may be found on the real estate broker's fact sheet on a property.

How Is It Used for Investment Decision? The capitalization rate when applied to the earnings of an investment determines its market value. The lower the capitalization rate, the higher the anticipated risk to the investor and the higher the asking price paid. In determining whether a piece of property is underpriced or overpriced, the investor should look at the capitalization rate of similar kinds of property in the marketplace. The investor must note two limitations with this appraisal approach. First, it is based on only the first year's NOI. Second, the method ignores return through appreciation in property value.

Also See: GROSS INCOME MULTIPLIER (GIM), REAL ESTATE RETURNS: NET INCOME MULTIPLIER (NIM)

HOME PRICE STATISTICS

What Are They? There are several measures reported monthly: New home activity, a monthly count of sales of newly constructed homes; home resale activity, a monthly check on sales of existing housing; and home affordability, a quarterly measure of prices versus income and interest rates.

How Are They Computed? New home sales, both average price and sales volume, are reported by the U.S. Commerce Department. Sales figures are adjusted to reflect the seasonality of activity. Both sales and price figures are reported on both a national and regional basis.

Home resale activity, both average price and sales volume, are reported by the National Association of Realtors (NAR). Sales figures, too, are adjusted for seasonality. Both sales and price figures are reported on a national and state basis as well as for many major metropolitan areas.

The NAR's affordability index shows how likely it is for an average American family to afford to buy an existing home, considering current home prices, income levels, and mortgages rates. For example, if the index is 110.4, this means that a family earning the median income of $36,414 had 110.4% of the income needed to qualify for a mortgage covering 80% of a median-priced home using a loan rate of 9.41%. NAR uses a composite of both fixed-rate and adjustable-rate mortgages.

Where Are They Found? Such housing figures are published regularly in newspapers such as the *New York Times*, *USA Today*, and the *Wall Street Journal*. A sample report as it appears in the *Orange County Register* is presented in Figure 65.

Figure 65: Home Price Statistics

ORANGE COUNTY HOME SALES	1992	1991
Ave. resale home price (Aug.)	$263,204	$270,692
Ave. new home price (Aug.)	$309,710	$322,577
Ave. resale condo price (Aug.)	$170,503	$172,384
Ave. new condo price (Aug.)	$180,279	$184,823
Total sales count (Aug.)	2,272	3,351
Residential building permits (Aug.)	331	301

Source: *Orange County Register*

How Are They Used for Investment Decisons? These figures can be used to judge the health of both the overall economy as well as the housing industry.

New home sales figures, particularly volume, are seen as a key barometer of future economic growth, since the housing and construction sector often leads the nation out of an economic slump. They also can be viewed as a way to determine the potential for home builders' shares as an investment.

Existing home sales figures, notably price changes, are seen more as an indicator of consumer sentiment, another key factor since individuals purchase two-thirds of the nation's goods and services. Rising volumes, as well as strong price showing, make homeowners feel better about their own economic outlook and motivates them to spend.

The affordability index is a way to judge current and future potential for the housing industry. Low affordability can foreshadow upcoming problems for housing as more potential buyers stay out of the market.

A Word of Caution: Housing figures can be fairly erratic and are highly regionalized. That makes them difficult to extrapolate to major national trends. And on a local level, the small sample base—only a tiny portion of homes in any market changes hands in a year—makes sales price figures difficult to use for an individual home.

NET INCOME MULTIPLIER (NIM)

What Is It? The net income multiplier (NIM) is a method to determine the price of income-producing property.

How Is It Computed? The multiplier equals the asking price (or market value) of the commercial property divided by the current net operating income (NOI). NOI equals the gross rental income less allowances for vacancies and operating expenses, except for depreciation and interest on debt.

Assume that net operating income is $20,000 and the asking price is $200,000. The NIM equals:

$$\frac{\$200,000}{\$\ 20,000} = 10$$

If similar commercial property in the locality is selling for "8 times annual net," the value would be taken as $160,000 (8 x $20,000). This means that the property is overvalued and should *not* be bought.

Where Is It Found? The NIM for commercial property in an area may be ascertained by inquiring with real estate agents and reading published real estate information. The real estate broker's fact sheet on a property typically provides the NIM. The investor also should obtain an understanding of the real estate market in the locality by asking around and finding out what similar property has been selling for in the market.

How Is It Used for Investment Decisions? The NIM method is used by the investor to determine the approximate market value of a property. It is superior to the gross income multiplier (GIM) approach because it considers vacancies and operating expenses. A property may be purchased when it is undervalued. However, if the investor currently owns the property, he should sell it if it is overvalued before the property declines in price. For example, if the property's NIM is "8 times annual net" but the going market rate is 5 times annual net, it is overpriced and should be sold.

Also See: REAL ESTATE RETURNS: CAPITALIZATION RATE (CAP RATE, INCOME YIELD), GROSS INCOME MULTIPLIER (GIM)

REAL ESTATE PERFORMANCE AVERAGES — RUSSELL-NCREIF PROPERTY

What Is It? These averages, developed by Frank Russell Co., Tacoma, Washington, and the National Council of Real Estate Investment Fiduciaries (NCREIF), are market-value property performance averages broken down by building type and geographic region.

How Is It Computed? The index measures investment results over time for nonleveraged investment-grade warehouse-research-and-development-office facilities, retail properties, office buildings, and apartment buildings. Properties in the index are all held in pension investment pools. There are subindexes for each. There are also two distinct parts to the index and its subindexes: one measures income, the other appreciation. In addition, national and eight subregional indexes are compiled.

A determination is made through appraisals of the average market values of property in selected major geographic areas. The average income generated from the properties also is determined by the company.

The index started December 31, 1977. The apartment return index began in 1988.

Where Is It Found? It is published in *Barron's*. A sample report is presented in Figure 66.

Figure 66: Sample of Russell's Real Estate Performance Averages

Annual Performance—Years Ending June 30

Period	Total(%)	Income(%)	Capital(%)
1979	18.58	8.85	9.12
1980	20.43	8.87	11.06
1981	17.30	8.26	8.53
1982	13.91	7.84	5.74
1983	9.31	8.05	1.20
1984	15.68	7.40	7.85
1985	10.60	7.42	3.02
1986	8.96	7.46	1.42
1987	4.68	7.04	-2.24
1988	6.99	7.05	-0.08
1989	8.69	6.91	-0.20
1990	5.37	6.58	-1.15
1991	-1.10	6.81	-7.53

Source: National Council of Real Estate Investment Fiduciaries and the Frank Russell Co., 1991.

How Is It Used for Investment Decisions? The investor can use this information to decide lucrative areas in the country for real estate investment. Further, the data may be used to identify negative trends that would prompt a sell decision now before property values deteriorate further. The index also can be used to view broader trends in real estate prices, notably for those considering a real estate investment trust (REIT).

A Word of Caution: The appraisal of what a property is worth is subjective. Further, property values and income thereon may drastically change depending on economic and demographic conditions.

84. SAFETY AND TIMELINESS RANKING

What Is It? Investment advisory services monitor and rate hundreds of securities in terms of safety and timeliness. Value Line has a good track record.

How Is It Computed? Value Line uses a financial model directed toward determining a company's profit growth and estimates what earnings will be over the next year. The computerized model then projects which stocks will perform the best or worst in terms of price over the next 12 months. A risk rating is assigned to each security based on its historical fluctuation in price compared to a market index. This is measured by beta. Industries also are ranked.

Where Is It Found? The rankings of stocks and industries may be found in Value Line's *Investment Survey* publication.

How Is It Used and Applied? Value Line assigns one of the following rankings based on the timeliness and safety of the company's stock:

1. best
2. above average
3. average
4. below average
5. worst

How Is It Used for Investment Decisions? The investor may use the Value Line information as a basis to buy or sell a stock. A company rated number 1 may be an attractive buy. However, a number 5 category stock should be avoided or sold if currently held.

Besides ranking companies and industries, Value Line includes other information including corporate financial data, institutional percentage of ownership of the company, and insider transactions.

A Word of Caution: The safety and timeliness ranking may be used along with beta, the price-earnings ratio, and other data such as the institutional percentage of ownership of the company, and insider transactions.

Also See: BETA FOR A SECURITY, *INVESTOR'S BUSINESS DAILY*'s "INTELLI-GENT TABLES"

85. SHARE PRICE RATIOS

BOOK VALUE PER SHARE

What Is It? Book value per share is the net assets available to common stockholders divided by the shares outstanding, where net assets is stockholders' equity less preferred stock. It is what each share is worth based on historical cost.

How Is It Computed?

Book value per share of preferred stock equals:

$$\frac{\text{Liquidation value of preferred stock + preferred dividends in arrears}}{\text{Preferred shares outstanding}}$$

Book value per share of common stock equals:

$$\frac{A - (B + C)}{D}$$

where, A = Total stockholders' equity
B = liquidation value of preferred stock
C = preferred dividends in arrears
D = Common shares outstanding

Care must be taken in computing the liquidation value of preferred stock. Some companies have preferred stock issues outstanding that give the right to significant liquidation premiums that substantially exceed the par value of such shares. The effect of such liquidation premiums on the book value of common stock can be quite material.

Example: The following information is given:

Total stockholders' equity	$4,000,000
Preferred stock, 6% dividend rate, 100,000 shares, $10 par value, $12 liquidation value	
Common stock, 200,000 shares, $20 par value	
Preferred dividends in arrears for 3 years	
Liquidation value of preferred stock = 100,000 shares x $12	$1,200,000
Preferred dividends in arrears equals:	
Par value of preferred stock 100,000 x $10	$1,000,000
Preferred dividend rate	x 6%
Preferred dividend per year	$60,000
Number of years	x 3
Preferred dividend in arrears	$180,000

Book value per share for preferred stock equals:

$$\frac{\$1,200,000 + \$180,000}{100,000 \text{ shares}} = \frac{\$1,380,000}{100,000} = \$13.80$$

Book value per share for common stock equals:

$$\frac{\$4,000,000 - \$1,380,000}{200,000 \text{ shares}} = \frac{\$2,620,000}{200,000} = \$13.10$$

Where Is It Found? Book value per share is usually reported in financial advisory service publications (e.g., *Value Line Investment Survey, Standard & Poor's Stock Guide*) and brokerage research reports. *Barron's* publishes the book value per share of stocks in Dow Jones Averages. It is often disclosed in a company's annual report. It also may be calculated by the investor because all needed information is contained in the annual report.

How Is It Used for Investment Decisions? A comparison of book value per share with market price per share gives an indication of how the stock market views the company. If market price per share is significantly below book value per share, the investment community is not favorably disposed toward the company's stock. However, the stock may be undervalued if the investor believes the company has future potential. Thus, it may be a buying opportunity.

A Word of Caution: Book value per share may not come close to the market value per share.

Also See: SHARE PRICE RATIOS: EARNINGS PER SHARE, SHARE PRICE RATIOS: PRICE-BOOK VALUE RATIO

CASH PER SHARE

What Is It? Cash per share is the per share cash earnings of the company. Earnings are of higher quality if they are backed by cash. Cash may be used to pay debt, buy back stocks or bonds, buy capital assets, pay dividends, and so on.

How Is It Computed?

$$\text{Cash per share} = \frac{\text{Cash flow from operations}}{\text{Total shares outstanding}}$$

Cash flow from operations equals:
  Net income
  Add: Noncash expenses (*e.g.*, depreciation)
  Less: Noncash revenue (*e.g.*, amortization of deferred revenue)
  Cash flow from operations (cash earnings)

Cash flow from operations may be approximated by the investor by adding back to net income depreciation.

Compute the ratio of cash earnings to net income. The trend in this ratio should be thoroughly examined. A higher ratio is desirable since it means that the net income is supported by the internal generation of cash. This is a cost-free source of financing.

Where Is It Found? Cash earnings per share may be found in some brokerage research reports and financial advisory servies (e.g., the *Value Line Investment Survey*). The investor also can compute it from information readily available in the company's annual report. Depreciation is simply added to net income and then divided by the shares outstanding at year-end.

Example: A company's net income for 19X1 is $5,700,000, which includes depreciation expense of $300,000. There are 1,000,000 shares outstanding. The cash earnings per share equals:

$$\frac{\$5,700,000 + \$300,000}{1,000,000} = \$6 \text{ per share}$$

How Is It Used for Investment Decisions? Net income backed by cash is important since it represents a liquid source of funds. The investor should place a premium on a company's earnings that are supported by cash. Such earnings are worth more and should be reflected in a higher market price per share.

A Word of Caution: Cash per share may be artificially high when there are few shares outstanding even though the company's cash position is weak. Further, cash per share does not necessarily reflect a company's profitability as depicted by the earnings per share.

Also See: SHARE PRICE RATIOS: EARNINGS PER SHARE

EARNINGS PER SHARE

What Is it? Earnings per share (EPS) is the amount of the company's earnings to each share held by the investing public.

How Is It Computed? Dual presentation of EPS is made as follows:

$$\text{Primary EPS} = \frac{A - B}{C + D}$$

$$\text{Fully diluted EPS} = \frac{A - B}{C + D + E}$$

where   A = Net income
    B = Preferred dividends
    C = Weighted-common stock outstanding
    D = Common stock equivalents
    E = Other fully diluted securities

Weighted-average common stock outstanding takes into account the number of months in which those shares were outstanding.

Common stock equivalents are securities that can become common stock at a later date including stock options, stock warrants, and convertible securities (when the yield is less than 2/3 of the average Aa corporate bond yield at the time of issuance).

Other fully diluted securities are convertible securities with a yield equal to or greater than 2/3 of the average Aa corporate bond yield at the time of issuance.

Where Is It found? A company's earnings per share is reported in its quarterly and annual reports. In addition, brokerage reports and financial advisory services (e.g., the *Value Line Investment Survey*) report the company's earnings per share. Earnings per share of stocks in the Dow Jones Averages is published in *Barron's*.

How Is It Used for Investment Decisions? The investor is interested in earnings per share as a measure of the profitability of the company. A company with a high earnings per share has been successful in its operating performance. A higher earnings per share will likely result in higher dividends per share and market price per share. On the other hand, a declining or negative earnings per share infers financial problems negatively impacting the attractiveness of the company's stock.

The trend (momentum) in earnings per share should be examined as an indication of the company's earning power (see SHARE PRICE RATIOS: GROWTH RATE).

A Word of Caution: The earnings per share statistic should be used in conjunction with other ratios such as cash per share and dividend payout.

Also See : SHARE PRICE RATIOS: CASH PER SHARE

GROWTH RATE

What Is It? The growth rate of a business may be expressed in terms of earnings, dividends, sales, market price, and assets. A higher premium is assigned to a company that has a track record of growth.

How Is It Computed? Growth rate in earnings per share equals:

$$\frac{\text{Earnings per share (end of period) - earnings per share (beginning of period)}}{\text{Earnings per share (beginning of period)}}$$

Assume that earnings per share for 19X1 and 19X2 were $1.25 and $1.50 per share, respectively. The annual growth rate in earnings per share equals:

$$\frac{\$1.50 - \$1.25}{\$1.25} = 20\%$$

A 20% growth rate in earnings from 19X1 and 19X2 is favorable.

The same approach may be used in computing the growth rate in dividends per share. Other measures of growth also may be used, such as the change in sales.

Growth rate may be expressed in terms of a compounded annual rate equal to:
Compounded annual rate of growth = F_n = P x FVIF (i, n)

where F_n = future value amount

P = present value amount

FVIF (i, n) = future value factor based on the interest rate (i) and number of periods (n)

Solving this for FVIF, the investor would obtain:

$$FVIF\ (i,\ n)\ =\ \frac{F_n}{P}$$

Assume that a company has earnings per share of $2.50 in 19X1 and ten years later the earnings per share has increased to $3.70. The compound annual rate of growth in earnings per share equals:

$$F_{10}\ =\ \$3.70\ and\ P\ =\ \$2.50$$

Therefore,

$$FVIF\ (i,\ 10)\ =\ \frac{\$3.70}{\$2.50}\ =\ 1.48$$

From a future value of $1 table, a FVIF of 1.48 at 10 years is at $i = 4\%$. The compound annual rate of growth is therefore 4%.

Figure 67 presents a future value of $1 table.

Where Is It Found? The investor may find earnings per share, dividends per share, and sales in the company's annual report. From these published figures, the investor may compute the appropriate growth rates. In addition, brokerage research reports and financial advisory publications (e.g., the *Value Line Investment Survey*) often publish growth rates in earnings per share and dividends per share for companies analyzed.

How Is It Used for Investment Decisions? The growth rate of the company should be compared over the years. In addition, the company's growth rate should be compared to competing companies and industry norms.

The rate of growth in stock price, earnings, and dividends will help determine whether to buy a particular stock. A company with a higher growth rate is theoretically worth more than a company with a low or negative growth rate.

The value of a stock is the present value of all future cash inflows expected to be received by the investor. The cash inflows are dividends and the future sales price.

The growth rate in dividends is a component in Gordon's formula to determine the theoretical value of a stock. If there is a constant growth rate of g every year [*i.e.*, $D_t = D_0 (1+g)^t$], then the model is:

$$P_0\ =\ \frac{D_1}{r\ -\ g}$$

where P_0 = current market price of stock
D_1 = dividends per share in year 1
r = required rate of return
g = constant growth rate in dividends

Assume that a common stock paid a $3 dividend per share last year and is expected to pay a dividend each year at a growth rate of 10%. The investor's required rate of return is 12%. The value of the stock would be:

$$P_0\ =\ \frac{D_t}{r-g}\ =\ \frac{\$3.30}{.12\ -\ 10}\ =\ \$165$$

A Word of Caution: When selecting a stock, risk should be considered along with the growth rate.

Figure 67: Future Value of $1 Table

Period	1%	2%	3%	4%	5%	6%	7%	8%	9%	10%
1	1.010	1.020	1.030	1.040	1.050	1.060	1.070	1.080	1.090	1.100
2	1.020	1.040	1.061	1.082	1.102	1.124	1.145	1.166	1.188	1.210
3	1.030	1.061	1.093	1.125	1.158	1.191	1.225	1.260	1.295	1.331
4	1.041	1.082	1.126	1.170	1.216	1.262	1.311	1.360	1.412	1.464
5	1.051	1.104	1.159	1.217	1.276	1.338	1.403	1.469	1.539	1.611
6	1.062	1.126	1.194	1.265	1.340	1.419	1.501	1.587	1.677	1.772
7	1.072	1.149	1.230	1.316	1.407	1.504	1.606	1.714	1.828	1.949
8	1.083	1.172	1.267	1.369	1.477	1.594	1.718	1.851	1.993	2.144
9	1.094	1.195	1.305	1.423	1.551	1.689	1.838	1.999	2.172	2.358
10	1.105	1.219	1.344	1.480	1.629	1.791	1.967	2.159	2.367	2.594
11	1.116	1.243	1.384	1.539	1.710	1.898	2.105	2.332	2.580	2.853
12	1.127	1.268	1.426	1.601	1.796	2.012	2.252	2.518	2.813	3.138
13	1.138	1.294	1.469	1.665	1.886	2.133	2.410	2.720	3.066	3.452
14	1.149	1.319	1.513	1.732	1.980	2.261	2.579	2.937	3.342	3.797
15	1.161	1.346	1.558	1.801	2.079	2.397	2.759	3.172	3.642	4.177
16	1.173	1.373	1.605	1.873	2.183	2.540	2.952	3.426	3.970	4.595
17	1.184	1.400	1.653	1.948	2.292	2.693	3.159	3.700	4.328	5.054
18	1.196	1.428	1.702	2.026	2.407	2.854	3.380	3.996	4.717	5.560
19	1.208	1.457	1.753	2.107	2.527	3.026	3.616	4.316	5.142	6.116
20	1.220	1.486	1.806	2.191	2.653	3.207	3.870	4.661	5.604	6.727
21	1.232	1.516	1.860	2.279	2.786	3.399	4.140	5.034	6.109	7.400
22	1.245	1.546	1.916	2.370	2.925	3.603	4.430	5.436	6.658	8.140
23	1.257	1.577	1.974	2.465	3.071	3.820	4.740	5.871	7.258	8.954
24	1.270	1.608	2.033	2.563	3.225	4.049	5.072	6.341	7.911	9.850
25	1.282	1.641	2.094	2.666	3.386	4.292	5.427	6.848	8.623	10.834
30	1.348	1.811	2.427	3.243	4.322	5.743	7.612	10.062	13.267	17.449
35	1.417	2.000	2.814	3.946	5.516	7.686	10.676	14.785	20.413	28.102
40	1.489	2.208	3.262	4.801	7.040	10.285	14.974	21.724	31.408	45.258
45	1.565	2.438	3.781	5.841	8.985	13.764	21.002	31.920	48.325	72.888
50	1.645	2.691	4.384	7.106	11.467	18.419	29.456	46.900	74.354	117.386

PRICE-BOOK VALUE RATIO

What Is It? The ratio compares the market price of a stock to its book value.
How Is It Computed?

$$\frac{\text{Market price per share}}{\text{Book value per share}}$$

Book value per share = Total stockholders' equity divided by total shares outstanding

Market price per share is based on current prices while book value per share is based on historical cost. Market price per share should typically exceed book value per share because of inflation and good corporate performance over the years.

Assume that a company's market price per share is $30 and its book value per share is $50. The price-book value ratio equals:

$$\frac{\$30}{\$50} = 0.6$$

This company is not doing well because its market price of stock is 60% of its book value. The company's stock has not kept up with increasing prices. Furthermore, the company's earnings and growth may be deficient. Perhaps the market is saying that the assets are overvalued.

Where Is It Found? The price-book value ratio may be found in financial advisory service publications such as Standard & Poor's. Brokerage research reports sometimes refer to it. If not, the investor can obtain the market price of stock by referring to price quotations in financial newspapers. The book value per share appears in financial advisory publications and typically in the company's annual report.

How Is It Used and Applied? The analytical implication may be that a company has not been performing well when its market price per share is below its book value per share. The company may be experiencing financial difficulties.

A high price-book value ratio is desirable since it shows that the stock market places a higher value on the company.

The ratio often depends on the industry. For example, many banks have book values that exceed their market price per shares.

How Is It Used for Investment Decisions? The investor may have a buying opportunity when book value per share is above market price per share because the stock may be undervalued. On the other hand, if the investor believes the market price per share is too high relative to book value per share, the stock should be sold.

A comparison also should be made to peer groups.

A Word of Caution: Other financial ratios have to be considered besides the price-book value ratio in selecting a stock. It is just one indicator that should be confirmed by other measures such as the trend in market price per share.

Also See: SHARE PRICE RATIOS: BOOK VALUE PER SHARE, SHARE PRICE RATIOS: PRICE-EARNINGS RATIO (MULTIPLE)

PRICE-EARNINGS RATIO (MULTIPLE)

What Is It? The price-earnings (P/E) ratio is a company's market price per share divided by its earnings per share, also called earnings multiple. It is an indicator of a company's relationship to its stockholders.

How Is It Computed?

$$\text{Price-earnings ratio} = \frac{\text{Market price per share}}{\text{Earnings per share}}$$

Assume that the market price per share of X Company's stock was $50 and $80, respectively, for 19X1 and 19X2. The earnings per share for those years are $5 and $6, respectively. The price-earnings ratios are computed as

		19X1	19X2
Price-earnings ratio =	$\dfrac{\text{Market price per share}}{\text{Earnings per share}}$	$\dfrac{\$50}{\$5} = 10$	$\dfrac{\$80}{\$6} = 13.3$

The increase in the price-earnings ratio by 33% (3.3/10) reflects a better perception of the company in the marketplace.

Where Is It Found? The price-earnings ratios of a company is listed in financial advisory reports (e.g., Standard & Poor's, Moodys, and Value Line) and in the financial pages of daily newspapers (e.g., *Investor's Business Daily*, the *New York Times*, and the *Wall Street Journal*). In July 1993, some price-earnings ratios of companies were:

Loews	49
Mattel Toys	16
Philip Morris	9

Figure 68 shows price-earnings ratios, yields, book value, and so on for major indexes, as published in *Barron's*.

Figure 68: Indexes' P/Es and Yields

	Last Week	Prev. Week	Year Ago Week
DJ Ind. P/E	56.6	56.4	23.3
Earns Yield, %	1.77	1.77	4.28
Earns, $	57.69	57.69	130.39
Divs Yield, %	3.16	3.17	3.01
Divs, $	103.12	103.12	91.48
Mkt to Book, %	251.10	250.06	228.58
Book Value, $	1301.31	1301.31	1331.52

Source: *Barron's*, August 31, 1992.

How Is It Used and Applied? An increase in the price-earnings ratio may indicate one or more of the following:

- Investors are more confident in the company. This may be due to the company's improved financial position (*e.g.*, better cash flow, superior earnings, improved liquidity and solvency), increase in growth rate, enhanced stability, diversification reducing risk, economic prosperity, new patented products, favorable political environment, and quality management.
- The company's net income may be understated or have a high quality associated with it. This will put a premium on such earnings.

Some companies have high price-earnings multiples that reflect high earnings growth expectations. Young, fast-growing companies typically have high price-earnings stocks with multiples over 30.

The price-earnings ratio varies among companies in one industry as well as varying among companies in different industries.

How Is It Used for Investment Decisions? The price-earnings ratio should be examined by potential investors in deciding whether to invest in the company. A high price-earnings ratio is desirable because it indicates that investors highly value a company's profits. On the other hand, a steady decline in the price-earnings ratio reflects decreasing investor confidence in the business.

Some investors believe that if a company's price-earnings ratio is relatively too low the stock is undervalued and should be bought. On the other hand, some investors believe that if the price-earnings multiple is relatively too high the stock is overvalued and should be sold. One strategy calls for an investor to buy a company's stock with a low price-earnings ratio and sell the stock when it reaches a high price-earnings ratio. However, this strategy does not always work. A low price-earnings stock may deteriorate further because the business is not doing well.

A Word of Caution: The company's price-earnings ratio must be compared over the years and to the price-earnings ratios of competing companies in the industry. The price-earnings ratio is only one consideration in making an investment decision. Other factors must be taken into account such as product line, risk, quality of assets, contingencies, and management philosophy.

Also See: SHARE PRICE RATIOS: EARNINGS PER SHARE, SHARE PRICE RATIOS: PRICE-SALES RATIO (PSR)

PRICE-SALES RATIO (PSR)

What Is It? The price-sales ratio compares the market value of a company's outstanding shares to its sales.

How Is It Computed?

$$PSR = \frac{\text{Market price per share} \times \text{shares outstanding}}{\text{Sales}}$$

Example: ABC Company stock has a market price of $5 per share, outstanding shares are 1.5 million, and sales are $15 million.

$$PSR = \frac{\$5 \times 1.5 \text{ million}}{\$15 \text{ million}} = \frac{\$ 7.5 \text{ million}}{\$15.0 \text{ million}} = .50$$

Where Is It Found? PSR information on companies can be found in *Forbes* and *Kiplinger's Personal Finance Magazine*. It also can be computed from information contained in the annual report.

How Is It Used for Investment Decisions? PSR reflects a company's underlying financial strength. A company with a low PSR is more attractive while one with a high PSR is less attractive. As a rule of thumb, investors should avoid stocks with a PSR of 1.5 or more. Further, investors should sell a stock when the PSR is between 3 to 6.

A Word of Caution: The PSR approach to investing is a long-term strategy. Stock should be held for about three to five years because in many cases the investor is dealing with a turnaround situation.

Also See: SHARE PRICE RATIOS: PRICE-EARNINGS RATIO (MULTIPLE)

86. SHARPE'S RISK-ADJUSTED RETURN

What Is It? The *Money* magazine's risk-adjusted grades compare funds by five-year, risk-adjusted return. This measure is based on a measure developed by William Sharpe. The fund manager is thus able to view his excess returns per unit of risk.

The index concentrates on total risk as measured by the standard deviation of returns (6).

How Is It Computed?

$$\text{Sharpe measure} = \frac{\text{Excess returns}}{\text{Fund standard deviation}} = \frac{\text{Total fund return} - \text{Risk-fee rate}}{\text{Fund standard deviation}}$$

Example: If a fund has a return of 10%, the risk-free rate is 6%, and the fund standard deviation is 18%, the Sharpe measure is .22, as shown below.

$$\text{Sharpe measure} = \frac{10\% - 6\%}{18\%} = \frac{4\%}{18\%} = .22$$

Where Is It Found? It appears in *Money's* annual mutual fund ratings.

How Is It Used for Investment Decisions? In appraising the performance of an investment portfolio, an investor must consider return and risk. The Sharpe index of portfolio performance my be used for this purpose.

An investor should rank the performance of his mutual funds based on Sharpe's index of portfolio performance. The funds would be ranked from high to low return. For example, a fund with an index of .6 would be far superior than one with an index of .3.

Sharpe's index should be compared with other trends as well as with the average market. The larger the index, the better the performance.

A Word of Caution: The index should be used by investors with some mathematical knowledge.

Also See: PERFORMANCE AND RISK: JENSEN'S PERFORMANCE MEASURE (ALPHA), PERFORMANCE AND RISK: TREYNOR'S PERFORMANCE MEASURE

87. SHORT SELLING

SHORT-INTEREST RATIO (SIR)

What Is It? Short selling occurs when investors believe that stock prices will drop. Technical analysts look at the number of shares sold short. Short interest measures the number of stocks sold short in the market at any given time which have not yet been repurchased to close out short positions.

How Is It Computed? The short interest ratio is the latest reported short interest position for the month divided by the daily average trading volume. The SIR is more closely watched than the trading volume of shares sold short.

A high ratio is bullish and a low ratio is bearish. In the past, the ratio for all stocks on the NYSE has hovered between 1.0 and 1.75. A ratio above 1.8 is considered bullish while a ratio below 1.15 is deemed bearish. For example, a ratio of 2 represents 2.0 days of potential buying power. The SIR works best as a bullish indicator after a long-term decline in prices instead of after a long upturn.

Where Is It Found? The amount of short interest on the NYSE, AMEX, and NASDAQ is published in *Barron's*, the *New York Times*, the *Wall Street Journal*, and other financial publications. The exchanges publish short interest figures on about the 20th day of each month.

How Is It Used and Applied? Looking at short sales is often called a contrary opinion rule. Some believe that an increase in the number of short sellers indicates a bullish market. It is believed that short sellers get emotional and overreact when they are proven wrong and will quickly buy the short-sold stock. Increased short sales and increased market activity will create additional market supply. Then, when the market goes down, the short sellers will buy back their shares, and this will produce increased market demand.

Some believe, however, that increased short selling reflects a downward and technically weak market that results from investors' pessimism. The short seller, in fact, expects a downward market.

Short interest information does have two limitations, however: Some studies have shown that short interest follows the same pattern as market price changes, and data are sometimes not available until two weeks after the short sale occurs.

How Is It Used for Investment Decisions? By monitoring overall short interest, the investor can foresee future market demand and determine whether the market is optimistic or pessimistic. A very substantial short interest in a single stock should make the investor question the value of the security.

The investor also should examine odd-lot short sales. It is believed that many odd-lotters are uninformed. An odd-lotter short sale ratio of around .5% indicates optimism; a ratio of 3.0 or more reflects pessimism.

Specialists make markets in securities and are considered "smart money." Investors should watch the ratio of specialists' short sales to the total number of short sales on an exchange. For example, if specialists sell 100,000 shares short in a week and the total number of short sales is 400,000 the specialists' sales constitute 25% of all short sales. Specialists' short sales are a bullish indicator. The specialists keep a book of limit orders on their securities so they are knowledgeable as to market activity at a particular time. However, if most of their short sales are covered, this is a bullish sign. A normal ratio is about 55%. A ratio of 65% or more is a bearish indicator. A ratio less than 40% is bullish.

A Word of Caution: Short-sellers may be right that the market is headed downward.

Also See: SHORT SELLING: SHORT SALES POSITION, SHORT SELLING: SPECIALISTS/PUBLIC SHORT (S/P) RATIO

SHORT SALES POSITION

What Is It? Shares are borrowed from a broker in order to sell shares the investor does not own. In short selling, the investor hopes to sell high and to buy back the stock low at a later date. The shares are then returned to the broker. If the stock falls, the investor makes money. If it rises, the investor loses money. It is a speculative form of investment involving considerable risk.

How Is It Computed?

$$\frac{\text{Selling price} - \text{Purchase price}}{\text{Gain (or loss)}}$$

where, Selling price = shares sold × selling price per share, and
Purchase price = shares bought × cost per share

Example: Assume that the investor sells short 50 shares of stock with a market price of $25 per share. The broker borrows the shares for the investor and sells them to someone else for $1,250. The brokerage house holds on to the proceeds of the short sale. Later on, the investor buys the stock back at $20 a share, earning a per share profit of $5, or a total of $250.

How Is It Used and Applied? A short seller must set up a margin account with a stockbroker. If the price suddenly rises, the investor can buy back the stock to minimize his losses. The Federal Reserve requires a short seller to have in a margin account cash or securities worth at least 50% of the market value of the stock sold short. Another requirement is that a stock can be sold short only when the stock price has risen. An investor cannot sell short a listed stock that drops steadily from $50 to $30, for example. Stocks traded over-the-counter, on the other hand, can be sold short any time. Short sellers pay brokerage commissions on both the sale and repurchase.

Where Is It Found? Information on short sales appears in the financial section of newspapers and financial magazines such as *Barron's* and the *Wall Street Journal*. It's also available on *The Source*, an on-line database service.

How Is It Used for Investment Decisions? The investor may use the following short-selling strategies:

- The investor sells short because he thinks the stock price is going to decline.
- The investor sells short if he wants to postpone making gain and paying taxes on it from one year to the next. Assume, for example, that 100 shares of Apple were bought at $10 per share and are now selling for $35 each. The investor would like to sell the stock and take the profit. If the investor sells now, he will have to pay income taxes on the gain by next April 15. If the investor wants to postpone the gain until the following year, he can instruct the broker to short the stock against the box. Against the box means that the investor is selling short shares he owns. The broker keeps the stock certificate in a vault and sells it short. Because the investor owns the stock and has sold it short, he has a hedge against increases or decreases in the price of Apple stock. If Apple rises to $50 a share by the time it's sold in January, the investor will have an additional $15-a-share gain on the stock he owns but a $15-a-share loss on the stock he sells short. If, on the other hand, Apple falls back to $10, he will have no gain in the stock he originally purchased but a $25-a-share gain on the stock he sold short.
- The investor sells short to protect himself if he owns the stock but for some reason cannot sell. If, for example, an investor buys stock through a payroll purchase plan at the end of each quarter but does not get the certificates until several weeks later, it may make sense for him to sell the shares short to lock in the gain.

A Word of Caution: A short seller can incur a significant loss if the stock sold short appreciably increases in market price.

Also See: SHORT SELLING: SHORT INTEREST RATIO, SHORT SELLING: SPECIALISTS/PUBLIC SHORT (S/P) RATIO

SPECIALISTS/PUBLIC SHORT (S/P) RATIO

What Is It? This ratio is used with the assumption that the speculative public makes an error at market turns and speculators who sell short are among the least astute. What short selling is not done on the exchange by members is by definition done by the public (which may include a few institutions but they are not really active in short selling). This is one of many so-called smart money rules under which specialists might provide unusual insight into the future.

How Is It Computed? It is derived by dividing the specialists shorts by the public shorts.

Where Is It Found? It is found in the Market Laboratory section of *Barron's*.

How Is It Used for Investment Decisions? It is recommended to smooth the ratio over a 4-week average. A ratio of around 3.5 (especially greater than 4.0) is interpreted as a bearish signal since it is a reflection of too much optimism. An S/P ratio below about 1.8 (especially near 1.0) indicates considerable pessimism and tends to be bullish.

A Word of Caution: Any indicator can fail at times. Investors should weigh all the evidence.

88. STANDARD & POOR'S (S&P) INDEXES

What Are They? The S&P indexes are industrial (400 companies called S&P 400), financial (40 companies), transportation (20 companies), public utility (40 companies), and composite (500 companies). The S&P 500 is broad-based and looks at the performance of 500 large, widely held common stocks in 95 industrial sectors. It is composed primarily of NYSE-listed companies with some AMEX and over-the-counter issues. The S&P 500 constitutes about 80% of the market value of issues traded on the NYSE. The S&P 100 Index (a condensed version of the S&P 500) is comprised of 100 highly capitalized stocks that have options listed on the Chicago Board of Trade. The S&P also has indexes for consumer and capital goods companies as well as low-grade and high-grade common stocks. It introduced the S&P Mid Cap Index in 1991.

How Are They Computed? The S&P indexes compare the present price as a group of stocks to the base prices (established in 1941-1943). The indexes are capitalization (value) weighted to take into account the stock price and the number of outstanding shares. A value-weighted index is based on the aggregate market value of the stock (price times number of shares). The indexes are adjusted to include the reinvestment of dividends (cash and stock) and stock splits. A limitation of the index computation is that large capitalized stocks, those having many shares outstanding, heavily influence the index value.

The S&P Mid Cap Index is a market valued index that tracks the market behavior of 400 medium-sized U.S. companies having a median market capitalization of $610 million. Market capitalization equals stock price multiplied by outstanding shares. Approximately, 62% of the companies in the Mid Cap Index are listed on the NYSE, 35% on the NASDAQ, and 3% on the AMEX.

Where Are They found? The S&P indexes are published by Standard & Poor's. The S&P indexes as well as stock index futures prices can be found in the financial pages of newspapers and business magazines such as *Barron's*, the *New York Times*, and the *Wall Street Journal*. The indexes also may be accessed through the computerized Standard & Poor's on-line database. Also, the S&P 500 is reported on Prodigy. Charles Schwab and Company's The Equalizer is an on-line data service that also may be accessed. Figure 69 shows the S&P indexes as they appear in the *New York Times*.

How Are They Used for Investment Decisions? The performance of the S&P index is an indication of the health of the overall stock market and specific industry groupings (*e.g.*, utilities, transportation, financials). For example, the S&P 500 is widely used to measure institutional performance and gives an indication of total returns on major U.S. equities. The S&P indexes may be used by the investor to gauge market direction and strength. An upward increase in the S&P index is a sign of a bull market while a downward trend is an indication of a bear market. If the overall market is improving, the investor may now view it as a time to buy.

The S&P Mid Cap Index fills a void for the investor because it provides a new analytical tool for a potentially lucrative but volatile sector of the market. The investor may find good values in small- and medium-sized company stocks because they have lower price-earnings (P/E) ratios and high growth rates.

The investor may buy a stock index futures contract tied into a broad stock market index such as the S&P 500 or S&P 100. The latter involves a smaller margin deposit. Stock index futures allow the investor to participate in the general change in the overall stock market. The investor can buy and sell the "market as a whole" rather than specific securities. If the investor anticipates a bull market but is unsure which particular stock will rise, he should buy (long position) a stock index future. There are high risks involved so trading in stock index futures should be used only for hedging or speculation.

Also See : DOW JONES INDUSTRIAL AVERAGE, NYSE INDEXES, STOCK INDEXES: OTHER: VALUE LINE AVERAGES

Figure 69: Standard & Poor's Indexes

	High	Low	Close	Chg.
Indust	487.82	485.90	487.72	+1.75
Transpt	313.99	311.07	313.87	+2.44
Utilities	157.30	156.80	156.97	-0.08
Financl	35.16	35.01	35.15	+0.11
MidCap 400	142.86	142.42	142.69	+0.89
500 Stocks	414.95	413.38	414.84	+1.31
100 Stocks	385.38	383.70	385.38	+1.35

Source: *New York Times*, August 29, 1992.

89. STOCK/BOND YIELD GAP

What Is It? A stock/bond yield gap measures the difference in yield between securities.

How Is It Computed? Normally, it measures yield spread between the average quarterly yield on Moody's Composite (average long-term Corporate Bond Series—AAA, AA, A, and BAA) and the quarterly (seasonally adjusted) dividend yield on Standard & Poor's 500 Industrial Stock Price Index).

Where Is It Found? Financial information services such as Bloomberg Business and White, Weld & Co. compute and chart the yield gap on a regular basis.

How Is It Used for Investment Decisions? Stock yields are typically higher than bond yields, given the greater risk associated with stocks. If bond yields are higher than stock yields, the yield gap becomes negative and is known as the "reverse" yield gap. This negative gap is a direct result of growing investor confidence in stocks—investors are considering stocks less risky.

A Word of Caution: This gap is viewed as a long-term indicator of market valuation. Investors need to detect a long-term trend of the gap. For example, if the gap is negative (*i.e.*, bond yields are higher than stock yields) for some time, it is usually indicating a bull market in equities. A positive gap is normally associated with a bear market.

Also See: ECONOMIC INDICATORS AND BOND YIELDS, YIELD CURVE

90. STOCK INDEXES: OTHER

CHICAGO BOARD OPTIONS EXCHANGE (CBOE) 250 STOCK INDEX

What Is It? This is a broad-based index of stock prices of the major companies traded on the NYSE.

How Is It Computed? It is a capitalized weighted index of 250 of the NYSE issues with the highest market value. The market value constitutes more than two-thirds of the total market value on the NYSE. The elements in the index are updated every three months on a cycle basis. A base level of 100 was assigned in 1982. Some major companies included in the index are General Electric, General Motors, Merck, and Philip Morris.

Where Is It Found? The index can be obtained from the Chicago Board Options Exchange. It appears in *Barron's*.

How Is It Used for Investment Decisions? The index can be used to examine the difference between the spot prices on commodities and the prices of short-term future commodity contracts.

RUSSELL 1000, 2000, 3000

What Are They? Russell 1000, 2000, and 3000 are a series of indexes, developed jointly by the Frank Russell Company and the New York Futures Exchange (NYFE) to represent investment-grade equities. They are all capitalization-weighted indexes and were designed to help measure money manager performance.

How Are They Computed? All three indexes are capitalization-weighted, and adjustments are made for cross-ownership. For example, if IBM owns 20% of Intel, the index includes only 80% of Intel's outstanding shares. The indexes are updated annually each June.

Whereas the S&P 500 represents approximately 75% of the investment-grade stocks held by most institutional investors, the Russell 1000, 2000, and 3000 indexes track almost 99% of the stocks included in portfolios of institutional investors.

All three indexes, however, exclude non-U.S. stocks—both American Depository Receipts (ADRs) and the ordinary shares that are traded on U.S. stock exchanges. The base level for all three indexes was set at 100 in 1979.

Where Are They Found? Russell indexes appear in major daily newspapers as well as in *Barron's* and the *Wall Street Journal*.

How Are They Used for Investment Decisions? Russell indexes can be used to detect the first and second tier market, together accounting for 99% of the U.S. market.

Although there are more than 6,000 publicly traded U.S. stocks, the Russell 3000 Index confines itself to the 3,000 most actively traded shares and is divided into the Russell 1000 and Russell 2000 subindexes. The 3000 index has an average market capitalization of $1 billion.

The Russell 1000 Index represents the prices of the top tier of the domestic equity market—companies with market values greater than $400 million, which typically represent approximately 90% of the market. Its average market capitalization as of May 1991 was $2.8 billion.

The Russell 2000 Index represents the second tier of U.S. equities—companies with market values between $20 million and $400 million, which account for approximately 8% to 9% of the total market. Its average market cap was $100 million as of May 1991.

Russell also compiles indexes suited to measure a money manager's style with its Earnings Growth (growth) and Price-Driven (value) indexes plus a Mid-Cap Index that tracks the 800 smallest stocks in the Russell 1000.

A Word of Caution: Russell indexes track specific groups of the market and should therefore be interpreted as such.

Also See: DOW JONES INDUSTRIAL AVERAGE, STANDARD & POOR'S (S&P) INDEXES, WILSHIRE 5,000 EQUITY INDEX

VALUE LINE AVERAGES

What Are They? Value Line indexes of the overall stock performance of most issues are based on both geometric and arithmetic averages. There are also averages for utilities and railroads.

How Are They Computed? The Value Line Composite Index is a broad one covering about 1,750 securities (included in the *Value Line Survey*) traded on the NYSE, AMEX, and over-the-counter markets. It constitutes more than 90% of the capitalized value of all U.S. stocks. It is a geometric average of market prices with each stock having the same weight.

The component stocks in the index remain intact unless the company has failed, been acquired, or gone private.

Criteria established by Value Line for inclusion in the index include:

- Investor interest as evidenced by requests for information from Value Line about the security.
- The stock must be actively traded.
- The stock must have a determinable and appropriate market value.

A 100 base level was established in 1961.

The Value Line Arithmetic Average is the same as the Composite Index except that it is based on an arithmetic average rather than a geometric average. As a result, the Arithmetic Average is less volatile and higher in amount than the Composite Average.

Value Line also publishes an Industrial Average (about 1,500 industrial companies), Utility Average (about 175 utilities), and a Railroad Average (about 15 railroads).

Where Are They found? The indexes are published by Value Line. The Geometric Index and the Arithmetic Index appear in *Barron's*. The Geometric Index also is found in the *Wall Street Journal*. Information also may be obtained from CompuServe, an on-line database service.

How Are They Used for Investment Decisions? The Value Line Averages are a basis to evaluate the performance of the stock market and certain segments within. Some investors use these indexes because they more closely correspond to the variety of stocks that small investors may have in their portfolios. A bullish market may represent a time to buy if the peak has not been reached. On the other hand, a bear market may be a time to unload securities if the bottom has a way to go.

VALUE LINE CONVERTIBLE INDEXES

What Are They? The indexes measure the performance of convertible bonds and preferred stocks. Convertible securities can be converted (exchanged) into common stock at a later date.

How Are They Computed? The index is equally weighted and measures the price performance of 575 convertible securities including preferred, bonds, and Euro-convertibles. The Value Line Total Returns Index includes the income on the issues. The Value Line Warrant Index is equally weighted and measures price performance of 85 warrants. The base, as of March 1, 1982, is 100. Both are computed by Value Line.

Where Are They found? The indexes are found in financial newspapers such as *Barron's*.

How Are They Used for Investment Decisions? The investor examines the indexes to see how well convertibles are doing in price and yield. If the investor believes that convertible security prices are undervalued, a buying opportunity exists.

Also See: LIPPER MUTUAL FUND INDEXES

91. STOCK SPLITS

What Are They? Stock splits occur when a corporation decides to alter its capitalization by either issuing new shares to existing shareholders or, most commonly, will issue new shares at a set rate per share owned. In a reverse stock split, the company reduces the number of shares outstanding. The shares will have the same market value immediately after the reverse split. In other words, the number of shares owned will be less but will be worth more per share.

How Are They Computed? The numerology of stock splits can be confusing. In a 2-for-1 split, for example, a current shareholder with 100 shares will have 200 shares after the split is completed. As a result, this investor's 100 shares that were priced at $60 each, will now be 200 shares worth $30 a piece. A 3-for-1 split means that 100 shares become 300 (at $20 on a $60 stock) while a 3-for-2 means that 100 shares become 150 (at $40 on that same $60 issue).

On the reverse side, a 1-for-10 split means that a shareholder with 1,000 shares will have 100 afterward. The 1,000 shares priced at $1 will become 100 shares at $10.

Financial data calculated on a per share basis will need to be recalculated to reflect the changed number of shares and altered share price.

Where Are They Found? Lists of stock splits are published in many major daily newspapers such as the *Los Angeles Times* and the *Wall Street Journal*. Figure 70 shows how the *Orange County Register* reports this data.

How Are They Used for Investment Decisions? Companies say that they make stock splits to keep their share prices in a marketable range—typically between $20 and $50. That keeps a 100-share round lot affordable to many small investors, or so goes the logic.

Reverse splits have become more common as regulators have cracked down on investment schemes involving penny stocks—shares that trade under $5. Such negative publicity has hurt the lure—even the shares of legitimate but very low-priced firms.

A Word of Caution: While many investors like stock splits as a sign that a company believes that its stock price will be rising higher, there is little empirical data to suggest that such splits actually provide any long-term boost to share prices. Nevertheless, they often give a short-term boost to a stock's price and, given the public's approval of the splits, can be viewed as a positive for a company's shares.

Figure 70: Stock Splits

Declared stock splits	*Stock splits last week*
Amnex Inc 1-for-10 reverse	Command Credit Cp 1-for-20 rev
Brainerd Intl 1-for-10 reverse	First Northern Savings 2-for-1
CSF Holdings 3-for-2	Health-Mor Inc 3-for-2
Check Express 1-for-2 reverse	Indep Entertain Grp 1-for-10 rev
Comm Credits 1-for-20 reverse	Sealed Air Corp 2-for-1
Computer Concepts 1-for-4 reverse	Synalloy Corp 3-for-2
Consumat Systems 1-for-3 reverse	Value Health Inc 3-for-2
Convoy Capital 1-for-5 reverse	Werner Enterp 2-for-1
Dev Tech 1-for-3 reverse	
Fst Ntl Bncp GA 3-for-2	
Koala Techs 1-for-3 reverse	
Medcross Inc 1-for-15 reverse	
Nth Carol NaturGas 3-for-2	
Reading Bates 1-for-5 reverse	
Ryan, Beck 5-for-4	

Source: *Orange County Register.*

92. SUPPORT AND RESISTANCE LEVELS

What Is It? A support level is the lower end of a trading range; a resistance level is the upper end. At the "support" level, there is support not to have a further decline in price while at the "resistance" level there is resistance to a further price decline. These levels are considered in technical investment analysis.

How Is It Prepared? A chart may be prepared showing the price over time of an individual stock or overall market. The support and resistance prices based on the historical trend are depicted along with the breakout points. Support and resistance lines are actually trend lines drawn through high and low prices. Figure 71 is an illustrative diagram.

When prices go to the support level, actual or potential buying in sufficient volume is expected to stop the downward price trend for a sustained period of time. When prices go to the resistance level, actual or potential selling in sufficient volume will halt an upward price trend.

Where Is It Found? A chart for a company or market containing support and resistance levels may appear in brokerage research reports prepared by technical analysts such as Bear Stearns and Kidder Peabody. The investor also can prepare this chart for a company's stock by tracking price over a desired time period.

How Is It Used and Applied? Support may occur when a stock goes to a lower level of trading because new investors may now want to purchase it. If so, new demand will occur in the market. Resistance may take place when a security goes to the high side of the normal trading range. Investors who purchased on an earlier high may view this as a chance to sell the stock at a profit. When market price goes above a resistance point or below a support point (in a "breakout"), investors assume that the stock is trading in a new range and that higher or lower trading volume are imminent.

How Is It Used for Investment Decisions? If the company's stock price is within the support and resistance levels, the stock should be kept. If the stock penetrates the resistance

Figure 71: Support and Resistance Levels Chart

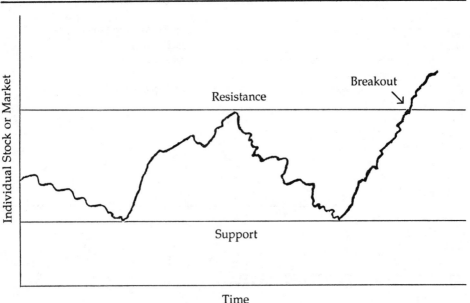

line, there is a buying opportunity. If the support line is broken, there is a selling situation. The investor also should consider volume in addition to price. If a breakthrough in the support or resistance levels is accompanied by heavy volume, this is a stronger indicator.

A Word of Caution: A stock's market price may break through the support or resistance level.

93. TICK AND CLOSING TICK

What Is It? A tick is a measure of movement in closing stock prices. A positive (+) tick means that prices were rising at the end of the day, while a negative (-) tick means that prices were falling. Tick closing prices provide insight into how strong the market was near the close. These tick statistics show the number of stocks whose last price change was an increase less those whose last move was a downtick.

How Is It Computed? The closing tick nets all stocks whose last trade was higher than the previous trade (+) on the exchange against all stocks whose last trade was lower (-). It is computed for the NYSE, the AMEX, and for the 30 stocks in the Dow Jones Industrial Average.

Example: A closing tick of +41, for example, means that 41 more stocks were rising than falling at their last trade.

Where Is It Found? It is published in *Barron's*. TV networks such as CNBC, The Business Channel, and Nightly Business Report report closing ticks daily.

A sample of one type from the *Wall Street Journal* is presented in Figure 72.

Figure 72: Tick & Closing Tick

DIARIES

NYSE	FRI	THUR	7/23 WK
Issues traded	2,598	2,587	2,735
Advances	1,026	767	1,019
Declines	865	1,208	1,333
Unchanged	707	612	383
New highs	51	72	247
New lows	36	40	119
zAdv vol (000)	113,968	78,811	510,533
zDecl vol (000)	66,626	143,573	538,712
zTotal vol (000)	218,065	248,085	1,210,243
Closing tick[1]	+300	−9	. . . .
Closing Arms[2] (trin)	.69	1.16	. . . .
zBlock trades	4,742	5,670	27,333

Source: *Wall Street Journal*, July 23, 1993.

How Is It Used for Investment Decisions? High positive figures indicate strength while negative figures indicate weakness. In general, the object is to look for positive or negative trends. For example, if the reading went from a negative reading such as -100 to a positive reading such as +200, it would be construed to be a short-term bullish sign. However, extremely high readings supposedly signify a short-term overbought condition and signal a reversal to the downside. By the same token, extremely low tick readings could indicate a short-term oversold condition and are viewed as bullish in the near term.

A Word of Caution: Tick readings must be interpreted with extreme caution since this is not an exact science.

Also See: ARMS INDEX (TRIN)

94. TOTAL RETURN

What Is It? Total return is the most complete measure of an investment's profitability. It is based on both price changes of the assets plus dividends or interest payments made by the security's issuer. By including appreciation and income, total return allows for fair evaluations of disparate assets.

How Is It Computed? Total return reflects the price of an investment or portfolio at the start of a period and the end plus any cash payouts the investment may have generated. Often the calculation assumes that dividends and/or interest payments were immediately reinvested into more shares of that investment.

Examples:

For a stock investment:

An investor bought a stock for $5,000 plus a brokerage commission of $100. After holding it for one year, during which time he received a dividend of $260, he sold it for $5,500 less commissions of $150. The table below shows how to figure the total return:

Net proceeds	($5,500 - $150)	$5,350
Minus net cost	($5,000 + $100)	-$5,100
Plus dividend income		+$260
Total return		$510
As a percentage of initial investment	($510 ÷ $5,100)	10%

For a bond investment:

An investor bought a bond for $9,900 plus a brokerage commission of $100. After holding it for one year, during which time he received interest at an 8.08% rate, he sold it for $9,500 less commissions of $100. Here's how to figure the total return:

Net proceeds	($9,500 - $100)	$9,400
Minus net cost	($9,900 + $100)	-$10,000
Plus dividend income		+$800
Total return		$200
As a percentage of initial investment	($200 ÷ $10,000)	2%

For a mutual fund investment:

An investor bought 2,000 shares of a no-load fund at $10. After three months, he received $400 in income distributions and $700 in capital gains distributions that were automatically reinvested at $11, giving him another 100 shares. Six months later, he received the same distribution only this time he took them in cash. Three months later, he sold the 2,100 shares at $12. Here's how to figure the total return:

Net proceeds	(2,100 × $12)	$25,200
Minus net cost	(2,000 × $10)	-$20,000
Plus unreinvested distributions		+$1,100
Total return		$6,300

As a percentage of initial investment	($6,300 ÷ $20,000)	31%

Where Is It Found? Total return is discussed in many forms, though most commonly it is used among bond traders and when comparing mutual funds.

In bond markets, interest payments can be wiped out by bad trading, so total return is key. Total return is less frequently talked about when the issue is stocks because dividends are a smaller part of an investor's expected returns.

Services like Lipper Analytical Services of New Jersey and Morningstar of Chicago publish total return figures for funds regularly.

Many stock and bond indexes are calculated on a total return basis. This enables the investor to see the combined effect of appreciation and payouts in such investment benchmarks.

How Is It Used for Investment Decisions? Total return is a way to produce a level playing field to compare various investments. It is a simple way to check an investment's performance.

Over longer periods of time, total return figures also help investors learn the power of compound interest. Simply looking at price appreciation may not adequately reflect an investment's profitability, especially if dividends are routinely reinvested.

Also See: LIPPER MUTUAL FUND RANKINGS, MORNINGSTAR MUTUAL FUND RANKINGS

95. TRADING VOLUME

What Is It? Trading volume is the number of shares traded on a stock exchange or for an individual security for a specified period of time, usually daily. Program trading is the simultaneous purchase or sale of at least 15 different stocks with a total value of $1 million or more.

How Is It Computed? A tabulation is made of the number of shares transacted for the day.

Where Is It Found? Trading volume of the overall market and individual stocks can be found in the financial pages of newspapers (e.g., *Barron's*, *Investor's Business Daily*, and the *Wall Street Journal*) and other financial publications. A "net volume" service for major listed stocks is published by Muller and Company. Program trading activity can be found in the *Wall Street Journal* based on information furnished by the NYSE.

How Is It Used and Applied? Trading volume trends indicate the health of the market. Price follows volume. For example, increased price can be expected on increased volume.

Market volume of stocks is based on supply demand relationships. Real and psychological factors influence stock buyers and sellers. A strong market exists when volume increases as prices rise. The market is weak when volume increases as prices decline.

If the supply of new stock offerings exceeds the demand, stock prices will decrease. If the demand exceeds the supply of new stock offerings, stock prices will increase. Supply/demand analysis is concerned more with the short term than with the long term.

Volume is closely related to stock price change. A bullish market exists when there is a new high on heavy trading volume. A new high with light volume, however, is viewed as a temporary situation. A new low with light volume is considered much better than one with high volume because fewer investors are involved. If there is high volume with the new low price, a very bearish situation may exist.

When price goes to a new high on increased volume, a potential reversal may occur where the current volume is less than the prior rally's volume. A rally with declining volume is questionable and may foreshadow a reversal in price. A bullish indicator exists when prices increase after a long decline and then reach a level equal to or greater than the preceding trough. It is a bullish indicator when volume on the secondary trough is less than the first one. When price declines on heavy volume, a bearish indicator exists pointing to a reversal in the trend.

A selling climax takes place when prices decrease for a long period at an increased rate coupled with increased volume. After the selling climax, prices are expected to go up, and the low at the point of climax is not expected to be violated for a long time. A selling climax often occurs at the end of a bear market.

When prices have been rising for several months, a low price increase coupled with high volume is a bearish sign.

An upside/downside index illustrates the difference between stock volume advancing and decreasing and is usually based on a 10-day or 30-day moving average. The index is helpful in predicting market turning points. A bull-market continues only where buying pressures remain strong.

An exhaustion move is the last stage of a major rise in stock price. It occurs when trading volume and prices drop rapidly. It usually points to a trend reversal.

When net volume increases, accumulation is occurring. When net volume decreases, distribution is taking place. When the net volume line increases or stays constant while the price drops, accumulation under weakness is occurring and a reversal is anticipated. On the other hand, a decrease or constant net volume during a price rise indicates distribution under strength and an impending reversal.

How Is It Used for Investment Decisions? The investor should consider increasing price of a stock on heavy volume to be a much more positive sign than increasing price on light volume. Similarly, decreasing price on heavy volume is a more ominous sign than decreasing price on low volume. Tracking volume indicates the strength or weakness of the security. For example, the investor may have a buying opportunity when a company's stock price begins to rise with increasing volume. This may indicate that the investment community looks favorably upon the stock.

If program trading accounts for a high percentage of share volume, it means that institutional investors (*e.g.*, brokerage firms) are very active. This may have a pronounced effect on the price of stock in either direction. The investor must realize that when a stock is widely held by institutions, price may vary greatly as the institutions buy or sell. The investor should try to determine why the company's stock is being bought or sold significantly by institutions. What do the institutions know?

The investor also should consider secondary distributions, which are the number of new stock issues by already public companies. A high number indicates an overheated market.

A Word of Caution: Trading volume does not always correlate to the magnitude of stock price change. For example, trading volume may be high but the Standard & Poor's 500 index may change only modestly by one or two points.

Also See: BREADTH (ADVANCE-DECLINE) INDEX, TRADING VOLUME GAUGES: SPECULATION INDEX

96. TRADING VOLUME GAUGES

LOW-PRICE ACTIVITY RATIO

What Is It? The ratio compares high risk (speculative) stocks to blue chip (low risk) stocks.

How Is It Computed?

$$\frac{\text{Volume of low-priced speculative securities}}{\text{Volume of high-quality securities}}$$

Example: The volume of low-priced speculative stocks and high-quality stocks are 15 million shares and 140 million shares, respectively. The ratio is 10.7%.

Where Is It Found? This measure is published in *Barron's*.

How Is It Used for Investment Decisions? The market top may be indicated when the volume of low-priced securities increases compared to the volume of blue chip stocks. A ratio of less than about 3% indicates a market bottom, which is the time to buy since increasing stock prices are expected. However, a ratio about 7.6% indicates a market peak, which is the time to sell securities.

A Word of Caution: The investor's definition of a blue-chip or speculative stock is subjective. What is speculative to one person may not be for another person.

NET MEMBER BUY/SELL RATIO

What Is It? The ratio is the volume of shares purchased compared to the volume of shares sold by members of the stock exchange. These members include specialists in securities and floor traders.

How Is It Computed?

$$\frac{\text{Volume of securities bought by members}}{\text{Volume of securities sold by members}}$$

Example: If shares bought and sold by members of the stock exchange are 60 million and 45 million respectively, the ratio is 1.33.

Where Is It Found? The net member buy/sell statistic may be found in *Barron's*.

How Is It Used for Investment Decisions? Members of the stock exchange are considered "smart money" who have significant expertise in securities. If they are net buyers (buyers minus sellers), this is a bullish sign. If they are net sellers, this has a bearish connotation.

The trend over time in member activity is a reflection of the direction of market confidence.

A Word of Caution: The specialists and floor traders in a stock may be wrong in their investment decisions. They are not infallible. For example, they did not expect the stock market crash in October of 1987.

ODD-LOT THEORY

What Is It? An odd lot is a transaction involving fewer than 100 shares of a security. It is usually done by small investors. Odd-lot trading reflects popular opinion. The odd-lot theory rests on the rule of contrary opinion. In other words, an investor determines what others are doing and then does the opposite.

How Is It Computed? An odd-lot index is a ratio of odd-lot purchases to odd-lot sales. This ratio usually is between .40 and 1.60. The investor also may look at the ratio of odd-lot short sales to total odd-lot sales, and the ratio of total odd-lot volume (buys and sells) to round-lot volume (units of 100 shares each) on the NYSE. These figures serve to substantiate the conclusions reached by the investor in analyzing the ratio of odd-lot selling volume to odd-lot buying volume. Figure 73 shows a chart of the ratio of odd lot purchases to sales (plotted inversely).

$$\text{Odd lot short ratio} = \frac{\text{Odd-lot short sales}}{\text{Average of odd-lot purchases and sales}}$$

Example: In one period, odd-lot purchases were 1,500,000 shares while odd-lot sales were 3,000,000 shares. The odd-lot index is therefore .50. The index last period was 1.2. The investor should now buy securities because odd-lot traders, who reflect popular opinion, are selling.

Where Is It Found? Odd-lot trading data are published in *Barron's*, *Investor's Business Daily*, the *New York Times*, and the *Wall Street Journal*. Volume is typically expressed in number of shares instead of dollars. The Securities and Exchange Commission Statistical Bulletin, another source of data, refers to volume in dollars. Figure 74 shows odd-lot trading as published in the *Wall Street Journal*.

How Is It Used and Applied? According to the odd-lot theory, the small trader is right most of the time but misses key market turns. For example, odd-lot traders correctly start selling off part of their portfolios in an up market trend but, as the market continues to rise, the small traders try to make a killing by becoming significant net buyers. This precedes a market fall. Similarly, it is assumed that odd-lotters will start selling off strong prior to a bottoming of a bear market. When odd-lot volume rises in an increasing stock market, the market is about to turn around.

How Is It Used for Investment Decisions? The investor should buy when small traders are selling. Similarly, the investor should sell when small traders are buying.

A Word of Caution: Stock market research does not fully support the odd-lot theory.

Figure 73: Ratio of Odd Lot Purchases to Sales (Plotted Inversely)

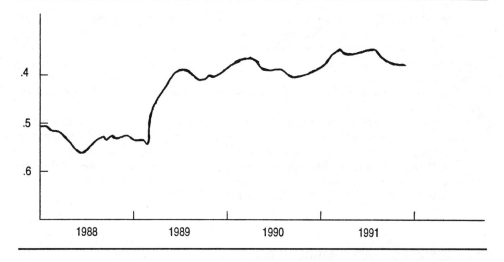

Figure 74: Odd-Lot Trading

New York - The New York Stock Exchange specialists reported the following odd-lot transactions (in shares):

	Customer Purchases	Short Sales	Other Sales	Total Sales
August 26, 1992	675,038	39,359	582,833	622,192

Source: *Wall Street Journal*, August 28, 1992.

SPECULATION INDEX

What Is It? The speculation index is the ratio of the AMEX volume divided by the NYSE volume.

How Is It Computed?

$$\frac{\text{AMEX volume}}{\text{NYSE volume}}$$

Where Is It Found? The ratio may be computed easily from total volume information available in financial newspapers such as *Barron's* and the *Wall Street Journal*.

How Is It Used for Investment Decisions? Speculation is growing when trading on AMEX stocks (which are typically more speculative) increases at a faster rate than trading on NYSE stocks (typically higher-quality issues).

A Word of Caution: The investor should be cautious when there exists a lot of speculation by traders because of the potential for greater losses.

What Is It? The up-to-down ratio looks at the number of advancing issues relative to declining ones. It is used in technical investment analysis.

How Is It Computed? The upside/downside index is the ratio of stock volume advancing to the stock volume decreasing. It is usually based on a 10-day or 30-day moving average.

Where Is It Found? The up-to-down volume ratio may be found in *Barron's* and the *Wall Street Journal*.

How Is It Used for Investment Decisions? The ratio aids in determining whether accumulation or distribution is occurring. It is helpful in predicting market turning points. For example, a bull market continues only where buying pressures remain strong.

A Word of Caution: Although the up-to-down ratio is increasing, the market still may be headed for future falloff in stock prices due to an overvalued situation.

Also See: BREADTH (ADVANCE-DECLINE) INDEX

97. TREYNOR'S PERFORMANCE MEASURE

What Is It? The index can be used to measure portfolio performance. It is concerned with systematic (beta) risk.

How Is It Computed?

$$T_p = \frac{\text{Risk premium}}{\text{Portfolio's beta coefficient}}$$

Example: An investor wants to rank two stock mutual funds he owns. The risk-free interest rate is 6%. Information for each fund follows:

Growth fund	Return	Fund's Beta
A	14%	1.10
B	12%	1.30

$$T_A = \frac{14\% - 6\%}{1.10} = 7.27 \quad \text{(First)}$$

$$T_B = \frac{12\% - 6\%}{1.30} = 4.62 \quad \text{(Second)}$$

Fund A is ranked first because it has a higher return relative to Fund B.

Where Is It Found? The index can be computed based on information obtained from financial newspapers such as *Barron's* and the *Wall Street Journal*.

How Is It Used for Investment Decisions? The index can be used to rank mutual fund investments in terms of return performance considering risk.

Also See: SHARPE'S RISK-ADJUSTED RETURN, PERFORMANCE AND RISK: JENSEN'S PERFORMANCE MEASURE (ALPHA)

98. VALUE AVERAGING

What Is It? Value averaging is a new investment strategy developed by Michael E. Edleson. The premise of value averaging is to make the value of an investor's stock holdings increase by $1,000 (or some other preset amount) each investment period instead of investing a fixed dollar amount as is done with dollar-cost averaging. This way, investors will realize higher returns at lower per share prices. Edleson claims that this strategy beats dollar-cost averaging about 90% of the time.

How Is It Computed? With dollar-cost averaging, an investor automatically buys more shares when prices are low and fewer shares when prices are high. But buying is all he does. With value averaging, an investor would sell part of his investment if the value goes up too high.

Example: If, after four months, our investor's investment was worth $5,000, he would sell $1,000 worth of shares the fifth month to bring the account value down to $4,000. In other words, value averaging forces him to sell high.

How Is It Used for Investment Decisions? There is no decision involved. Value averaging is an investment strategy that takes emotions out of the investment process. As with dollar-cost averaging, an investor can invest without worrying whether this is the right time to buy or sell.

A Word of Caution: Value averaging works well for a fund that stays fully invested in stocks, such as one that tracks the S&P's 500 index. In fact, it works best with no-load index funds that charge no commission to buy or sell.

As for drawbacks, value averaging requires more work and will probably result in more taxable transactions.

Also See: DOLLAR-COST AVERAGING

99. WILSHIRE 5,000 EQUITY INDEX

What Is It? The Wilshire 5,000 is the broadest weighted index of all common stock issues on the NYSE, AMEX, and the most active issues on the over-the-counter market. Approximately 85% of the securities are traded on the NYSE. The index's value is in billions of dollars. It includes about 6,000 stocks (not 5,000 as its name would suggest) so it is representative of the overall market.

How Is It Computed? The stocks included in the index are weighted by market value. It covers total prices of all stocks with daily quotations. The base period is December 31, 1980, at which time the total market value of all stocks in the index was $1,404,896 billion.

Where Is It Found? The Wilshire index is published by Wilshire Associates (Santa Monica, California). The index is reported weekly in *Barron's* and in each issue of *Forbes*. It is reported daily in many newspapers such as *Investor's Business Daily*, the *New York Times*, and the *Wall Street Journal*.

Figure 75 shows the index as reported in the *New York Times*.

How Is It Used for Investment Decisions? The investor should use the Wilshire 5,000 index as a barometer of the overall stock market condition. In a bull market the index will be increasing, but in a bear market the index will be decreasing. A stock may be bought if the index is on an upward move and the investor feels that prices will continue

Figure 75: Wilshire 5,000 Index

INDEXES

	Last	Chg.
Value Line		
Geometric	246.20	+0.58
Arithmetic	347.59	+0.93
Wilshire 5,000	3,991.83	-11.74
Russell 2,000	188.82	+0.46

Source: *New York Times*, August 29, 1992.

moving up. However, if stock conditions are deteriorating as evidenced by a declining index, the investor should sell the stock if he believes that conditions will worsen.

A Word of Caution: The equity index may have increased in a day but a component element of the index (e.g., AMEX issues) may have decreased.

100. YIELD CURVE

What Is It? While basically a graphic representation of bond yields versus bond maturities, the yield curve's shape is often quoted by analysts as a description of the bond market's condition. The curve breaks bonds into three categories by maturity—short (less than 5 years in length), intermediate (5 to 10 years), and long (10-plus years).

How Is It Computed? The curve is drawn by graphing the various maturities of one type of bond, from shortest to longest (typically from overnight to 30 years), against the yields those bond maturities are currently producing. The curve is then sometimes compared to yield curves of other securities or of the same securities at earlier times.

Where Is It Found? On a daily basis, readers can find the yield curve in *Investor's Daily* and the *Wall Street Journal*. Many other publications and newsletters, such as the *Bond Fund Report* or *Grant's Interest Rate Observer*, as well as reports from investment houses typically discuss and chart the yield curve.

How Is It Used for Investment Decisions? The slope of the yield curve and relative changes in the shape can help investors understand bond market conditions.

When the yield curve is steep—short-term rates low, long-term rates high, which is consider the normal shape—rate-seeking investors must take on the added risk of owning long-term bonds to boost their returns. Long-term bond prices are most volatile because their fixed payouts can be dramatically hurt if, for instance, inflation was to rise and erode that income stream's buying power.

An inverted yield curve creates the difficult choice for investors. Should lower long-term rates be locked in? Or can investors take the chance that the currently more attractive short-term rates will stay? This often occurs in times of economic difficulty.

Then there's a flat yield curve when passbook rates might be the same as mortgage rates. This is often seen as a signal of an upcoming dramatic change in the interest rate environment.

A Word of Caution: Yield is not the only consideration when it comes to buying a bond. The price risk of holding long-term bonds should be studied. Credit quality is another important factor—a high current yield is not a valuable holding after an issuer defaults.

Also See: BOND RATINGS, DURATION, ECONOMIC INDICATORS AND BOND YIELDS, INTEREST RATES: 30-YEAR TREASURY BONDS, INTEREST RATES: THREE-MONTH TREASURY BILLS

101. YIELD ON AN INVESTMENT

ANNUAL PERCENTAGE RATE (EFFECTIVE ANNUAL YIELD)

What Is It? The annual percentage rate (APR), also known as the effective annual yield, is the true (effective) rate of interest earned on savings that reflects the frequency of compounding.

How Is It Computed? APR is computed as follows:

$$APR = (1 + r/m)^m - 1.0$$

where r = the stated, nominal, or quoted rate

m = the number of compounding periods per year

Example: If a bank offers 6% interest, compounded quarterly, the APR is:

$$
\begin{aligned}
APR &= (1 + .06/4)^4 - 1.0 \\
&= (1.015)^4 - 1.0 \\
&= 1.0614 - 1.0 \\
&= .0614 \\
&= 6.14\%
\end{aligned}
$$

This means that one bank offering 6% with quarterly compounding and another bank offering 6.14% with annual compounding would both be paying the same effective rate of interest. Figure 76 shows how much difference compounding can make on the rate of interest paid.

Figure 76: Nominal and Effective Interest Rates with Different Compounding Periods

Nominal Rate	Annually	Effective Annualized Yield Semiannually	Quarterly	Monthly	Daily
6%	6%	6.09%	6.14%	6.17%	6.18%
7	7	7.12	7.19	7.23	7.25
8	8	8.16	8.24	8.30	8.33
9	9	9.20	9.31	9.38	9.42
10	10	10.25	10.38	10.47	10.52
11	11	11.30	11.46	11.57	11.62
12	12	12.36	12.55	12.68	12.74

Where Is It Found? Banks competing for deposits, such as certificates of deposit (CDs), usually spell out their true (effective) annual yields, along with their nominal interest rates in their advertising, inside bank offices, or disclose them over the phone.

How Is It Used for Investment Decisions? Different types of investments use different compounding periods. For example, most bonds pay interest semiannually. Some banks pay interest quarterly. If an investor wishes to compare investments with different compounding periods, he needs to put them on a common basis. APR is used for this purpose.

A Word of Caution: Yield is one thing; risk is another. Furthermore, in the case of CDs, investors should ask about other provisions such as the penalty for early withdrawal. For example, the so-called brokered CDs—CDs purchased through brokerage firms—allow investors to cash out of CDs without paying an interest penalty.

CURRENT YIELD ON A BOND

What Is It? It's the measure of what the coupon payments on a bond are worth when the market value or last-trade price of the bond, rather than the par value or principal value of the bond, is considered. If a bond is selling at par, its coupon rate and current yield will be the same.

How Is It Computed? A simple formula:

$$\text{Current yield} = \frac{\text{Coupon payments per year}}{\text{Market price}}$$

Example: A $1,000 par value bond pays a 9% coupon rate. It is currently selling for $1,075.

Current yield = $90/$1,075 = .0837 = 8.37%

However, this simple current yield formula does not take into account the maturity of the bond. To do that, an investor must calculate the yield to maturity, or at least a close approximation, by using the following formula:

$$\text{Yield to maturity} = \frac{\text{Annual coupon payment} + \dfrac{(\text{Face value} - \text{market price})}{\text{Years to maturity}}}{(\text{Face value} + \text{market value})/2}$$

Example: Using the same bond, assuming a 10-year maturity.

$$\text{Yield to maturity} = \frac{\$90 + (\$1,000 - \$1,075)/10}{(1,000 + \$1,075)/2}$$

$$= \frac{\$82.50}{\$1,037.50}$$

$$= .0795$$

$$= 7.95\%$$

Where Is It Found? The typical bond listing in newspapers such as *Barron's*, the *New York Times*, and the *Wall Street Journal* contains yield to maturity information along with coupon rate and last-trade prices. Computerized securities industry databases such as Quotron and Reuters, available at most brokerage houses, also contain such data.

How Is It Used for Investment Decisions? By using the current yield, an investor can more accurately see the value of the income stream being generated by a specific bond. The investor can then properly compare it to other income-producing investments.

But by going the extra step and calculating the yield to maturity, the investor can get an even better picture of the value of an income stream. This is particularly important when investors are buying bonds at a premium price above the par value.

A Word of Caution: Yield is not the only decision an investor must consider when buying a bond. Credit quality, the callability (or early payoff), and a bond's sensitivity to interest rate swings are also important factors.

Also See: BOND RATINGS, DURATION

CURRENT YIELD ON A STOCK

What Is It? Current yield on a stock is a way to evaluate the income stream created by a dividend on a common or preferred stock as it relates to the market price of those shares. Dividends are paid to shareholders out of the profits a company makes.

How Is It Computed? Using a simple formula, investors combine dividend information and share price.

Dividend yield = Dividend paid last 4 quarters / Latest share price

Example: Flood City & Co. pays a quarterly dividend of 25 cents. Its shares last traded for $24.

Dividend yield = ($0.25 + $0.25 + $0.25 + $0.25) / $24
= .0417
= 4.17%

Some investors, however, like to calculate the yield of a stock based on their original cost, not current selling prices. To do that, they just substitute the purchase price for the last trade. In the previous example, the investor paid $20 for his shares.

Dividend yield = ($0.25 + $0.25 + $0.25 + $0.25) / $20
= .050
= 5.0%

Where Is It Found? The stock tables of publications, such as *Barron's* and the *Wall Street Journal* contain current yield information on common and preferred stock. Computerized securities industry databases such as Quotron, Reuters, and Bloomberg, available at most brokerage houses, also contain such data.

How Is It Used for Investment Decisions? The current dividend yield gives an investor the chance to compare the cash-generating ability of income-producing stocks to other investments.

The yield also can be used as a measure of the market's outlook for a particular issue. When a stock yield is near an all-time high, analysts might say either that the stock is underpriced or that the dividend is in danger of being cut. When a stock yield is near a low, the stock may be overvalued or the chances of a dividend increase are remote.

A Word of Caution: Many stocks particularly so-called growth issues of younger companies that reinvest their profits back into their business do not pay dividends or pay very small ones. Dividend yield is only one part of the equation when choosing a stock to buy.

DIVIDEND PAYOUT RATIO

What Is It? The dividend payout ratio measures the percentage of net income paid out in dividends.

How Is It Computed?

$$\text{Dividend payout} = \frac{\text{Dividends per share}}{\text{Earnings per share}}$$

Example: Assume the following:

	19X1	19X2
Cash dividends	$ 200,000	$ 500,000
Net income	1,000,000	1,100,000

The dividend payout ratios are 20% in 19X1 and 45.5% in 19X2, respectively. The investor would look upon the increase in dividend payout favorably since a higher dividend distribution is typically associated with the company performing better. The investor usually likes to receive more dividends because it is available cash and is associated with less uncertainty about the business.

Where Is It Found? The dividend payout ratio often appears in financial advisory service publications (e.g., the *Value Line Investment Survey*), brokerage research reports, and *Business Week's* Corporate Scorecard. The investor also can determine it from readily available data in a company's annual report since dividends per share and earnings per share are always presented. Dividends per share of stocks in the Dow Jones Averages is published in *Barron's*. The week's dividend payments also appear in *Barron's*. *Forbes* lists stocks with strong or laggered dividends.

How Is It Used for Investment Decisions? A decline in dividend payout will cause concern to the investor since fewer earnings are being distributed in the form of dividends. Perhaps the company is running into financial difficulties forcing it to cut back on its dividends. A "red flag" is raised when a company pays out in dividends more than its earnings.

Some industries, such as utilities, are known for their stable dividend records. This is attractive for an individual such as an elderly investor who relies on fixed income.

A Word of Caution: A company should retain earnings rather than distribute them when the corporate return exceeds the return that investors could obtain on their money elsewhere. Further, if the company obtains a return on its profits that exceed the cost of capital, the market price of its stock will be maximized.

Also See: SHARE PRICE RATIOS: BOOK VALUE PER SHARE, CURRENT YIELD ON A STOCK, SHARE PRICE RATIOS: EARNINGS PER SHARE, SHARE PRICE RATIOS: PRICE-EARNINGS RATIO (MULTIPLE)

TAX-EQUIVALENT YIELD

What Is It? The tax-equivalent yield shows what a saver would have to earn on a taxable income-producing investment before taxes to equal tax-free bond payouts.

How Is It Computed? First, an investor must figure his marginal tax rate, that is, what he pays on each extra dollar of income. That can be difficult when finding the marginal rate for double tax-free investments, those free of both state and federal taxes. The formula:

$$\text{Tax-equivalent yield} = \frac{\text{Tax-free return}}{1 - \text{Marginal tax rate}}$$

Example: A municipal bond pays an interest rate of 6%. The investor's tax rate is 34%. The equivalent rate on a taxable instrument is:

$$\frac{.06}{1-.34} = \frac{.06}{.66} = 9.1\%$$

Where Is It Found? Tax-equivalent yield is widely used in marketing and promotional materials for tax-free investments, often in large, dramatic type. Legally, the assumptions used to calculate the tax-equivalent yield must accompany it. They are often found in very small type at the bottom of such sales devices. See Figure 77.

Figure 77: Tax Equivalent Yield

Comparison of State Tax Exempt Yields with Equivalent State Taxable Yields

City/State	Massachusetts	New York City & State	Hawaii	California	New York State
City/State Highest Marginal Tax Rate:	12.00%[1]	11.275%[2]	10.00%[3]	9.3%[4]	7.875%[5]
State Tax Exempt Yield:		*State Tax Equivalent Yields*			
6.00% =	6.82%	6.76%	6.67%	6.62%	6.51%
6.50% =	7.39%	7.33%	7.22%	7.17%	7.06%
7.00% =	7.95%	7.89%	7.78%	7.72%	7.60%
7.50% =	8.52%	8.45%	8.33%	8.27%	8.14%
8.00% =	9.09%	9.02%	8.89%	8.82%	8.68%
8.50% =	9.66%	9.58%	9.44%	9.37%	9.23%

[1] For individual and joint taxpayers. Based upon Massachusetts Personal Income Tax Rate Schedules for 1990.
[2] For individual and joint taxpayers with NYC taxable incomes of $60,000 and $108,000 and greater, respectively. Based upon New York City and State Personal Income Tax Rate Schedules for 1990.
[3] For individual and joint taxpayers with taxable income of $20,500 and $41,000 and greater, respectively. Based upon Hawaii Personal Income Tax Rate Schedules for 1990.
[4] For individual and joint taxpayers with taxable incomes of $26,000 and $52,760 and greater, respectively. Based upon California Personal Income Tax Rate Schedules for 1990.
[5] For individual and joint taxpayers with taxable incomes of $13,000 and $26,000 and greater, respectively. Based upon New York State Personal Tax Rate Schedules for 1990.

Source: United Services Funds.

How Is It Used for Investment Decisions? It is a way to compare tax-free bond yields to taxable returns. It must be used carefully, however. Experts remind investors that the tax status of an investment should not be the only reason to buy it.

Tax-free investments come in various credit qualities. The investor must use a taxable investment of equal safety—both from a credit quality and maturity perspective—when making such comparisons.

In addition, a saver's tax rate is important. According to Internal Revenue Service (IRS) statistics, 1 in 6 investors with tax-free income does not earn enough to have a tax bill sufficiently large to make tax-free investments outperform their taxable counterparts.

A Word of Caution: Municipal bonds rarely are comparable to U.S. Treasury issues or government-insured bank accounts, as far as credit worthiness, although these investments are frequently used as comparisons by tax-free investment brokers.

INDEX OF INVESTMENT TOOLS

One-of-a-Kind Investment Information Guide

It took a seasoned financial planner a mere five minutes of leafing through this book's 400-plus pages to recognize its enormous potential value for both financial beginners and old pro's.

For her client, an admitted neophyte, *SOURCE: The Complete Guide to Investment Information, Where to Find It and How to Use It* provides a painless education in how to discover the most pertinent investment information and how to employ it—not to mention how to better understand what the financial planner and her stockbroker are talking about. For more experienced investors, it offers the one-stop convenience of up-to-date source information; as such, it's a first-of-its-kind tool.

SOURCE is an investment information handbook designed for students of finance and investments as well as for practical investors. *SOURCE* shows where to find information and advice on different types of investment instruments and how to read and interpret those sources. *SOURCE* breaks down the information into an overview, a look at how to choose the right type of security in each investment category, how to read related information given for each source. From the most common and accessible daily newspaper or radio report to the most sophisticated and often costly investment newsletter, no information source is overlooked.

SOURCE, by Jae K. Shim and Joel G. Siegel, who also co-authored the best-selling *The Vest Pocket MBA*, is an invaluable one-of-a-kind investment decision making tool for both beginning and experienced investors.

Send me _____ copies of *SOURCE: The Complete Guide to Investment Information, Where to Find It and How to Use It*, by Jae K. Shim and Joel G. Siegel at $29.95 each (hardcover).

Name_____

Address_____

City / State / Zip _____

Here is my check made payable to International Publishing Corporation. I have added $2.00 for each book to cover postage and handling. (In Illinois, I have also added 8.75% sales tax.)

Payment $ _____, or charge my VISA/Master Card # _____ Exp. date_____

Signature_____

MAIL TO: International Publishing Corp., Inc., 625 N. Michigan Ave., Suite 1920, Chicago, IL 60611 or call 1-800-488-4149 for faster service.

Earn Higher Investment Returns with Lower Costs

Now in its second edition, revised, and made even more practical than before, *Value Averaging: The Safe and Easy Strategy for Higher Investment Returns:*

- shows you how to make the buying and selling of investments nearly automatic, relieving you of emotional anxiety and the need for market-timing and stock picking skills;
- recommends investments best suited for value averaging;
- tells you how to build real wealth easily and consistently over time;
- demonstrates in detail how to use both dollar cost averaging and value averaging for specific investment goals, such as college tuition for your children or your own retirement.

Here's what reviewers said about the last edition:

"The latest wrinkle in automatic investing . . . Compared over time with dollar cost averaging, value averaging will always lower your total cost per share, and it will typically provide a rate of return that's about one percentage point higher . . . "
Kiplinger's Personal Finance Magazine

" 'Today's Best Way to Invest' The smartest strategy today is not to shun stock—but to add money a little at a time. . . . The most familiar such technique is dollar cost averaging. . . . But a lesser-known version called value averaging can get better results by forcing you to make an extra investment in a month when stocks are down and to invest less—or actually a little less—when stocks advance."
Money Magazine

"Value averaging takes dollar cost averaging one step further. Besides buying low, you sell shares when the markets soar." *The New York Times*

- -

Please send me _____ copies of *Value Averaging: The Safe and Easy Strategy for Higher Investment Returns,* 2nd ed., revised, by Michael E. Edleson, PH.D., at $22.95 for each copy.

Name_____

Address_____

City / State / Zip Code _____

Here is my check made payable to International Publishing Corporation. I have added $2.00 for each book to cover postage and handling. (In Illinois, I have added 8.75% sales tax.)

Payment $_____, or charge my VISA/Master Card # _____ Exp. date _____

Signature_____

MAIL TO: International Publishing Corp., Inc., 625 N. Michigan Ave., Suite 1920, Chicago, IL 60611 or call 1-800-488-4149 for faster service.

- -